MARRIAGE CUSTOMS IN MANY LANDS

MARRIAGE CUSTOMS
IN MANY LANDS

REV. H. N. HUTCHINSON, B. A., F. G. S.

GYAN

Published by

Gyan Publishing House
5, Ansari Road
Daryaganj, New Delhi-110002
Phone: 011-47034999, 9811692060
E-mail: books@gyanbooks.com

Distribution Network
gyanbooks.com
India, USA, Canada, UK, Australia, France

ISBN: 978-81-212-8368-7 (PB)
First Published, 1897

2nd Impression 2023

Printed at: Gyan Press, Delhi.

MARRIAGE CUSTOMS IN MANY LANDS
Author: H. N. HUTCHINSON

MARRIAGE CUSTOMS IN MANY LANDS

MARRIAGE CUSTOMS
IN MANY LANDS

REV. H. N. HUTCHINSON, B. A., F. G. S.

GYAN

Published by

GYAN

Gyan Publishing House
5, Ansari Road
Daryaganj, New Delhi-110002
Phone: 011-47034999, 9811692060
E-mail: books@gyanbooks.com

Distribution Network
gyanbooks.com
India, USA, Canada, UK, Australia, France

ISBN: 978-81-212-8368-7 (PB)
First Published, 1897

2nd Impression 2023

Printed at: Gyan Press, Delhi.

MARRIAGE CUSTOMS IN MANY LANDS
Author: H. N. HUTCHINSON

MARRIAGE CUSTOMS IN MANY LANDS

BY THE SAME AUTHOR

THE STORY OF THE HILLS. 5s.
Seeley & Co.

THE AUTOBIOGRAPHY OF THE EARTH. 7s. 6d.
Stanford & Co.

EXTINCT MONSTERS. 6s.
Chapman, Hall & Co.

CREATURES OF OTHER DAYS. 6s.
Chapman, Hall & Co.

PREHISTORIC MAN AND BEAST. 10s. 6d.
Smith, Elder & Co.

HINDOO BRIDE AND BRIDEGROOM. *From a Photograph by Bourne & Shepherd.*

MARRIAGE CUSTOMS

IN MANY LANDS

BY THE

REV. H. N. HUTCHINSON, B.A., F.G.S.

Author of "Extinct Monsters," "The Story of the Hills," "Prehistoric Man and Beast," &c.

WITH MANY ILLUSTRATIONS

LONDON

SEELEY AND CO. LIMITED

38, GREAT RUSSELL STREET

1897

PREFACE

THE Marriage Customs of the World, if treated exhaustively, would fill a good many volumes, and the compilation of such a work might occupy the best part of a lifetime. The present writer's object is to present to general readers a careful account of quaint and interesting customs derived from information scattered through innumerable volumes, not to discuss scientific questions connected with the origin of marriage and the human family, which have been dealt with by well-known writers like Sir John Lubbock, Professor Tylor, Professor Robertson Smith, Westermark, and McLenan.

The present age, with its marvellous facilities for travel and consequent bringing together of peoples and races, is not favourable to the preservation of old customs. In fact, they are fast dying out everywhere, and, ere long, most of them will be as dead as the mammoth, or other extinct monsters. Hence, it is highly desirable that the old customs connected with betrothal and marriage should be brought together and presented to the public in some convenient and compact form. Although much has been written on marriage, there is no modern book of this kind. In the year 1822, Lady Augusta Hamilton published a book entitled "The Marriage Rites, Customs, and Ceremonies of all Nations," but the facilities for such a compilation were then but few in comparison with the wealth of material now available. The number of books of travel published since that date is truly enormous, and it is to such works that the writer is chiefly indebted. But he has used other sources, and gleaned much from periodicals, from the "Gazetteer of India" (over 40 volumes), Hunter's "Cyclopedia of India," and records of Missionary labour. Nearly ninety separate works on Africa were examined, and on India more than fifty, including the two just mentioned. "The Wedding Day in all Countries and all Ages," by E. J. Wood, appears to be the only other English work of this kind. It was published nearly thirty years ago, is somewhat too brief, and now out of print.

The illustrations have been carefully selected from a large number collected by the author from various sources. Some are photographed from life, others are drawn or painted by artists well acquainted with the scenes which they depict, or are based on trustworthy materials.

The writer is particularly indebted to Mr. Thos. Child, of Chelsfield, Kent, for his excellent photograph of a Chinese bride; to Lieut. Chas. Fox (Bedfordshire Regiment), for a photograph of an Indian Mohammedan bridal party; to Messrs. Bourne and Sheppard, of Bombay, for their excellent photograph which forms the frontispiece; to Mrs. Rigg for the photograph of a Brahmin wedding party; to Mr. Percy Bigland for permission to reproduce his picture, "A Quaker Wedding," as well as to Mr. J. R. Reid for similar permission with regard to his "Mate of the Mermaid's Wedding"; to Prof. Douglas for a Chinese illustration of a bridal chair, from his book "Society in China" (Innes & Co.), and for finding the Japanese native drawing, "Bringing home the presents." Acknowledgment is also due to Mr. E. D. Cuming and to his publishers, Messrs. Osgood, McIlvaine & Co., for permission to quote the graphic description of a Burmese marriage from "With the Jungle Folk in Burma."

London, *September*, 1897.

CONTENTS

LIST OF ILLUSTRATIONS

MARRIAGE CUSTOMS

CHAPTER I

India

IT is doubtful whether the Vedas and other ancient sacred books of the Hindus countenance the polygamy which prevails among the richer classes in India, and against this degradation of the sex Hindu marriage ceremonies, which have descended from remote ages, make their constant, albeit useless, protest. The whole spirit of their marriage ritual is opposed to plurality of wives, and inculcates firm and undeviating allegiance between man and wife. The peasants and the poorer inhabitants of towns are necessarily restricted to one wife, and among them married life is often very happy. Neither do the sacred writings appear to sanction the child-marriages which are so prevalent and so injurious.

In Hindu law the marriage-tie is very binding, and may only be broken for some grave reason. If the wife is drunken, or unfaithful to her spouse, or excessively extravagant, or if, after eleven years she bears him no son, he may take a second wife; but, even then, his first wife still rules the house. There are at least five things essential to the marriage ceremony, viz., the betrothal, the gift of the virgin, the acceptance, the seizure of the hand, and the seven steps, or *sapta-padi*.

As the girl's father, or guardian, gives her away he must say, in the presence of the Brahmins, to the bridegroom's father, "I give you, for your son, my beautiful virgin daughter: accept her therefore." The father of the youth must reply, "With my hand, with my voice, and with my body I joyfully accept thy daughter for my son, and religiously receive her among my own kindred." The girl's father then declares his tribe, and gives grains of rice tinged with red, and leaves of the betel plant to the bridegroom, declaring again that he gives him his daughter and promises to defray all the expenses of the marriage. He usually gives a present of cows as well, and especially a certain stone which is used as a charm. It is hardly necessary to point out that in a great country like India, with a population of nearly three hundred millions, and a very large number of different races, the customs and ceremonies attending marriage vary very considerably; we shall presently give a few selected examples of curious customs, but at present we are dealing with the case of an ordinary or typical Hindu wedding.

Addressing the assembled Brahmins, or priests, the

father says, "O Brahmins, to this youth, learned in the Vedas, I give my daughter, dressed in gay apparel, and adorned with gems." They answer, "So let it be." The father-in-law, having taken the hand of his daughter, now puts it into the hand of the bridegroom and pours over them water, sacred to Vishnu, which has been previously blessed by a priest. This is perhaps the most solemn and important of all the marriage ceremonies; for the pouring of water, according to Eastern custom, makes a gift irrevocable. Another important rite is the tying on of the *tali*, a jewel set in gold, on the neck of the bride. In India all Hindu married women wear this ornament as a sign of their being in the married state. It is fastened by a short string dyed yellow with turmeric, and composed of many fine threads. To the guests, sandal-wood, paste, perfumes, and flowers are offered: the couple receive congratulations from the assembly as they prostrate themselves at their parents' feet to receive a blessing. In Northern India, part of the ceremony consists in tying a string or thread round the wrist of the bride; and with many of the races of India the man and the woman, or the boy and the girl, as the case may be, are tied together by the corners of their garments and made to walk through the village, to signify to all that they are tied together for life. In order to impress upon the bride the duty of complete submission to her husband, the wooden yoke of a bullock is laid lightly for a moment on her head. A veil is then held up between her and the bridegroom and certain prayers, or verses, are recited. In these they call upon the gods, the saints, the trees and the rivers, to witness the union.

Then follows the *honam*, or offering to Agni, the god of fire, in which the bride and bridegroom take together the seven steps, or *sapta-padi*, amidst the loud chanting of the Vedas. This is an important piece of symbolism, for the action implies eternal friendship.

In India, as in so many other countries, marrying a wife means buying one. The father-in-law, of course, gets the highest price he can for his daughter. The young man must stipulate to pay a certain sum of money. The bride, being only a child, has no voice in the matter, and everything is arranged for her. The young man thinks chiefly of the purity of her caste, while her relations are more anxious about his wealth, and the disposition of his mother; a very important matter, for the poor little bride, when she comes to her new home, is entirely under the rule of that important person the mother-in-law. If, after the marriage has taken place, the bridegroom does not pay up "like a man," as the saying is with us, he is liable to be brought into court by an angry father-in-law. Or, more probably, the young wife has to be sent home as a pledge until the money is all paid. In other words, she is pawned! Among the poor people of India there is much litigation over such matters. Among the rich the money received by the father is laid out in jewels which become the bride's property, and can on no account be disposed of by the husband.

There is, of course, no courtship. But, if a young man takes a fancy to a little girl, he must get some friend to visit her parents and ascertain whether his suit would be favourably received. If they have no objections, he selects a fortunate day to visit them and ask for her hand. She *may* give him her heart some day, long after, but that is all a matter of chance. The presents he brings with him are usually a cloth, cocoanuts, bananas, and some saffron. The Hindus are great observers of omens. Thus, if the man, while on his way, should meet a cat, a fox, or a serpent, and it should cross the road before him, he would instantly return home and postpone the journey to a more fortunate day. In like manner the girl's father defers his answer until one of those little lizards which creep on the wall, making now and then a small shrill cry, gives a favourable augury by one of its chirps. Not until "the lizard has spoken" (as the people say) will he take any of the steps necessary for the betrothal.

Marriages take place only in March, April, May, or June. Second marriages, however, may be made in November or February. The months from March to June are very hot, and country labour is then suspended and the harvest has been gathered in; these appear to be the reasons for the above limitation.

The various ceremonies of a Brahmin wedding are very elaborate, and are spread over five days. First, the bride and bridegroom are placed under the alcove, or canopy, with twelve pillars. This is a common and useful appendage to the principal houses in India, being erected before the door and covered with boughs of trees, as a shelter from the heat of the sun. Under this alcove, gorgeously decorated for the occasion, the young couple are seated with their faces turned to the east. The married women then advance and wave lighted camphor before an image to avert the "evil eye": this ceremony, called *arati*, may be otherwise performed. All the Hindu gods are invited to the wedding, and requested to remain the whole time. The same prayer is made to the god's ancestors, which rather suggests that the gods are only deified heroes. The god of obstacles is an important person and greatly feared, since his displeasure might cast some impediment in the way of a happy ending. So they place his image under the *pandal*, or alcove, in order that all may be well.

The bridegroom must be able to show that he is "pure," or free from sin, but these little matters are easily settled in a country where ceremony counts for so much, and he is merely called upon to offer, on the second day, a gift of fourteen flags to one of the Brahmins.

Then follows a little piece of acting, which must strike the Western mind as very absurd, but is probably connected with Brahmin notions of ceremonial purity. The bridegroom professes an eager desire to quit the village, upon a pilgrimage to Benares, in order that he may wash in the sacred waters of the Ganges. He

A BRAHMIN WEDDING. *From a Photograph.*

equips himself as a traveller, and being supplied with provisions for the journey, departs with instruments of music sounding before him, and accompanied by several of his relations and friends, as if he were really proceeding on that holy adventure. But, no sooner has he got out of the village than, upon turning to the east, he meets his future father-in-law, who, of course, begs him to give up his good intention, and offers him his daughter. The would-be pilgrim readily accepts the conditions, and they return together to the house. The bridegroom has done the right thing in offering to go, so the father takes the will for the deed, and the Brahmins doubtless are satisfied.

The ceremonies are then allowed to proceed, and the next thing is the tying on of the thread, which is fastened to the right wrist of the man and the left one of the bride, to show that they are now tied together for life. Then the young man being seated with his face to the east, his father-in-law approaches, and, looking steadily at him, fancies that he beholds in him the great god Vishnu himself, and with this impression actually makes an offering to him.

The father of the bridegroom must next fix his thoughts on all the gods of the Hindus, naming each one separately; and he even adds the month, the day, the cardinal points of the compass, the woods, the mountains, and many other things. This is followed by the pouring of water over the couple, and the tying on of the *tali*, as described above. The ornament is so highly honoured that they even offer incense to it.

Just before the tying on of the *tali*, the Brahmins put a screen of silk between the bride and bridegroom, while certain prayers are being recited.

Next, fire is brought in, and the *honam*, or sacrifice to Agni, the god of fire, is performed ; the man and the woman, hand in hand, walk seven times round the fire, and so make "the seven steps" together—symbol of everlasting friendship. Lastly, the man touches the woman's ankle with a small stone, called the stone of sandal, and in so doing he must fix his thoughts on "The Great Mountain of the North," the native place of the ancestors of the Brahmins. This little ceremony will be specially interesting to students of ethnology and etymology because the Sanscrit language affords evidence that the original Hindus, or some of them, came from the north.

We must not omit to mention the eating together, which is so important a ceremony among many peoples. According to the late Abbé Du Bois, to whose book we are indebted, another ceremony is the sprinkling with rice of the bride and bridegroom, each standing in a basket made of bamboo, while the one throws rice over the other. This ceremony appears to be symbolical of fertility and abundance of temporal blessings.

On the third day, the astrologer points out to the newly-married pair the star *Arundhati*, to impress upon them the duty of faithfulness. The bridal procession takes place at night, the bride being covered with jewels and precious stones. Friends and relations come out of their houses to hail the young couple, and women endeavour to avert the "evil eye" by the ceremony of *arati*, or waving a lamp over the heads of the bride and bridegroom.

The youthful wife is taken back to her father's house, to live there until she has grown up and can keep house for her husband.

When this epoch of her life arrives, it is made the occasion for much feasting and rejoicing, and many of the ceremonies above described are performed again.

In bygone days women were sometimes allowed to choose their own husbands. Occasionally a prince or king would hold a *swayámvar*, or tournament, at which the fair princess would choose some knight who took her fancy and showed great prowess. There is an old Indian fairy tale illustrating the marriage-choice ceremony: the fair princess placed a garland on the neck of the young man who had won her heart.

In old days the "Brides of Venice" were all married on the same day, and so also in some parts of India young people may have to wait for years before they can get married. Thus, with the Kadava Kumbi of Gujerat an interval of nine, or even twelve, years elapses between one marriage season and another. When nine years have passed the priest consults the goddess, to see if he can obtain her consent. This is the way they proceed: two bits of paper, one containing the word "Yes" and the other the word "No," are thrown before her, and a virgin is asked to take up one of them. Should she take up the one with the word "Yes," it is interpreted as a consent for the celebration of marriages that season. But if unfortunately it is the one with "No" written on it, the goddess is supposed to withhold her consent. In that case they must wait two years before consulting her again. But if, after that interval, she again appears to refuse, their patience becomes fairly exhausted, and they go on throwing the paper until a favourable answer is obtained.

There are in India, as every one knows, a large number of Mohammedans; but their marriage ceremonies will be described under the head of Turkey. Our illustration shows the bringing home of a Mohammedan bride; the bearers have set down their burthen, and are taking a rest.

With the princes, rajahs, and the rich people weddings are very expensive affairs, and presents are given on a princely scale. Thus, when Prithi-raj carried off the daughter of Jye-chand, her father nevertheless gave him the richest gems, which he had won in victory, pearls, elephants, and dyes. And when the same rajah married the daughter of Dahima of Biana, her father gave him 8 beautiful damsels, 63 female slaves, 100 Irak horses, 2 elephants, 10 shields, a pallet of silver for the bride, 100 wooden images, 100 chariots, and 100 pieces of gold! The desire of marrying into a higher family is so great with them (as it often is in our own country and America) that a father is willing to make great sacrifices to mark his sense of gratitude to a son-in-law for his condescension in marrying his daughter. It

A MOHAMMEDAN WEDDING IN INDIA. *From a Photograph by Charles Fox, Esq.*

seems that a dread of marriage expenses and pride of race are among the causes leading to infanticide. The Kadava Kumbis have invented an ingenious device by means of which the expenses of a wedding may be very much reduced. If the parents fail to find a rich husband for their daughter *she is solemnly married to a bunch of flowers*, which is afterwards thrown into a well! The girl is now a widow, so when next time she really is married it counts as a second marriage, and these alliances can be done cheaply! Another way they have is to marry the girl to some man who is already married, on the distinct understanding that as soon as the ceremony is over he will divorce her. She can then be given in second marriage to any man who wants to marry her. People who are determined to do things "on the cheap" can generally find ways of doing so!

In Kangra, a district in the Lieutenant-Governorship of the Punjab, is a hill people with fair complexion and good features, whose neighbours are polyandrous. Here it is not an uncommon thing for a man to sell his wife to another man; and it is said that such agreements are sometimes executed on stamped paper and presented at the courts for registration! Among some of the people of India a wife is reckoned among a man's "available effects," and can be turned into money, as the saying is. So, if a man owe money to his neighbour he can, if hard pressed, pledge his wife (or his daughter) to the creditor, who may either accept them or pass them on to some one else. On the debt being paid, the man may claim his wife, and any children born in the interval!

Among the Kol tribes, and others, the price of a wife is sometimes as high as forty head of cattle; the result is that a girl may have to wait a long time before finding a husband. Old maids therefore are plentiful.

These tribes have a ceremony called by some writers Plant-marriage, the meaning of which is, however, obscure. When an old maid is married, she clasps a mahwa tree, and the bridegroom a mango tree, and, at the close of the ceremonies, the bridesmaids pour a jar of water over the heads of the pair, who then retire to change their wet garments.

In the hills of North and South Arcot and the Salem districts (Madras Presidency) are the Malayalis, a timid and harmless people, who have a most remarkable custom. A man who has young sons, mere children, takes new wives for himself, who are, however, called his sons' wives, and the children they bear to him are called his sons' children. And so it goes on from one generation to another. This appears to be a relic of what is called the Matriarchal system, which still prevails in various countries, as once in India.

"Marriage by capture" was the rule of old, and relics of this are to be found in various places. The Mahi Kantha is a group of native states under the political agency of the Government of Bombay, but subject to a number of chiefs. The Posina Fair in the North gives the Bhíls of these parts a great matrimonial opportunity, for if a Bhīl succeeds in taking the woman he wants to marry across the river without being discovered, their respective parents agree to the match. But if, on the other hand, he is found out before they can cross the river, he is severely handled by the girl's father. The Kolis also have customs which appear to be survivals from the old days of violence. The father generally finds a bride for his son; but, even when all has been peacefully and properly arranged, the young man must go through the form of starting to find a bride. When matters have been settled, the girl's father asks the young man and his father to come and dine. During the ceremony the women of the family strew grains of corn on the threshold, and as the boy's father is leaving the house they rush at him as if to beat him, and he, making for the door, slips, and falls down. So important is this little ceremony on his part that, without it, no marriage would be considered lucky or prosperous! Only it is curious that the girls should show signs of combat and resistance to the father and not to the bridegroom.

The Kurmis and others celebrate the marriage by a pretended combat. The bridegroom sometimes marks his forehead with blood, and here we seem to have the origin of a singular and nearly universal custom in India, namely, the marking of the bride's forehead with vermilion. We find it cropping up among the Ooraons, who celebrate a child-wedding somewhat after this fashion. The uncles, who are very important personages, pick up the bride and bridegroom and set them astride on their backs—just as older people in England sometimes play with their young ones. One takes the little girl and the other the boy, and thus burdened they pretend to be "gee-gees," and paw the ground, as if impatient to start off at a gallop. They exchange their burdens and begin a sham quarrel, which ends in a prance of reconciliation. The young people, who have been well rubbed with oil, are presented with a lighted lamp—emblem of conjugal love—the flame of which must be fed by the husband. Then follow two important ceremonies. First, the bridegroom presses his toe upon the bride's heel, while she throws herself backwards, her head touching his shoulder. Secondly, he marks her brow with a red stain from a drop of his blood, a solemn act, which those outside announce by the discharge of firearms. The parents present the "cup of love," out of which the two drink. These three symbols—the loving-cup, the crimson mark, and the conquering toe, are to be found in nearly every region of India. Two of them are clearly relics of the old way of "marriage by capture."

In central India we meet with a curious little custom which perhaps serves to explain our habit of giving presents to bridesmaids. The Kurku girls pretend to resist the removal of the bride. When they get near enough to the young man they pelt him with balls of boiled rice, then coyly retreat, followed of course by the men. At the door of the bride's house they make

A Cingalese Wedding: joining the Thumbs. *By* J. Williamson.

a final stand, only suffering the men to enter when they have paid toll in the form of presents to themselves.

Among the Gonds we see marriage by capture still in force. A young man, having seen in some neighbouring village a girl whom he would like to marry, goes with some friends to the place where she is working, and makes a rush to seize her. But his companions will not aid him to carry her away by force unless he succeed, unaided, in touching her hand before she reaches the shelter of her village. The women often contest every inch of ground with their pursuers, and sometimes beat them off; but, if once the man can touch the girl's hand, it is considered a match. Doubtless it lies with the girl herself to decide whether he shall do so or no, and in this way she can exercise her own choice. Writing of the Khand race in Orissa, Sir John Campbell says that on one occasion he heard loud cries proceeding from a village close at hand. Fearing some quarrel, he rode to the spot, and there he saw a man bearing away upon his back something enveloped in an ample covering of scarlet cloth. He was surrounded by some twenty or thirty young fellows, and by them protected from the desperate attack made upon him by a party of young women. On seeking an explanation of this novel scene, he was told that the man had just been married, and his precious burden was his blooming bride, whom he was thus conveying to his own home! Her young friends were seeking to regain possession of her, and hurled stones and bamboos at the head of the devoted bridegroom until he reached the confines of his own village.

If a man and a woman have been living together, and the man dies, the woman is so loth to be considered unmarried that she is willing to go through *some* kind of ceremony by which she may be, as it were, sealed to him before his body is committed to the earth—at least among the Komati caste. And so it occasionally happens that a marriage is performed between the living and the dead! The sad intelligence of her man's death is communicated to the neighbours; a *guru*, or priest, is summoned, and the ceremony takes place at once. According to a writer who once witnessed such a proceeding, the dead body of the man was placed against the outer wall of the verandah of the house in a sitting posture, attired like a bridegroom, and the face and hands besmeared with turmeric. The woman also was clothed like a bride, and adorned with the usual tinsel ornament over the face, which, as well as the arms, was daubed over with yellow. She sat opposite the dead body of her late lamented partner—we cannot say husband, for the ceremony is not yet done. Now she spoke to it in light unmeaning words, as seems customary on such occasions, and then she chewed bits of dry cocoanut and squirted them on the face of the dead man. This continued for hours, and not until near sunset was the ceremony brought to a close. Then the head of the corpse was bathed and covered with a cloth of silk, the face was rubbed over with some red powder, and betel leaves placed in the mouth. Now she might consider herself married, and the funeral procession started.

The cruel treatment of widows among the Hindus is the result of ancient superstition. The horrible practice of Suttee, or burning alive, was only suppressed by the Indian Government about the year 1830, and cases have occurred within the reign of Queen Victoria. The custom was certainly ancient, though not so old as some of the native codes. Diodorus relates how the two widows of Geteus, an Indian general of Eumenes, disputed the honour of being burned with the body of their late husband. His description corresponds in every detail with the ceremony as performed in recent times. One of the wives, he says, could not be burned because she was about to become a mother. The other advanced to the funeral pile crowned with myrtle, adorned as for a wedding, and preceded by her relatives, who sang hymns in her praise—all of which no doubt would be very comforting, but hardly likely to diminish the pain of such a cruel death to any great extent. Having bestowed her jewels on friends and servants, she lay down by the side of her husband's body and died without uttering a cry! Early in the last century, at the funeral of the Prince of Marava, all his wives, to the number of forty-seven, were burned on the pyre with his body. The prince was eighty years of age when he died, and his body, richly adorned, was placed in a large grave filled with wood. The unfortunate victims were covered with precious stones, and at first appeared very brave, but as soon as the flames reached them they uttered loud cries and rushed on each other. Then the onlookers endeavoured to diminish their suffering by stunning them with pieces of wood which they hurled at them. When all was over, and these poor wretches had joined their lord and master in the spirit world—for that was the idea in all such sacrifices—their bones and ashes were gathered up and thrown into the sea. In time a temple was erected to their honour on the site where they perished. These hideous and revolting practices were *not* compulsory, *i.e.*, the law did not enforce them, but it was considered a point of honour for the widow to die on the funeral pyre of her husband, even when her relations endeavoured to dissuade her from so doing. Death, however painful, was considered preferable to living in a kind of disgrace. What will not mortals do to avoid contempt?

In Bengal the woman was bound firmly to the corpse, and the two bodies were covered with bamboos. In Orissa the widow threw herself on the pile, which was in a pit or grave. In the Deccan she sat on the pile, and placed the head of her husband on her knees. Sometimes she was overthrown by the fall of heavy logs of wood attached with cords to posts placed at the four corners of the pile. The smoke from the burning logs often suffocated the victim before the flames reached her, and it is said that, in some provinces, she was previously intoxicated with opium. But, if none of these precautions were taken, it might happen that she would rush madly out of the flames, in which case the spectators cruelly thrust her back!

In Burma there are no child-marriages, and the people seem happy in their domestic affairs. Although girls are considered to be the property of their parents, they are very seldom constrained to marry a man against their will. The young men, too, make love pretty much where their fancy leads them, obtaining first the consent of the parents, which is generally given, unless there is any doubt on the score of their character. Courtship does not now last as long as it did formerly. The period of day between eight in the evening and midnight is called courting time; in Burmese it is "*Loo-byo-lai-thee-kala*," which seems somehow to have a romantic ring about it, or is it only the soothing sound of these words, so strange to our ears? A lamp placed in the casement intimates that the young lady is "at home" and prepared to receive bachelors. It is all very correct and proper, for the mother is looking on not far off. Moreover, the damsel probably receives as many as five or six together, on the principle of safety in numbers. The Burmese mother is a great match-maker, but she uses persuasion rather than compulsion. If, however, she should try constraint, it would probably be in vain, for in that case either the girl elopes with the lover of her choice, or she goes and hangs herself. The women carry on most of the trading and shopping, and are excellent housekeepers, as Mr. Rudyard

Kipling shows in one of his short stories of Indian life. It cannot be said that there is any true marriage ceremony, but the following account condensed from "With the Jungle Folk in Burma," a most readable and interesting book by our friend Mr. E. D. Cuming, will give the reader a good idea of how these affairs are managed :—

"You know the purpose of our coming ?" said the young man's father, as one who knows he is welcome.

"We are pleased to see you," said the girl's father, and his wife murmured words to the same effect, though, properly speaking, the woman should say nothing on this occasion.

"Our son loves your daughter, and wishes to make her his wife."

"We are honoured — much honoured," was the reply of the girl's father, who went on to say : "I believe, good neighbour, I am sure, that your admirable son is of good blood ; that in his family, on either side, has never been any taint of slave-blood. That none of his forefathers have been king's slaves ?"

"There is no slave-blood in our family," was the reply.

"No, surely not," murmured the assembled friends and relations.

"And we are also sure that he has in his veins no taint of the Grave-digger class ?"

"Neither the ancestors of myself nor of my woman have had any strain of Grave-digger caste."

"Surely not," again murmured the friends and relations.

"He is a fine young man. We feel sure he is healthy?"

To which his parents reply, "Our son does not suffer from leprosy, nor scrofula, nor from other evil disease that is properly held disgraceful. He is clean and healthy."

"We are sure of it."

"Well, then, good neighbour, in the presence of our friends and neighbours we consent to your excellent son's marriage with our daughter; and we shall pray that long life, fertility, and much happiness attend their union."

"It is good."

Then the headman said—

"We all wish the young people freedom from accidents, diseases, and misfortunes, and very great happiness."

After this the conversation became general, and everybody agreed that the match was most suitable, and sure to be a happy one. But, of course, they all expressed surprise (as was proper), and professed not to have had any idea that such a thing was impending!

On returning home, the young man's mother said to him, "You will marry to-morrow, I expect."

"Yes, to-morrow, good mother."

Next morning, before the sun was hot, a cart with all the bridegroom's belongings arrived at the bride's house, the young man himself leading the way, returning with smiles the good wishes of the neighbours, who stood on their verandahs to see him pass, the bullock-cart squeaking and groaning behind him.

Mah Pan, the bride, wore her best tamein, a white silk jacket, and a new pink silk handkerchief about her shoulders, carefully arranged that it might not hide her necklet.

Pho Lone, the bridegroom, stepped into the house, where he was greeted by his father-in-law with the words, "The rice is ready, my son." Meanwhile, the bride's mother has set on the floor a new lacquer tray with a little boiled rice.

Pho Lone, sitting, ate a mouthful, and Mah Pan, taking her place beside him, did the same. They smiled at one another.

"It is done," said the headman; "they are man and wife."

At night, the young bachelors came and silently threw stones thick and fast upon the thatch, just to prove their envy.

Irish "wakes," we know, are far from dismal affairs, but no one ever heard of their being turned into occasions for courtship and love-making in a public manner, and by a considerable number of young people. Collective courtship, however, appears to be the distinguishing characteristic of funerals among the Karens. These are a people who live, for the most part, among the mountains of Burma, though some of them have come down

A Burmese Bride and Bridegroom.
From a Photograph by Surgeon-Captain McDermott.

to the plains. Under ordinary circumstances they are a quiet and peaceable people, but one branch of them, the Red Karens, are the most brutal savages, committing every atrocity except cannibalism.

When one of the Karens dies, the probability is that his relations are too much engrossed in other matters to conduct the funeral rites and ceremonies. Perhaps the harvest has not been gathered in, or the weather is too cold or too wet, in which case the girls would not think of turning out in their finery, as they are wont to do on these occasions, that they may be wooed collectively by the village swains. To the western mind this might seem rather an awkward dilemma, but the Karens have solved the difficulty in a delightfully simple manner. The man is buried temporarily, to be dug up again and "waked" at some more convenient season! Therefore, when a Karen dies, he is promptly stowed away in a hole in the ground, and the spot marked by stakes or a fence of cactus. If a rich man, his body is burned—a safer plan, because the dogs cannot then get at it. The final ceremony may take place within six months, if there are a large number of young women waiting to be married; but otherwise there may be a delay of two or three years, or even more!

When the time has at last arrived, a platform of bamboo is erected in front of the house where the deceased lived, and his bones are dug out of their temporary grave. On this platform, or stage, barbarously adorned with pieces of cloth, a linen sheet is placed, on which the remains are laid.

People from neighbouring villages come in large numbers; but, although certain funeral rites are performed, these are postponed till the young men and maidens have done their courting and chosen their partners for life. And so the occasion partakes more of the nature of a public courting than of a funeral. The proceedings are somewhat after this fashion. The young men and the girls separate into two choirs and seat themselves on opposite sides of the remains. Family jewels are displayed in great profusion. The young men begin with a chorus celebrating the beauties of the Karen maidens, their charm of movement, and modest demeanour. To this the girls respond in a falsetto of the usual drawling character, accepting the eulogy of their graces. These overtures are usually set pieces, handed down from antiquity, or rendered into the Karen tongue from some popular Burmese play. Then the young bachelors begin, each in turn, and sing love-stricken solos, calling on the name of some particular damsel. Among an Eastern and poetic people, flowery language is only what might be expected on such an occasion; so we need not be surprised to learn that the girl is compared to a star, a flower, or a ruby. No painter could possibly do justice to her charms; she would ruin the peace of mind of a hermit! When rejected, the suitor becomes plaintive—perhaps in the belief that "pity is akin to love"—saying that he can neither eat nor drink, and will assuredly die before the morning! Far from feeling embarassed, the Karen maidens appear to be pleased at such expressions of devotion. Their answers are usually of a somewhat stereotyped character. The girl will declare that it is a shameful thing not to be married, but that to be divorced afterwards is much worse—"to be like a dress that has been washed." Another will declare that she is not going to give herself away too cheaply. She lets the suitor know that she is not like a day dim with the heat-haze, nor like a diamond that has lost the foil below to set it off, nor like a peacock's tail draggled in the wet. All this means that the wrong man has applied, and the lucky swain will be a great fool if her eyes do not let him know that, when his turn comes, the answer will be favourable. A girl seldom says "No" outright; they prefer a more indirect and less crushing mode of refusal, expressed in some such terms as "Come to me when the full moon appears on the first day of the month," or "Eat your rice before it is cooked and come before daylight." But these cases are exceptional; for, as a rule, the girl has made up her mind which young man she will accept, and the others will look elsewhere. The young people have met before, and so matters are considerably simplified. When all the courting is over, they retire and are married forthwith. Then the elders go on with the funeral rites!

Marriages in Siam take place at an early age. An English traveller, Sir P. J. Bowring, states that he has seen as many as five generations gathered round the head of a family! As in India and China, "go-betweens" or "match-makers" are employed. A wedding procession in this country is a very picturesque affair, and one which might well tempt an artist to choose the subject for his canvas. When the negotiations have been nearly completed, the bridegroom travels by water to the house of the bride-elect in a large boat, gaily adorned with flags, and laden with presents, such as garments for his future wife, plates, fruits, betel-nut, &c. In the centre is a huge cake, in the form of a pyramid, and decorated with bright colours. The musicians on board play as the boat glides along. Arrived at his destination he lands, makes his way to the house in order to make the final arrangements and fix the happy day. There is no religious ceremony: only a great feast, at which the musicians again perform.

Among the Jakûn tribes of the Malay Peninsula an entertainment takes place on the wedding-day at the house of the bride's father, where the whole tribe are assembled. The dowry, given by the man, is delivered in their presence. A dance follows, in the midst of which the bride-elect darts off into the forest, followed by the bridegroom; a chase ensues, during which, should he fall down or return without her, the match is declared to be "off," and the unhappy youth meets with nothing but jeers from the whole party. But, if the tribe should happen to live on the shores of a lake, the damsel is given a canoe and a paddle, and allowed a start of some distance. The lover then goes off in pursuit, and he *must* overtake her, or give up all claim to her hand. The girl, it need hardly be remarked, usually knows her own mind, and becomes a willing captive. Sometimes there is no stream or lake conveniently near; in that case a circle is formed, the damsel is stripped of all but a waistband, and given a start of half the circle. She must run three times round without being caught, or else become the man's wife.

Among the Sinambau Dyaks of Borneo there are ways of courting not unknown in European countries. For instance, when a young girl has taken the fancy of some man, he shows his preference by helping her in her daily labour in a chivalrous manner only too rare in Eastern countries. One day he will carry a load of wood for her; another day he performs some other useful task. Occasionally she receives a present from her admirer. When this state of affairs has lasted for some time, he resolves to declare his passion; for this purpose he steals out at night to the house where his lady-love lives, and gently awakes her as she sleeps. Her parents sleep in the same room; and if they approve of the suitor take no notice, pretending to be asleep. If they have any objection to him he is promptly told to depart. He brings with him betel nuts and other food. Should the young woman accept these, it is equivalent to saying she fancies him; but if it is otherwise, she tells him to stir the fire, or to light the lamp, which is only a polite way of bidding him beat a retreat.

The marriage ceremony opens with a little bit of symbolism. The bride and bridegroom are brought out and made to sit on two bars of iron previously laid down on the ground. This act implies that the two are being bound together with the iron band of matrimony. The priest gives to each a cigar and and some betel nuts, which they hold in their hands while he waves two fowls over their heads, and in the course of a lengthy address invokes every blessing upon them. The bridegroom then places the betel nut in the mouth of the bride, and the cigar between her lips, and in this way he publicly acknowledges her to be his wife. The two fowls are then killed, and omens taken from their blood. As among the Kaffirs and others, the husband must never pronounce the name of his father-in-law.

Among the Aheta of the Philippine Islands, when a man wishes to marry a girl, her parents send her before sunrise into the woods. She has about an hour's start, after which the lover goes off to seek her. If he succeed in finding her and bringing her back before sunset, the marriage is acknowledged. If not, he must abandon all claim to her.

These are not to be regarded as instances of "marriage by capture" pure and simple, as we see it at the present day among the Esquimaux or the aboriginal Australians, but as ceremonies in imitation of it and, as it were, commemorating the days when it actually did take place. We shall see how mock combats take place among the Druse people of Palestine and elsewhere. Examples might easily be multiplied. Thus, with the greater part of the nomads of Central Asia, and especially Turcomans, the young girl, clothed in her bridal costume, mounts a horse, and gallops off with a lamb or kid just killed at the saddle. The man and his party pursue her on horseback in hot haste, while she endeavours to out-distance them, and prevent them seizing the animal she has with her.

CHAPTER II

China

THE lives of the Celestials, as the Chinese style themselves, are very much ruled and influenced by certain notions with regard to spirits and the spirit-world. Their passionate desire for male children is essentially a religious sentiment. Not only do they consider, as the Jews of old did, that a man with a large family is highly blessed, but they believe that the spirits of the departed are rendered happy by the homage received at the hands of their male posterity. The worship of ancestors and parents is a very essential part of their religion, and particularly interesting as illustrating a primitive phase in religious ideas. The young people are taught that it is a sacred duty to marry and bring up children, *i.e.*, *male* children. At first sight this seems all very well; but unfortunately it is one of the reasons why the rich are allowed to have more than one wife—a custom undoubtedly tending towards that degradation of women which is one of the saddest features of Chinese life. Parents expect all their children to marry, whatever may be the state of their health. Archdeacon Gray, in his well-known "History of China," records the case of a young man belonging to a most influential family in Canton, whose parents were informed by the family physician that he had but a very short time to live. They therefore at once selected a day for his marriage. On that day his bride-elect was brought to the house with all the pomp and parade attending a wedding. The ceremony was no sooner over than the bridegroom was led back to his sick chamber where, in a few days, he died.

The Chinese now marry very young, though this appears to be contrary to the usages of antiquity and their Book of Rites. Here it is laid down that a man at twenty is not at his best; his reason is not fully developed—a truth which seems obvious enough, when we remember what undergraduates at our own Universities are at this age. The age recommended is thirty. At forty a man may be a magistrate in a small way; and at fifty he may be entrusted with some very responsible post. No lady may marry until she is fourteen years of age, but to be still unmarried at twenty-three is considered very wrong. It is a common thing for parents to arrange marriages for their children during infancy: and there are cases where two friends make a solemn promise, or take an oath, to unite in marriage the children of different sexes that may be born to them. It may perhaps be thought that such an arrangement is entirely unknown in our own country, but such is not the case, for the writer has been informed on very good authority that the famous naturalist Waterton married the daughter of an intimate friend, to whom he was pledged before her birth! The marriage was a happy one while it lasted, but Mrs. Waterton died a year or so afterwards.

A mandarin is not allowed to marry a woman in the province over which he bears rule. This law was made to prevent one family from obtaining undue influence over other families in the same district. Should he disobey this rule, or even take a secondary wife in his own district, the marriage is forthwith declared void, and, what is worse, he is "liable" to receive eighty blows with the stick! Whether he actually receives so degrading a punishment, for a man of his rank, we will not undertake to say. The rule may be "more honoured in the breach than in the observance," and official life is so corrupt that he can probably find some back-door way of escape. Actors, policemen, boatmen, and slaves, are forbidden to marry out of their own class. Men and women may not marry during the time of mourning for a relative. Marriages take place at all times of the year, but the eighth month is considered the most favourable. There is therefore a marriage season, as in India. When this time comes round, books containing songs in honour of matrimony are to be seen in the bookstalls. The Chinese appear to be firm believers in the doctrine that "marriages are made in heaven"; the reason for this probably lies in the fact that they are thorough fatalists, and so it seems to them quite credible that parents, in arranging the marriages of their children, are acting under the influence of fate or the will of heaven.

Occasionally it happens that, when a marriage has been arranged for a young man by his family, the parents of the affianced lady delay to make the necessary arrangements for the wedding—perhaps on account of their poverty. The would-be bridegroom becomes impatient, and, if he considers that there is no good reason for such delay, takes the law (or rather the girl) into his own hands, and carries her off by main force. Thus we have another relic of the ancient usage of "marriage by capture." Certain relatives, or trusty friends, go with him, to help if their aid should be required. He *must* do it himself, and so, having obtained an ordinary sedan chair, he lies in wait near her house. A blanket is also considered necessary, and this is thrown over her as soon as she appears on the scene—possibly "by request." Having thus seized his bride, he quickly makes off to his own home. No one interferes, unless it be her parents or brothers, but they only do so in a half-hearted kind of way. The young people are betrothed, so it is all right.

In some cases a mere hint of abduction is sufficient to bring the reluctant parents to terms. On the arrival of the bride at her new home, the wedding is celebrated much in the usual way. There is, however, a danger lest he should carry off the wrong girl, especially as the marriages are all arranged by match-makers. It is highly necessary for him to be careful, for a mistake of that sort would lead to prosecution and a heavy punishment.

Although, as a rule, marriages in China are arranged between the respective families, and, in many cases, the bridegroom never sees his wife until the marriage day, yet every rule has its exceptions. Love-matches and what we call run-away marriages are not altogether unknown. Betrothed young ladies have been bold enough to elope with some other swain ; it may be the son of a next-door neighbour who has already won the girl's admiration—perhaps even her heart. But, alas ! the penalties of the prison-house await them if they are discovered. Considering how marriages are usually made, it is not surprising to find that peace and harmony seldom reign at home. To say nothing of the many causes of jealousy and discord arising from the presence of several secondary wives—except among the poor—it must be evident that two people who, before marriage, were total strangers to each other, cannot be expected to live in perfect happiness together. The poor women have indeed much to bear. They live in great subjection to their masters, who often become fearful tyrants. In some parts of the country, a man is so afraid of being considered "mild" that he will even beat his wife in public, just by way of showing to his friends and neighbours that he means to be master in his own house. The Abbé Huc, who was a Jesuit missionary in China for many years, and had special opportunities for studying the people and their ways, says that he once saw a young woman covered with blood and apparently dying. On making inquiries, he learned that her husband had been beating her because he imagined that the neighbours were laughing at him for not having done so before.

With regard to jealousy and intrigues, Archdeacon Gray confirms the testimony of M. Huc. "Many indeed," he says, "are the heartrending scenes which I have witnessed in such homes." Upon the false accusation of a rival, the Chinese husband frequently expels a wife from his house, or sells her to some one else. A few young women are so keenly alive to the hideous wrongs inflicted on their sex that, with a courage which is much to be admired, they altogether refuse to enter the bonds of matrimony. The same missionary says that in one street in a suburb of Canton, he knew four families in which there were ladies who refused to marry. Some become nuns, others even commit suicide. For example, during the reign of Taou-kwang, fifteen girls who were betrothed, met together and resolved to die. They flung themselves into a tributary stream of the Canton River near the village where they lived. Their tomb, near Fo-chune, is called "the tomb of the virgins." In 1873 eight young girls, arrayed in their best attire, similarly put an end to their lives in the darkness of the night. It is very likely that within the last thirty years or more, things may have somewhat improved owing to contact with European nations, and perhaps the influence of missionaries. But there can be little doubt that when M. Huc wrote his experiences some thirty years ago, the lot of most Chinese women was very unhappy. These are his words, "The condition of Chinese women is most pitiable; suffering, privation, contempt, all kinds of misery and degradation, seize on her in the cradle, and accompany her to the tomb. Her birth is commonly regarded as a humiliation and a disgrace to the family—an evident sign of the malediction of Heaven. If she be not immediately suffocated, a girl is regarded and treated as a creature radically despicable, and scarcely belonging to the human race."

The principle of co-operation, or mutual help, is not unknown in the Celestial Empire, where both weddings and funerals often involve poor people in a ruinous expense. When a family cannot command enough ready money to pay the cost of a wedding properly conducted in a style suitable to its social position, a kind of Society is formed for the purpose of collecting the necessary amount. A friend, or relative, interested in the case "takes the hat round," as we should say. The old English and Scotch "Penny Wedding" was also conducted on the principle of mutual help (see Scotland, p. 318).

On the Canton and other rivers a large population lives on floating islands of timber, or reeds skilfully twisted together. These people are possibly of a different race, but their origin is involved in obscurity. By the Chinese they are looked upon as "outsiders," or pariahs; their children are not allowed to attend the usual examinations. Their women are called *Suee-Ki*, or water-fowl; but, nevertheless, the despised women are of much finer physique. The marriages of these people are attended with much religious observance. Priests attend for three days and three nights chanting prayers to "the Nine Kings," to whom the children are dedicated shortly after birth. There is a great deal of feasting, and the parents of the bridegroom will spend the savings of several years on such an occasion.

Among the upper classes in China there are at least six principal rites connected with marriage, but with the poor there is less of ceremony. The first thing is to arrange for the marriage. This is done by go-betweens in a manner to be described presently. Secondly, the name of the young lady, as well as the day and month of her birth, must be inquired of her parents. Thirdly, diviners must be consulted in order to report a happy augury to the parents of the girl. Fourthly, presents are sent as pledges of the young man's intention. Fifthly, the wedding day is appointed; and lastly the bride must be conducted in procession to the bridegroom's house. These are only the preliminaries, for the actual marriage ceremonies, all regulated by a code of observances from which no departure is allowed, have yet to be performed. The missives which are sent from one family to another show how accomplished the Chinese are in the art of polite letter-writing. Thus, according to the Abbé Huc in his "Chinese Empire," the father, when the name of his daughter is asked, is required to answer in the following manner :—

"I have received with respect the marks of your goodness. The choice that you deign to make of my daughter to become the wife of your son shows me that you esteem my poor and cold family more than it deserves. My daughter is coarse and stupid, and I have not had the talent to bring her up well; yet I shall nevertheless glory in obeying you on this occasion. You will find written on another page the name of my daughter, and that of her mother, with the day of her birth."

When he receives the presents and the information that a day is fixed for the wedding, the young man's father replies in these terms:—

"I have received your last resolution. You wish this marriage to take place, and I am only sorry that my daughter has so little merit, and that she has not had all the education desirable. I fear she is good for nothing; yet, nevertheless, since the augury is favourable, I dare not disobey you. I accept your present, I salute you, and I consent to the day appointed for the wedding. I will take care to make due preparation."

These polite letters are of such peculiar interest, and so different from our modern matter-of-fact epistles, that we venture to put before the reader another specimen, couched in very flowery language. It is given by Archdeacon Gray as a specimen, and is one of two such documents which fell into his hands. His translation of it is as follows:—

"The sun has long since risen, and the brightness

of his rays illumines the house wherein resides the fair. At this hour, too, she, like the sun, has left her couch and attired herself in a costume becoming the hour of the day, and her rank and station in life. Her face has gazed upon the mirror, which has reflected back upon her the beautiful features of which it is possessed. Indeed, all nature has now assumed a beautiful aspect, and all creatures, as is designed by nature, are now pairing. I write this as an evidence of my respect and devotion. Permit me, therefore, respectfully to congratulate you, my venerable relative, whose honourable family has resided for so many ages in Seng-Moon, or Yut Hoee, where its respected members have ever been distinguished for their literary attainments, their essays being written in a style almost unparalleled. Further, the essay of your son in particular has obtained for him high literary honours; but no wonder, as your ancestors were one and all men of distinction, and your descendants, therefore, cannot be otherwise than men of renown. Your own rank is also great, and your son will prove a worthy successor of the same. I, for my part, have been from boyhood slothful and indigent. I wander through the world as one without any fixed purpose, and the rank which I hold is of a degree more honourable than I deserve. Your daughter is gentle and virtuous, and as for my son, he is so weak in intellect as to be unworthy of her. But, as you, upon hearing the words of the match-maker, or go-between, thought him worthy, and at once consented to the engagement, it is only right that the union should take place. There will be unbroken friendship between me and you after the celebration of the marriage rites of our children. This is the day appointed for me to give, and for you to receive the customary presents. I therefore beg to forward them herewith. They are, however, of a very ordinary kind, and of no value. Indeed, I only forward to you, together with a few simple things, a wooden hairpin, and I am in truth ashamed that I have no jewels, precious stones, and silk fabrics to present. You will, I am sure, readily excuse me. When these, the preliminary ceremonies, have been observed, we shall anxiously await the wedding-day."

The period immediately preceding the happy (?) day is one of lamentation for the bride elect, her sisters, lady friends, and attendants. She must frequently declare that the thought of leaving her parents is more than she can bear; death itself would be preferable! And when we consider what Chinese wives have to put up with, these demonstrations of grief may, after all, be partly genuine. Ten to fifteen days is the time usually allowed for such an expression of filial love, but sometimes it is prolonged for a whole month. The Jewish people of old had a similar custom, as the following text will show: "And she shall put the raiment of her captivity from off her, and shall remain in thine house, and bewail her father and her mother a full month" (Deut. xxi. 13).

On the night preceding a wedding the young lady's attendants make such loud demonstrations of grief as to disturb many of their neighbours. On some lucky day her parents send the trousseau and many articles of furniture to the bridegroom's house. This is done with considerable ostentation, for the father is anxious that everybody should be made aware of his generosity. The things are carried in procession through the streets by men in red tunics. On the marriage day a wedding breakfast is prepared at the young man's house. Tables are arranged at the east and west sides of the dining-hall. Four wine cups, usually made of gourds, are placed on a table near the door of the house. These are called *hop kun*, or "uniting cups." Another table in the courtyard contains refreshments for the bridegroom, who now appears in the visitors' hall. Here he kneels down and bows to his father, knocking his head on the ground six times, receives at his hands a cup of wine, and is told to send for his bride in the following words: "Go, my son, and seek your wife, and behave in all things with prudence and wisdom." Years ago the young man went to fetch his bride, or met her procession on the way to his house; but this is rarely done now. So he merely sends the palanquin, or sedan-chair, which is often richly carved and highly ornamented, and always coloured red. It is brought to her house (sometimes on the preceding day) in a gay procession of servants and musicians. Various emblems are here used, each of which has an appropriate meaning. One is a small orange-tree heavily laden with fruit, and with strings of money hanging from its branches, emblematical of a large family and much worldly wealth. A picture of the *kee-lun*, a fabulous quadruped, is borne under a canopy, and very often it figures upon the bride's chair also. This beast, they say, always appears when a "wise man" is born; and so it is hoped that a sage may be born from the union. Other signs are a goose and a gander, emblematic of conjugal faithfulness (compare the Japanese two pheasants), and a dolphin, which means wealth and rank. Men in red tunics carry red boards on poles displaying in letters of gold the titles of the bride and bridegroom's ancestors. Some of the attendants carry torches, others large red lanterns containing lighted candles (lights are believed to keep away evil spirits) and red umbrellas and fans. It is a picturesque affair.

Since marriage is held in such high honour, every one must make way for the procession, even mandarins; any one who does not is liable to be beaten.

"The friend of the bridegroom," or "best man," as we should say, bears a letter written on red paper to the bride, bidding her come. This she must carefully keep; it is regarded much as "marriage lines" are with us. The bride enters the visitors' hall, where her parents are waiting for her. To them she makes obeisance (or performs the *kow-tow*); a cup of wine is given her, out of which she drinks, first pouring out a few drops as a libation, after the manner of the Greeks and Romans. While still kneeling, the father exhorts her to obey the commands of her father and mother-in-law, and holds forth on the duties of husbands and wives. The mother does the same

A Chinese Bridal Chair. *From a Chinese Woodcut.*

thing, saying, "Take courage, daughter, and be always submissive to the will of your husband." She may well speak of courage, for it must require no small degree of fortitude on the part of the poor little bride to face the life of submission that now lies before her! Then the father goes to the door to receive the bridegroom's friend, who enters, holding a goose in each hand. The bride retires to her chamber and presently appears veiled in red silk, so that her features are invisible. She enters the chair, escorted by female attendants, and the bridal procession proceeds with much demonstration and noise—shall we say music?—to the house of the bridegroom. On her arrival the man who will soon be her husband taps with his fan at the door of the chair or palanquin, the bridesmaids, or female attendants, open it, and *voilà!* the bride steps out, but still veiled. Then follows a curious ceremony. She is placed on the back of a female servant and carried over a slow charcoal fire, on each side of which are arranged a pair of shoes for her husband (which she has brought with her). Meanwhile another female servant raises over her head a tray containing chopsticks, rice, and betel nuts.

The bridegroom, seated on a high stool to show his superiority, receives his future wife, who must prostrate herself at his feet. He now removes the red silk veil, and for the first time sees her face. The pair are then conducted to the ancestral hall, where they prostrate themselves before the altar, on which are arranged the ancestral tablets; but the formal worship of ancestors takes place later, as we shall see. Heaven and earth are also adored. This act is very important, so much so that when people wish to express that a certain person is married, they commonly say, " He has adored the heavens and the earth."

In the bridal chamber are the orange tree, with its strings of money and the burning tapers that formed part of the procession. The two salute each other and take food together, namely, tea and cake. At seven o'clock in the evening a grand feast is prepared by the bride, who waits on her new parents as a servant. Having presented a cup of wine to her father-in-law, she kneels at his feet and prostrates herself, knocking her head on the ground. So also to her mother-in-law. It is then her turn to be entertained with food. A cup of wine is presented to her by the mother-in-law, but before receiving it she duly makes her obeisance. In some parts of China the couple retire to their private chamber to dine.

In the districts around Canton they have a singular custom, according to which neighbours, friends, or even strangers, are allowed to come in and see the bride during the evening. This is a trying ordeal, and appears not to be inflicted on brides of good family or daughters of officials. The people who come in pass remarks about her with singular freedom, and in a loud tone of voice. The remarks are not always complimentary, and often in very questionable taste. But she must take no notice, and behave in all things with the greatest composure. Strangers and friends may ask her riddles, and whenever she fails to give a correct answer she must pay a forfeit of cakes. In this way the unfortunate bride is often kept up half the night. The husband is absent during the evening, for he would very likely take offence at some of the remarks passed upon his wife. In many districts of the province of Canton the bride and bridegroom separate after the ceremonies, and must wait about three years before they can live together.

On the third day, at an early hour, the newly-married couple worship their ancestors in the ancestral hall, where, on a table, are placed the ancestral tablets. Looking towards these, the husband's father pours out libations and reads aloud a letter to the spirits of the ancestors, which is somewhat as follows: "My son has married, and all the ceremonies attendant upon such an occasion having been duly observed, I now therefore give command to him and his wife to render you homage, in the hope of propitiating you and prevailing upon you to grant them many blessings." The husband and wife kneel before the tablets and prostrate themselves. They must also pay homage to the husband's parents, the uncles, and the aunts.

On the same day it is their duty to pay a visit of ceremony to the wife's parents, accompanied by numerous servants carrying boxes of cake and fruits, roasted pigs and fowls. These are very important, and doubtless must be regarded as relics of marriage by purchase. Such presents, in many parts of the world, are the chief part of a marriage ceremony.

It may, perhaps, not be out of place here to mention a very singular custom which is common both to the Tartars and Chinese. Marko Polo, in his famous book, says, speaking of the former people, that when a boy and girl die who are betrothed to each other (rather a rare occurrence) the parents nevertheless arrange a grand wedding between the lad and the lass, just as if they were alive, and make a regular contract! When the contract papers are made out, they put them in the fire, in order that the betrothed ones, now in the spirit world, may look upon each other as man and wife! The respective parents then consider themselves relations by marriage. A dowry is even given, and those who pay it cause it to be painted on pieces of paper and then put them in the fire, in the belief that in this way the dead person will get all the real articles in the other world. According to Navarete, this is also a Chinese custom. It was described to him by a Jesuit, F. Michael Trigautius, who lived several years in the province of Shansi. The parents send the usual presents with much ceremony and music, as if the young couple were alive. After this they put the two coffins together, hold the wedding dinner, and lay them together in one tomb. The respective parents, from this time forth, are looked upon, not merely as friends, but as relatives just as they would have been had their children really married in life. Gray, who witnessed such a ceremony, gives a somewhat different account. According to him the effigies of the young people in paper were burned.

If a Chinese girl die after or during her betrothal, and before marriage, the young man goes through a marriage ceremony at his own house, the bride being represented by a paper effigy made by her parents. This is burned by the bridegroom, who erects a tablet to her memory—an honour forbidden to an unmarried person. In so large an empire we are sure to find occasional differences in the local usages. The sad event we are now dealing with affords a case in point. Thus, according to another writer, they observe a custom called "asking for her shoes." Her *fiancé* goes to the house of her parents, and, with tears running down his cheeks, approaches the coffin in which she lies. He asks for a pair of shoes recently worn; these are, of course, given. He then proceeds home with them, having three lighted sticks of incense in his hands. Arrived there, he informs her spirit of the fact, and puts the incense in a censer. A room is then chosen in which he places a table and a chair, and the precious souvenir is placed on, or under, the chair. On the table he puts a pair of lighted candles, and the censer with the incense brought from her home. At this little shrine, or altar, incense is burned for two years, after which a tablet to her memory is placed in the niche containing the ancestral tablets of his family. In that way she is supposed to become his wife, and her afflicted parents are satisfied. Girls are of so little account that we may suppose that the parents are not particularly grieved. If, on the other hand, the young man should die, that is, of course, quite another matter! In that case, his *fiancée* must live as an old maid in the house of his parents till the end of her days! Should she live beyond sixty years, her friends and relatives hold her in great honour. It is then usual for them to mark their appreciation of her great virtue by erecting to her a monumental arch. The imperial Government contributes towards the fund established for this purpose.

A Chinaman calls his brother's male children his "sons," but his sister's children he calls his "nephews." A curious relic of bygone days is the ceremony of lifting the bride over the threshold of her new home. We find this also in Great Britain and other countries: it is supposed by some to be a relic of marriage by capture (see p. 104). No two persons of the same name may marry in China. Widows who refuse to marry again, or rather to be sold again, are held in great honour. A betrothed maiden whose *fiancé* dies, is much esteemed if she buries herself in a lifelong sorrow. But she can win far greater glory by committing suicide!—a custom which of course is *not* recommended for men. *They* are never considered superfluous! In order to encourage such exemplary and useful self-effacement, tablets are erected in the temples to the memory of young girls who have been so virtuous as to kill themselves on the tombs of their betrothed ones, and twice a year, certain mandarins make oblations in their honour. Even at the present time, widows are known to put an end to their lives, but those who do so are generally without children or relatives.

In 1857 the *Pekin Gazette* published a decree according a tablet to the memory of the wife of a mandarin who had poisoned herself on hearing of the death of her husband in a battle against the rebels. In a country where female infanticide is practised, one need not be surprised at such deeds. The Chinese are a terribly cruel nation, in spite of their highly literary education, and appear to take a delight in witnessing executions. These unfortunate widows, if desirous of obtaining high honour, are expected to kill themselves in public with great pomp and solemnity. A month before the fatal day, the widow parades the town in this fashion: Two executioners head the procession, then come musicians, then men dressed in coarse linen tunics with hoods, carrying parasols, little pagodas, boxes of perfumes, and streamers. After them, a third executioner, followed by another group bearing poles surmounted by fantastic animals. At the end of the procession is a mandarin's palanquin, surrounded by numerous servants, of both sexes, dressed in mourning, that is, in grey linen. The heroine or widow sits in the palanquin, dressed in red, and wearing a blue crown. Her robe of satin is richly ornamented. But all this to-do is merely preliminary, and by way of announcement or invitation. On the day appointed the tragedy takes place in the presence of a great crowd.

The manner in which a wife is selected for the Emperor furnishes a remarkable instance of the difference between Chinese and Western ideas. Girls are by no means desirous of being chosen for empress and wearing the crown! Parents also have no such ambition for their daughters: and for very good reasons—not that they fear a fate like that of the wives of Henry the Eighth, but because when a young woman has been chosen by the Emperor for his bride, and she has been crowned queen, he keeps her in such seclusion in his palace that her relations seldom or never see her. And, not unnaturally, they think that crowns are dear at the price. Also it brings them into a position attended with many serious drawbacks, and even dangers; hence there are difficulties in the way of a Manchu emperor obtaining a bride. He acknowledges no other king as his equal, and so no prince's daughter can be his wife. He must select his wife from "the people," which seems strange in a country where rank is of so much importance. It is recorded that in recent times, when it was necessary to select a bride for a young emperor, the two dowager empresses issued orders to all the chiefs who had daughters of the desired age to send them to the palace. But, strange to say, when the day came, very few presented themselves! All sorts of polite excuses were made by the parents. Some alleged that their daughters were crippled, others that they were blind. In some cases lameness was successfully imitated,

A CHINESE BRIDE. *From a Photograph by Mr. T. Child.*

or deformities artificially produced. To such an extent was this carried that the empresses gave express orders that the lame and the halt, the blind and the dumb, were to be sent to the palace. The result was that on the day fixed about six hundred or seven hundred girls appeared, and of these about fifty were selected after a first inspection. It is hardly necessary to add that none of them were halt or lame or blind or deaf! The names of all were taken and the character and position of their parents inquired into. Their horoscopes were carefully calculated—a very important matter. After the second inspection, thirty were chosen out of the fifty. These were honourably entertained at the palace, and watched so that their individual traits could be studied. After a short stay, ten were sent home, and then ten more. At last the number was reduced to two, and one of these was chosen. One would think even then the result might not be highly satisfactory. The daughter of some prince or noble would be far more likely to make a good empress than a total stranger to court life.

Golden and silver weddings are almost as much observed in China as among the Germans or in England.

Our portrait of a Chinese bride is from a photograph by Mr. Thomas Child, of Chelsfield, Kent, who has kindly permitted us to reproduce it. The young lady's father was fortunately a man of liberal ideas, and allowed her to be photographed without the usual veil that hides the features of a bride. The big emblem behind the chair is *Shi*, the Chinese symbol for Happiness, which occupies a very prominent place in weddings, everything being marked with it. It is usually doubled, to denote "Double Happiness," though not here.

According to a missionary who has worked of late years in Formosa, the savages who inhabit the mountains of that island are all "head hunters," and a man is not, as a rule, allowed to marry until he has brought in at least one Chinese head—just to give proof of his courage and skill! But if the Chinese are unusually careful about their heads, and keep beyond spear-reach of the most daring brave, the chief may grant a special dispensation to any man who has distinguished himself in the chase of the deer and the wild boar. There is very little if any ceremony at a wedding, but the bride is gaily decked out.

CHAPTER III

Japan

IT is with a feeling of relief that we turn from the cruel conventions of a decaying civilisation, such as that of China, to consider the marriage customs of the bright, happy, and intelligent people of Japan. They lead far more natural lives than the Chinese, and consequently there is often much happiness among them, especially in the country districts. But for all that Japan is not a paradise. To the "new woman" it would doubtless appear nothing short of an Inferno! Whatever freedom may be allowed to girls, when once they are married they make very faithful wives. Japanese husbands expect the most complete subjection and obedience from their consorts; and they certainly get it, for every girl is carefully taught from her childhood that some day she must be an obedient and faithful, hard-working housewife. The result is highly successful. Whether this is due to a natural submissiveness on the part of Japanese wives, or whether their remarkable amiability may be accounted for by the effect of generations of training and veneration for tradition, we cannot say.

European notions are being so rapidly absorbed by these clever and observant people that it would appear as if all their old ways may have died out ere another generation grows up. It is therefore all the more desirable to record the ceremonies used at their marriages.

They marry early; but as a *mésalliance* is held to be utterly disgraceful, even in the middle classes, people are not unfrequently reduced to the necessity of espousing those whom they have never seen. Thus, the treasurer of Nagasaki has no precise equal in the place, consequently his children cannot ally themselves with the young people in the town, their acquaintances and associates; but he must procure them wives and husbands out of the families of men of his own rank in distant cities or provinces. When no such obstacle prevents the course of true love from running smooth, and a youth has fixed his affections upon a maiden of suitable condition, he declares his passion by affixing a branch of a certain shrub (*celastrus alatus*) to the house of her parents. If the branch be neglected, the suit is rejected; if it be accepted, so is the lover. And if the young lady wishes to express reciprocal tenderness, she forthwith blackens her teeth. But she must not pluck out her eyebrows until the wedding has been celebrated. At present the choice of a wife depends, in most cases, on the will of the parents, hence there are not many love-matches. But, in old days, the following custom prevailed in the province of Ozu. Whoever took a fancy to a girl wrote his name on a small board, and hid it between the mats in the ante-chamber of her house. These boards showed the number of her lovers, and remained there till she took away that of the man whom she preferred. When the branch has been accepted, or if the respective parents have agreed to unite their children, a certain number of male friends of the bridegroom are appointed as marriage brokers. These persons meet and arrange the terms of the marriage contract; and when they have agreed upon these, they carefully select two auspicious days, the first for an interview between the young people, the second for the actual ceremony. The match-maker, or middleman, becomes through life a sort of godfather to the young people. Customs, of course, vary a good deal according to the locality; but in some parts of Japan, the parties are not entirely unknown to each other before the tying of the "fatal knot," because the match-maker arranges for a meeting. This is called a "mutual seeing," and takes place at the house of the match-maker, or at some private house agreed upon by the respective parents. That is the correct way of doing it; but, among the middle and lower classes, a picnic, a party to the theatre, or a visit to the temple will serve instead. Sometimes the man is even allowed to speak to the young lady, a privilege which must be highly prized! If she fails to please, the projected match comes to nothing; if, however, the young lady objects, that is a trifling matter which the parents can easily overrule. If both parties are pleased gifts are exchanged. This constitutes a betrothal, and is considered binding. The next step is for the future bridegroom to send presents, as costly as his means will allow, to the bride. She immediately offers them to her parents, in acknowledgment of their kindness in her infancy, and of the pains bestowed upon her education. Thus, although the Japanese girl is not subjected to the usual Oriental degradation of being actually or apparently purchased from her father by her husband, a handsome daughter is still considered as rather to the fortune of the family. The bride, however, is not transferred quite empty-handed to her new home. Besides sending a few trifles to the bridegroom, in return for his splendid gifts, the parents of the bride, after ceremoniously burning their daughter's childish toys, (in token of her being "grown up"), provide a handsome trousseau, and bestow upon her certain articles of household furniture, such as a spinning-wheel, a loom, and the necessary utensils for the kitchen. On the wedding-day the bridal equipment is conveyed in great state to the bridegroom's house, and there exhibited.

With regard to the marriage-rites, the authorities we have consulted give somewhat different accounts. Thus, Isaac Titsingh, in his "Illustrations of Japan," says that there is no religious ceremony, but here he may be wrong. It is easy to conceive that, in such a country as Japan, a foreigner might frequently be invited to attend the formal ceremonies with which the bride is installed in her new home, without ever witnessing, or even hearing, of the religious ceremony.

A JAPANESE WEDDING: BRINGING HOME THE PRESENTS. *From a Japanese Engraving.*

Again, there may be one custom for Buddhists, and another for Shintoists, whose religion is the older. Some say that the civil contract must be registered in the temple to which the young people belong. According to Mr. J. M. W. Silver, the following ceremony takes place there: "The pair, after listening to a lengthy harangue from one of the attendant priests, approach the altar, where large tapers are presented to them; the bride, instructed by the priest, lights her taper at the sacred censer on the altar, and the bridegroom, igniting his from hers, allows the two flames to combine and burn steadily together, thus symbolising the perfect unity of the marriage state; and this completes the ceremonial." The bride, covered from head to foot in a white veil, is seated in a palanquin and carried forth, escorted by the marriage-brokers, her family, and the guests invited to the feast. The men are all arrayed in their ceremonial dress, the women in their gayest gold-embroidered robes. The procession parades through the greater part of the town, affording a very pretty spectacle. On reaching the bridegroom's house, the bride, still veiled, is accompanied by two playfellows into the state room, where, in the post of honour, sits the bridegroom with his parents and nearest relations. In the centre stands a beautifully-wrought table, with miniature representations of a fir tree, a plum tree in blossom, cranes, and tortoises. The first is a symbol of man's strength, the second of woman's beauty, whilst the tortoise and the crane appear to represent length of life and happiness. And now it is time for them to drink the *saki*, or wine—this is really the principal part of the ceremony. This is done with endless formalities, and the wine is poured out by two young women who are called "The Male and the Female Butterfly," probably emblems of conjugal faithfulness, since butterflies appear to fly about in pairs.

Perhaps the description of an actual eye-witness will be more acceptable to our readers; we therefore take the liberty of quoting the account of a well-known traveller, Miss Bird, in her book entitled "Unbeaten Tracks in Japan."

"Two young girls, very beautifully dressed, brought in the bride, a very pleasing-looking creature, dressed entirely in white silk, with a veil of white silk covering her from head to foot. The bridegroom, who was already seated in the middle of the room, near its upper part, did not rise to receive her, and kept his eyes fixed on the ground. She sat opposite to him, but never looked up. A low table was spread in front, on which there was a two-spouted kettle full of *saki*, some *saki* bottles, and some cups, and on another were some small figures representing a fir tree, a plum tree in blossom, and a stork standing on a tortoise. After this, which was only a preliminary, the two girls who brought in the bride handed round a tray with three cups containing *saki*, which each person was expected to drain till he came to the god of luck at the bottom. [This reminds us of the Hindu custom of placing the god of obstacles under the canopy.]

"The bride and bridegroom then retired, and shortly reappeared in other dresses of ceremony, but the bride still wore her white silk veil, which one day will be her shroud. An old gold lacquer tray was produced, with three *saki* cups, which were filled by the two bridesmaids [the male and the female butterfly] and placed before the parents-in-law and the bride. The father-in-law drank three cups, and handed the cup to the bride, who, after drinking two cups, received from her father-in-law a present in a box, drank the third cup, and then returned the cup to the father-in-law, who again drank three cups. Rice and fish were next brought in, after which the bridegroom's mother took the second cup and filled and emptied it three times, after which she passed it to the bride, who drank two cups, received a present from her mother-in-law in a lacquer box, drank a third cup, and gave the cup to the elder lady, who again drank three cups. Soup was then served, and the bride drank once from the third cup, and handed it to her husband's father, who drank three more cups, the bride took it again and drank two, and lastly, the mother-in-law drank three more cups . . . After this the two bridesmaids raised the two-spouted kettle and presented it to the lips of the married pair, who drank from it alternately, till they had exhausted its contents. This concluding ceremony is said to be emblematic of the tasting together of the joys and sorrows of life. And so they became man and wife till death, or divorce, parted them. This drinking of *saki*, or wine, according to prescribed usage, appeared to constitute the "Marriage Service" to which none but relations were bidden. Immediately afterwards the wedding guests arrived, and the evening was spent in feasting and *saki* drinking, but the fare is simple, and intoxication is happily out of place at a marriage-feast."

At a marriage ceremony, neither bride nor bridegroom wears any clothing of a purple colour, lest their marriage-tie be soon loosed, as purple, with them, is the colour most liable to fade.

According to Titsingh, the bridegroom must find some man clever at letter-writing who will indite for him a letter to his father-in-law in some such terms as these :—

"I have the letter which you have sent me, in which you inform me that you are glad that all the ceremonies which were to take place up to this day are over. The vessel of *saki* and the tray of fish (or whatever the present may be) which you have sent me have been received by me in very good condition. I return you, with all my heart, my humble thanks for them. I flatter myself that we shall soon have an opportunity of speaking to one another. My father also presents you his thanks, through him, who has the honour to be, with the highest respect,"

(The name and signature).

(The date).

The bride also has with her a person acquainted with the usual wording of letters of this kind. Her epistle is to the same effect. It is a strict matter of etiquette that in these letters no other subject whatever should be introduced.

It is hardly necessary to say that there are many superstitions with regard to marriage observed by young girls ; one of them is that nothing will induce a girl to pour tea over a bowl of "red rice," for if she did so her marriage day would be sure to be rainy.

CHAPTER IV

Persia and Arabia

IN a country like Persia, where women are strictly veiled, love-matches are somewhat rare; in spite of all precautions, however, such things do occasionally take place. Although shrouded from head to foot in a great blue sheet, and wearing a calico or cambric veil a yard long, a little aperture partly covered by threads across the eyes enables the Persian belle to see other people. If inclined to flirt, she can do so, and will find some way to reward an admiring passer-by with a glance at her features. Hence it sometimes happens that a marriage is the result of some early attachment. Cousins frequently marry, and such unions are considered natural and proper because the young people have generally been brought up together, almost as brother and sister. In justice to the people of Persia let it be said at the outset that their women are hardly such down-trodden creatures as they are generally supposed by Europeans to be. The wife is not a slave to her lord, nor yet a mere toy, but his friend and counsellor, and, if a capable person, may rule his household. In most cases a young girl is betrothed to a man of her own class; if a merchant's daughter she marries the son of a merchant, and so on; but personal attractions are greatly sought after, and a poor girl, if exceptionally good-looking, may be as fortunate as Cinderella, though probably not so happy.

Married women have no objection to wearing the veil; in fact, they would not or dare not drop the custom. Without this protective covering they would be considered neither modest nor respectable. In the higher ranks of life women are often well educated; they delight in all domestic duties, such as cooking. Barring a taste for scandal, very little can be said against them, and they appear to win the love and admiration of their husbands and children.

When a wife becomes the mother of a son her position is greatly improved, and greater freedom is allowed to her. For example, she can then go about if accompanied by her child and her mother, or mother-in-law.

Betrothals are arranged by match-makers as in so many other countries. These are crafty old women who know how to drive a hard bargain, and they get a "commission" from the parents on each side.

Child-marriages are frequent. There is, first of all, a marriage contract or legal ceremony; the wedding itself may take place on the same day, in the evening, or, if the bride is a child, some years later. The former ceremony sometimes takes place in the open air, the women veiled; or it may be in a room, the bride being screened off by a curtain. A *mullah*, an official of the Mosque, reads out the contract which he himself has drawn up somewhat as follows: "It is agreed between Hassan the draper, who is agent for Houssein the son of the baker, 'that he Houssein hereby acknowledges the receipt of the portion of Nissa the daughter of Achmet the grocer." Then follows a list of the bride's property, in which a copy of the Koran and a certain amount of silk are always included. In case of her death or divorce the husband surrenders it all to her family or to herself. When both parties have given their consent to the bargain, in the presence of their relations and friends, the *mullah* thus pronounces them to be legally married:—

"Then, in the name of God, the Compassionate, the Merciful, and of Mahommed the prophet of God, I declare you A. and you B. to be man and wife." The document is then sealed. This is followed by a feast, at which no small amount of tobacco is consumed by the men, and of sweetmeats by the women (in their separate apartment). There is no music on this occasion.

On the wedding-day great preparations are made for the entertainment of a large party, both in the men's court and in that of the women.

The poor are not neglected on these occasions, but come in for a share of the good things. The entertainment takes place at the house of the bride's family. Great is the variety of the drinks consumed, tea, ices, and sherbets being the favourites. The latter are fruit-syrups delicately scented and sweetened, and may be made from roses, oranges, lemons, pomegranates, cherries, and other fruits. "All is ready; the master of the house, dressed in his best, gives a last anxious glance at the preparations, and has an excited discussion with his wife, or wives. He waves his hand to the musicians and hurries to a seat near the door, to be ready to welcome his guests; the music strikes up a merry tune (it is an air, barbaric but inspiriting). The tremendous din of the *dohol* (drum) is heard at intervals. Then in a loud scream rises the voice of the principal solo singer, who commences one of the sad love songs of Persia in a high falsetto voice. His face reddens with his exertions, which last through a dozen verses. His eyes nearly start from his head, the muscles of his neck stand out like ropes; but he keeps correct time on the big tambourine, which he plays with consummate skill. The rest of the musicians watch his every movement, and all join in the chorus of 'Ah! Lalla, Lalla, you have made roast meat of my heart!'

"The music is the signal to the invited guests; they now commence to arrive in crowds. The music and singing proceed, and go on unceasingly for some ten hours till the bride leaves for her husband's home. As the guests pour in the host receives them with transports of pleasure; all the extravagant compliments of Eastern politeness pass between them. 'May your wedding be fortunate!' 'You are indeed welcome; this is a never-to-be-forgotten honour to me your slave!'

"In they pour, the men in their best; the women, closely veiled, pass on unnoticed by the men into the *anderin*, where they unveil and appear to their delighted hostesses in their finest clothes, and all their jewelry, and, we are sorry to add, in most cases with their faces carefully painted."[1] Here buffoons and musicians are the only men allowed; the former bring performing bears, or monkeys, or even a wretched, half-starved lion, cowed by much beating.

Before dinner is served the bride goes to the bath accompanied by female relatives and friends. At night, as the procession of the bridegroom approaches, alms are distributed, and women and children look from neighbouring roofs. Loud cries from the women welcome the bridegroom on his arrival, while the bride, carefully veiled, mounts the horse awaiting her at the door. All the men who have been feasted and entertained join in the procession, in which lanterns are borne. The bride's departure is the signal for the discharge of fireworks and a great beating of the big drum. The final ceremony is similar to one observed by the Arabs and the Kopts, namely, the sacrifice of sheep; these are killed as the bride steps over the threshold of her new home. One wonders what is the idea underlying the sacrifices. Are they intended as acts of propitiation inherited from an earlier age, when people thus endeavoured "to appease the anger of the gods" or of the spirits of their ancestors? or is it

[1] "Persia as it is," 1887, by C. J. Wills, M.D., many years a resident medical officer in the country.

merely a way of sealing in blood an important act and covenant?

In October, 1867, the heir to the throne of Persia was married to his cousin, both of them being only sixteen years of age, and the wedding was celebrated with great pomp. The bride's cavalcade, on leaving her home, was preceded by about one hundred horses, mules, and camels, carrying servants, tents, carpets, &c.; then followed many led horses covered with rich trappings. The Princess's carriage, with the blinds down, was drawn by six horses, and followed by mules carrying palanquins closed with curtains, which contained the women of her suite. And lastly came a large number of officers and dignitaries on horseback. The players made music with their violins, trumpets, and tambourines. The journey took thirty-three days. On her arrival the Princess was temporarily lodged in a palace. Public rejoicings preceded the marriage, and on the wedding-day, three hours after sunset, the bride was conducted in a torch-light procession to the palace of the bridegroom.

The women of Afghanistan go about unveiled, and a young man may choose a partner for himself without the aid of a match-maker, or even of his parents. If some girl takes his fancy, all he has to do is to cut off a lock of her hair or throw a sheet over her, and proclaim the damsel his bride. He must then make a bargain with the father before he is allowed to take her to his home.

The Tartars who inhabit the highlands of Asia Minor have a peculiar custom. On the day when the bride enters her new home, she and her husband go to meet one another, each accompanied by their respective relatives on horseback. When the bridegroom is sufficiently near to the bride, he throws an apple, or orange, at her, and wheeling round his horse, gallops off to his own tent, while the men of the bride's party follow in hot pursuit, for whoever overtakes him before he reaches home is entitled to his horse, saddle, and clothes. When the bride arrives at her husband's tent, the women of her party implore her not to get down from her horse, while her husband's family entreat her to do so. Every male relative of his brings her a present, begging her at the same time to give up part of the dowry settled on her by her husband. The bride is usually too prudent to forego all of it, but for the sake of courtesy, gives up a small portion.

Some of the Kurds inhabiting the Eastern Highlands of Asia Minor, a hardy and brave mountain race, treat their wives very well. The marriage ceremony is nothing more than a few words uttered in the presence of a priest. One sect, the Zezidi, are less strict than others with regard to the importance of the marriage-tie, and the men do not forget the possibility of a divorce. For this reason it is said that the bridegroom, when pronouncing the marriage-oath, stands in running water, to signify that he thus washes away the binding nature of the promise, and therefore renders the breach of it less sinful. The ceremony takes place before a Sheikh of their creed, who, at its conclusion, receives from the bridegroom a loaf and gives him in return a consecrated one which the man and woman share between them.

Arabs entertain no very high opinion of women. They have a saying as follows: "Marriage is joy for a month, and sorrow for a life, and the paying of settlements, and the breaking of one's back (*i.e.* under the load of misery), and the listening to a woman's tongue!" It is not surprising, therefore, to find that Arab marriages are "arranged" as in so many other countries where "women's rights" have never yet been heard of.

The Arab marriage customs of present times are especially interesting inasmuch as they explain passages in Holy Scripture where weddings are referred to. For instance, in the plain on the coast of Palestine below Jaffa where the Philistines used to dwell, a marriage feast still continues for seven days, as that of Samson did, amidst songs, dances, and rough jollity, in which putting and answering riddles forms a prominent part. The wedding of this great strong man appears to have resembled one of the present day among the peasants of the Haurân. The scene was the open-air threshing floor, the company made up chiefly of "friends" of the bridegroom! We may picture bride and bridegroom crowned as king and queen of the sports, sitting on the threshing sledge on a mock throne. Quarrels often arise, as on that occasion, and sometimes lead to bloodshed.

A Bedouin always marries one of his own class. The sending of Eliezer to Mesopotamia to get a wife for Isaac was exactly what the Sheikh of an Arab tribe would do at this day. The reader will remember, also, how Rebekah got off the camel and veiled herself because she could not allow Isaac to see her face till she became his wife. And not until the wedding is over may the husband enter the tent where his bride awaits him and raise her veil. Women anxiously await outside, and when the bridegroom has announced to them that he is pleased with his bride set up a shrill cry of delight. To the Arabs this shout of the triumphant and satisfied bridegroom is one of the most delightful sounds that can be uttered. It is to this our Saviour alludes when He says, "He that hath the bride is the bridegroom; but the friend of the bridegroom, who standeth and heareth him, rejoiceth greatly *because of the bridegroom's voice.*"

Again at Nablus, the bride is brought home at night, as in the parable of the Virgins. Drums, fifes, shouts and rejoicings break the stillness as late as ten o'clock. Young and old run out to see the procession, the maidens in their best attire, the bridegroom and his friends, the bride, deeply veiled, the musicians, the crowd, and above all, the flaming lights, which give animation to the whole scene.

Mr. Burckhardt, the traveller, says that among the Aenezes the bridegroom comes with a lamb in his arms to the tent of the bride's father, and there cuts its throat before witnesses. As soon as the blood falls upon the ground the marriage ceremony is regarded as complete. Afterwards the men and girls amuse themselves with feasting and singing. Soon after sunset the bridegroom awaits the bride in his tent. The bashful girl meanwhile runs from the tent of one friend to another's, till at last she is caught and conducted by a few women to her lord and master. In Egypt the Kopts kill a sheep as soon as the bride enters the house of her husband, and she is obliged to step over the flowing blood on (to) the threshold (see p. 66).

Among the Bedouins of Mount Sinai, if a man wishes to marry a certain girl, he must call, accompanied by a few friends, on her father. On their arrival at the tent they are offered some refreshment. The suitor then explains that he would be glad if the man will have him for a son-in-law, to which the father replies, "I shall require (say) one hundred piastres of you as a dowry. This, the young man explains, with considerable animation, is a sum quite beyond his modest resources. When at last the father has consented to lower his terms to about half the sum mentioned, they agree and the bargain is concluded. When the young men of the party find that matters have been settled, they express great delight, and engage in trials of skill and various games. The public notary is then called in, who takes a piece of a certain herb and wraps it in the turban of the bridegroom. He ratifies the covenant between father and bridegroom in the following manner: Taking both their hands in his, he places between them the folded turban, and, pressing them closely together, thus addresses the father of the bride-elect, "Are you willing to give your daughter to"—mentioning the name. To which he replies, "I am." The bridegroom to be is also asked, "Do you take the girl to wife for better or worse?" On his replying, "I do take her," the notary says, "If you ill-treat her, or stint her in food or raiment, the sin be on your own neck." These questions and answers are repeated three times, after which the betrothal (if such it can be called!) is considered complete.

The girl until then is entirely ignorant of the fact that she is going to be given in marriage. If by chance she should find out what has happened, custom demands that she should at least make a pretence of escaping to the mountains. But she does not exactly do so, as we shall see, unless she entertains a strong dislike for her suitor. Therefore, if such is not the case, the girl continues to perform her daily labours as before. Supposing that everything has been carefully concealed from her, she is informed of the change that is in store for her in the following not very gentle manner: The notary, with the would-be bridegroom's mantle in his hands, come stealthily behind her, as she sits in the family tent in the evening on her return from tending the flocks, and suddenly throws it over her. Previously to this her relations have been surreptitiously burning incense or some lighted embers behind her to avert the dread influence of the "evil eye." On throwing the mantle over her, the notary says, "The name of God be with thee; none but such an one (naming the man) shall have thee!" Thereupon the girl starts up and tries to escape, calling upon her father and mother for help with loud cries and shrieks. Women collect round her and seize hold of her, repeating noisily the notary's words.

The next proceeding is to erect a tent for her in front of that of her father, to which she is conducted, and then sprinkled with the blood of a sheep sacrificed for the occasion. Here she abides for three days, and on the fourth day is led in procession by the women to some neighbouring spring where she washes herself. They then lead her to the tent of the bridegroom, who gives a great feast in her honour. The neighbours also kill a sheep as a contribution to the entertainment, and receive a small sum of money from the bride's father; who also gives the bridegroom a branch of a shrub, or something green, which he puts in his turban and wears for three days to show that he has married a maid and not a widow.

According to the late Professor E. H. Palmer, the distinguished Arabic scholar, whose death a few years ago was greatly lamented, the only tribe who depart in any degree from the customs here described are the Emzeineh Arabs; with them, the girl, instead of remaining three days in a tent near her father, does actually run away and hide in the mountains.

We have said that Arab marriages are always "arranged" and that is true; but, nevertheless, their women are not entirely unromantic. Occasionally it does happen that a young girl falls in love with a man she has met—it may be at some festival or at the tomb of a saint. In that case, if her parents should betroth her to another, she takes advantage of the three days' grace allowed and escapes to some neighbour, who will pity her and take her in · and she stays, obstinately refusing to leave until the man she so dislikes relinquishes his claim. Her relatives, not wishing to force her into the marriage against her will, make terms with the disappointed lover as best they can. The story of Jebel el Benát or "the Girls' Mount" affords an interesting example of these occasional romances. Two girls, who were betrothed to men they heartily disliked, found their way to the mountains and there perished of hunger rather than prove faithless to their lovers. Burckhardt says they twisted their hair together and threw themselves from the cliffs, but this part of the story is now forgotten in Sinai.

Mr. Layard, in his "Nineveh and Babylon," describing a marriage celebrated near Nimroud, says that the bride and bridegroom entered into a legal contract in the presence of witnesses. On the following day the bride, covered from head to foot by a thick veil, was escorted by her friends, with music, to the bridegroom's house. Here she was actually kept behind a curtain, in the corner of a darkened room, for three days! During all that time the guests were feasting. The courtyard of the house was filled with dancers and players. On the third day the bridegroom was led in triumph from house to house, and at each received some present. He was then placed within the circle of dancers, and the guests, wetting small coins, stuck them on his forehead. As the money fell it was collected in a handkerchief held open under the bridegroom's chin. Then followed a curious episode. A party of young men rushed into the crowd, and carrying off the most wealthy guests, proceeded to lock them up in a dark room until they paid ransom for their release, which they did without any ill-feeling. All the money collected was added to the dowry.

CHAPTER V

Turkey and Syria

THE ceremonies attending a Turkish wedding are thoroughly Eastern, and it would be easy to point out resemblances to customs which have been already described in our accounts of China, or Japan, Arabia and more especially Persia. The go-betweens or match-makers play an important part. They are generally old women who visit one harem after another hawking such articles of commerce as the fair ladies are likely to require, and so they have exceptional opportunities for arranging marriages. Nor are the harems their only happy hunting ground, for they sometimes look in at the schools. An English teacher once saw an old woman enter a class in a Turkish school, walk round the table, and look searchingly at the elder girls. On inquiry the teacher was told that the old lady was "looking out for a wife for somebody." When a mother wishes to get her son married she visits the harems with a match-maker and some of her relatives, and has a good look round. Having found a girl who seems suitable, she informs the mother, who is usually one of the inmates of the harem, and is received by her with the utmost courtesy. But if the girl selected should be a younger daughter it is the custom to offer the eldest first. We will suppose, however, in order to simplify matters, that she is the eldest. Presently the favoured one enters, arrayed in her best attire, and is presented to the honoured guests. She kisses their hands and offers them coffee. On her disappearance it is usual to make very complimentary remarks, such as, "What a beauty!" or to compare her to the full moon. The slightest criticism would be considered quite out of place. Then the young man's mother, who has the advantage because her son is not present, gives an exaggerated account of his character and position, stating at the same time the amount of the dowry to be settled on the young lady. She also makes inquiries with regard to the amount of her fortune, if any. On taking leave she remarks, "If it is their *kismet* (fate) they may become better acquainted." Should the negotiations proceed favourably, presents are exchanged between the two parties; the future mother-in-law visits the house bringing with her several yards of red silk and some sugar-plums. The silk having been spread out on the floor, the bride-elect steps upon it, kisses the hand of her future mother-in-law, and receives her blessing, also some sweets. One of these she bites in two, keeping the one half and returning the other as a love-token for her future husband. After a few days the young man sends a present of money as a contribution towards the wedding expenses. The civil marriage takes place eight days after the betrothal. A contract is drawn up in which the husband states the amount he settles on his wife in the event of his death, or if she should be divorced, and the document is duly witnessed. He declares before the priest (*imam*) three times his willingness to wed the young lady; and she replies three times, in answer to the priest's questions, stating her willingness to marry the man who has been chosen for her. But she is invisible, and her answers come from the door of the women's apartments. Thus is the civil marriage effected; but the bride and bridegroom are not allowed to meet until the marriage festivities are ended, and that may not be for several weeks—in some cases, many months.

A week before the wedding-day, the bridegroom sends the wedding-dress to the bride's house. The festivities begin on a Monday, and on that day the bride's parents (as in China) send the trousseau and a number of useful domestic articles to the future home of their daughter. These are borne in procession by porters. They also decorate the bridal chamber very elaborately. On Tuesday the bride is taken to the bath by her lady friends. On Wednesday her mother receives the female friends of the bridegroom, who are led into a room to which the bride is presently brought. She kisses

A TURKISH BETROTHAL ENTERTAINMENT; A FEMALE JESTER MAKING FREE COMMENTS ON THE BRIDE AND HER FUTURE HUSBAND. *From a Drawing by Sidney P. Hall.*

the hands of her mother-in-law and takes a seat by her side. The elder women give sugar to the mother-in-law and transfer it from her mouth to that of her daughter-in-law, as a symbol of sweet and pleasant relations between them. These friends then depart, and coins are scattered to the beggars who wait round the house; but they return in the evening to witness the ceremony of the *henna*. On their arrival a taper is given to one of the party, and a procession is formed with the bride at its head to the garden, where they wind in and out among the flower beds, while the gipsy-players make strange music and the dancing girls practise their graceful art. The effect is said to be most beautiful.

The *henna* ceremony, or application of the *henna* mixture then takes place; the mother of the bride applies the paste to her hands and feet, and when the skin has been stained to a deep orange colour, it is washed off. Meanwhile the guests look on at a certain dance called the *sakusum*. On the next day (Thursday) the bride leaves her home; just before departing her father puts a girdle on her, and both father and mother weep over her while she lies at their feet—apparently overcome with grief. Arrived at the bridegroom's house, she is expected, for the sake of appearances, to show great reluctance to enter. Some brides have been known to boast how much pressing they required on this occasion, and it is on record that husbands have had to wait for a whole hour! The bridegroom, after receiving her, returns to the men's quarters while the ladies inspect her trousseau, and then he attends the mosque. After the fifth prayer he may enter the harem and see his bride for the first time. It is said that, on proceeding to the women's apartments, he upsets a bowl of water on the stairs and scatters it in all directions. The bride is now expecting her husband, who is led to her, in the gaily decorated nuptial chamber, by a matron. This person raises the bride's veil from off her face and spreads it out on the floor, so that the husband may kneel on it while he offers up a prayer, the bride standing meanwhile on its edge and behind his back. It is said by a writer on Eastern life that on this occasion a curious little trick is played by the bride, and one which has its counterparts in China and in Russia ; for before her husband raises the veil to get a glimpse of her features, she slyly advances her foot and tries to tread on his toe. If she succeeds in so doing, it is considered that she will be the ruler at home ! From this it appears that the veil is not *always* raised by the old woman, as is stated above ; but there are sure to be little differences according to the locality. The matron has not yet departed, for she has another little ceremony to perform, namely, showing them their reflections in a mirror while she knocks their heads together so that the images may appear united. They then put lumps of sugar in their mouths and pass them to each other. At last, the old matron retires and they are left alone.

On the following day a reception takes place, and the

newly-married couple eat together at "the feast of the sheep's trotters."

The Armenians do not, as a rule, allow their daughters much freedom, and in consequence marriages are in most cases "arranged," the go-between being usually a priest. But in Smyrna and Constantinople, where young people are allowed to see more of each other, it need not be surprising to learn that they sometimes settle their own fate. Armenians believe in lucky times for marriages, and since these occasions are few and far between, it follows that a large number of couples are sometimes united in a single day. An English traveller once saw sixty bridegrooms at the altar rails awaiting their brides; and on that occasion a most unfortunate mistake was made. Two brides of similar height somehow changed places and were each married to the man engaged to the other. Divorce is not allowed in this country, and so a pretty but poor peasant maid became the wife of a comparatively rich middle-class man, while a wealthy but plain lady was united to a blacksmith!

The wedding celebrations usually begin on a Friday, the actual marriage taking place on the following Monday. As with Turks and others the bride is taken by her companions to the bath. Saturday is devoted to feasting, in which the poor are not forgotten. On Sunday there is still more feasting. The young men wait upon the girls, who sit down first; then the married couples and lastly the young men.

Monday evening is devoted to the religious ceremony. The bride's dress is very curious; her whole figure is enveloped in crimson silk, a silver plate resting on her head. Also a large pair of cardboard wings, covered with feathers, are fastened on to her head. The ring and wedding garments are blessed by the priest, as a precaution against the tricks of evil spirits, of which we shall have more to say presently. And now the disguised bride is conducted back to the reception room to begin the dance with her father, or nearest relative, while the others throw coins at her. Then the bridegroom, whose wedding garments have been consecrated, is led up to the bride by her mother, for the second betrothal, which may be thus briefly described. The priest, after reading the 89th Psalm, places the right hand of the bride in that of the bridegroom with these words:—

"When God presented Eve's hand to Adam, Adam said, 'This is now bone of my bone, and flesh of my flesh.' . . . What therefore God hath joined together let no man put asunder." A small cross is then tied upon their foreheads. Arrived at church, the first part of the ceremony takes place in the porch. The 122nd Psalm is read, and the bridal pair, after confessing their sins, receive absolution. An exhortation follows, after which the priest asks each separately whether he or she will remain faithful to the other, "though that one become blind, sick, crippled, or deaf," receiving the answer "yes." Joining their hands he then offers up certain prayers and leads them to the altar. The wedding mass is celebrated ; bride and bridegroom are crowned and receive the sacrament. On arrival at the bridegroom's house a sheep is sacrificed at the threshold, as among the Arabs, and the party step over its blood. Having taken their seats side by side on a sofa, the husband and wife now drink a cup of consecrated wine together. The guests come and offer their felicitations. The bride is still enveloped in her red silk, and now a baby boy is laid on her lap with the words, "May you be a happy mother." Then they all dance, the bride leading off with her husband.

For several days following, the newly-married pair must submit to the tedious ceremony of "wearing the crowns." This may last as long as eight days, but, as a rule, the priest removes the crowns (which have been worn day and night) on the following Wednesday evening. At this, the final ceremony, the priest brings their heads together till their foreheads touch, rests a sword and a cross upon them, gives a blessing, and warns them against unfaithfulness. The cross is the holy symbol of their religion, while the sword reminds them of the swift and sure punishment of God should they not keep true to their vows. Again consecrated wine is drunk, and now, at last, they are left alone.

Armenians have a curious custom with regard to the bride's father-in-law. A bride may not speak to any of her husband's relatives until she has first asked and obtained permission from the father-in-law, and on giving this permission he bids her lay aside the veil.

But it is *said* that this important person sometimes sternly refuses his consent, and that many a bride has gone through married life without ever speaking to the parents of her husband! Doubtless we have here a relic from prehistoric days when a father-in-law was "taboo" as he still is in certain countries. With regard to the custom previously alluded to of blessing the wedding garments, it appears that here also is a relic of prehistoric superstitions. These people—at least the peasants—seem to have a strong belief in evil spirits (*djins*), which are supposed to be particularly busy during the first forty days of married life. Also at night, so that newly married couples do not venture out after dark, unless accompanied by some responsible relative. Both Mussulmans and Armenians say that, unless a new garment is blessed, the *djins* will come and steal it, and of this they are quite convinced. There is a story to the effect that these mischievous beings once spirited away an old Turkish woman and kept her in an underground palace for three days. On her return she told her friends of the strange scenes she had witnessed, and assured them that the *djins* wore clothes stolen from human beings. It seems to the author that we have here legends based on facts which of late years have been brought to light by archæologists and others. There undoubtedly were once "little people" (fairies) living in underground dwellings, who stole whatever they could lay their hands upon and were very active at night. The author has dealt with this subject in his previous work entitled "Prehistoric Man and Beast," to which the reader, desirous of information, is referred.

Among the Druses of Mount Lebanon, when one of their Sheikhs wishes to marry, he sends a messenger to the father of the girl that takes his fancy, and demands his consent. On being accepted as son-in-law he sends the young woman presents of clothes and jewels as a pledge of fidelity. On the day appointed for the wedding, a contract is drawn up with the father and signed by witnesses. Before this contract is read out some passages from the Koran are recited in order to give a kind of religious sanction, according to the Mohammedan custom, to which religion the Druses outwardly conform.

The bride, veiled and mounted on horseback, and attended by a long train of attendants of both sexes, proceeds to the abode of her future husband. Here for a week or so festivities have been going on. As soon as the bride approaches, the entire body of tenants and dependants of the Sheikh advance to meet her, and the meeting takes place at a distance of a mile or two from the houses. Both parties being liberally supplied with blank cartridges, a mock fight takes place. Extending in skirmishing order the Druses now display all the tactics of guerilla warfare, both in attack and defence. Rocks, trees, and eminences of any kind are successively secured and abandoned until the bride-groom's party is gradually driven back to his village, which is vigorously defended. At length, amidst shouts of exultation, and a deafening discharge of musketry, the bride comes up and is borne along pell-mell into the harem. Some two or three thousand men are now collected on the scene; those on foot hastily arrange themselves on either side, while the Druse Sheikhs, on their high-bred Arab steeds, their spirit aroused by the mimic warfare in which they have been engaging, commence the game called *jereed* with great zeal. They are naturally anxious to exhibit their skill and prowess before the assembled vassals, and not altogether unconscious that from the high latticed windows of the harem many a dark eye is looking down upon them with no small admiration.

Meanwhile the bride, having received the caresses and congratulations of her new relations, is conducted to a separate chamber and placed on a divan with a large tray of sweetmeats and confectionery before her, after which the women all retire and she is left alone with a veil of muslin and gold over her head and shoulders. Presently she hears footsteps at the door; it opens, her husband approaches, lifts the veil from her face, takes one glance—and withdraws. Returning to the reception room he takes his seat among the guests. Pipes and coffee are handed round, and all present offer their good wishes. He, however, maintains an imperturbable silence, his mind is supposed to be entirely absorbed by one engrossing object—the bride. His brother, who sits by his side, makes the necessary acknowledgments.

When the Sheikhs have dined, others come in and are

hospitably entertained. Musicians come in the evening, and it is midnight before the party breaks up. All the Sheikhs make presents to the bride, according to their means. Lady Burton, who once witnessed a Druse wedding, says [1] that the women take a great delight in preparing the bride. The Turkish bath, the diet, the plucking of the eyebrows, the *henna*, and the hosts of cosmetics, are studies in which all the harem take the greatest interest. Old women are always employed in these matters, and they like to show how much they have learned. She also describes a most exciting romp which took place in the harem, where the wives screamed, and pinched and pulled one another about, just like a lot of school girls.

Dr. W. M. Thomson [2] describes how, on one of his journeys in the Holy Land, a little girl of twelve years, the daughter of his guide, accompanied his party on foot. She was a bride-elect, and her father was taking her to her future husband, who had purchased her for about forty dollars. Except a young donkey she had no companion or friend of any kind. Arrived at the camp, she was immediately taken to the harem of her lord and master, the Sheikh. She had no outfit, and even discarded the boots in which she started from her mother's tent.

Syrian ladies lead a life of great seclusion ; they are closely veiled from head to foot when they go abroad. As a rule, a man cannot eat with his wife and daughters,

[1] "The Inner Life of Syria, Palestine, and the Holy Land."

[2] "The Land and the Book."

because the meal is in a public room, and strangers may be there. Moslem women never join in the prayers at church ; they are accommodated with a part railed off, and a lattice shields them from the public gaze. The jealousy of their husbands goes to great lengths. For example, a Druse Sheikh, or wealthy Moslem, when he calls for a physician for any lady of his harem, makes a great mystery of the matter. Should the doctor ask to see the poor creature's tongue, there is much manœuvring to avoid exposure. Sometimes she thrusts her tongue through a rent in the veil made for the purpose. Again, it is considered quite improper for an unmarried lady to show any special regard for her future husband. Arabs give very poetic names to their daughters, such as sun, moon, star, rose, lily, diamond, or pearl. Married women think a great deal of ornaments and jewelry. They wear gay flowers, paint their cheeks, putting *kohl* round their eyes, as the Egyptians did of old, and stain both their hands and feet with *henna.* But unmarried girls are not allowed such vanities. So little are women esteemed that small boys often lord it over their mothers and sisters in a most insolent manner. Husbands rule their wives with the greatest severity, not even sparing the rod.

Among the Syrian Christians weddings usually take place on a Sunday. Friday is devoted to the ceremonies of the bath, and on Saturday all the neighbours come in to see the bride-elect, who is painted and gaily dressed, and to offer their congratulations. During the two previous days invitations to the wedding are conveyed to all friends—to the women by two women, and to the men by two men. Catholics attend the church, but Protestants are married in the bridegroom's house. The wedding day must be a trying ordeal for the bride ; she is placed on a chair, and her hands, being painted with *henna*, rest on a silk handkerchief spread out on her knees. Thus she must sit, arrayed in her gay wedding dress, for hours together in a room crowded to suffocation ; and it is not considered correct for her to open her eyes, even for a moment ! When, at last, the bridegroom sends for her, she starts off at once, accompanied by only two married women chosen by her mother. It is a sad day for the parents, who frequently display much real grief at parting with their child. The bridegroom sends two or three men and a number of women to fetch his bride ; should the distance to his house be considerable, she rides to her new home. If, however, the house is in the same village, or town, the bride walks, very slowly and crying all the way, a woman at each side supporting her, for it is considered proper for a bride to show the greatest reluctance to enter the house.

As a rule the procession takes place after dark, and then the accompanying crowd carry lighted candles. A temporary altar is erected at the bridegroom's house, and a priest, or bishop, performs the ceremony. The congregation of spectators, holding lighted candles in their hands, do not hesitate to indulge in conversation and even laughter during the service. Priest, bride, and bridegroom walk three times round the altar, and the crowns are placed three times on the heads of the man and woman. Everything is done "In the name of the Father, and of the Son, and of the Holy Ghost." The priest also blesses the bridal chamber. Feasting and rejoicing continue for several days. The old customs in Syria, as elsewhere, are rapidly changing ; and young men, instead of paying a sum of money to the parents, often seek in marriage some young lady who will bring them wealth.

CHAPTER VI

North Africa

THE marriage ceremonies of modern Egyptians resemble those of Turkey at the present day, so we need not repeat what has been already said of that country. If a maiden, in spite of the efforts of her parents, has not succeeded in being chosen, and desires to obtain a husband, tradition prescribes the following mode of procedure. She must go on a Friday to midday prayer—the most solemn service in the whole week—in the Mosque of the Daughters. When the believers prostrate themselves for the first time at the cry of the *Imam*, "*Allah akbar*" (God is Great), and while their foreheads touch the reed mats on the floor of the mosque, she must walk once up and down the space dividing two ranks of worshippers. Then, beyond doubt, within a year she will become a wife.

In Egypt girls are prepared for marriage with a great deal of ceremony. There are tirewomen who make the beautifying of brides their special profession. On the morning of the wedding the bride is attired in her wedding robes, her hair plaited with the Grecian plait, small pieces of gold leaf are stuck on her forehead, and great care is taken not to conceal any of the stars and spots tattooed on her face and chest in infancy. A little rouge is added. Travellers sailing up the Nile may sometimes see a large boat going across, with a gaily-coloured canopy containing a bride, and a merry party on board all going to the wedding.

The Mahdi, whose cruel and despotic rule in the Sudan has caused so much misery, has often a good deal to do with the matrimonial affairs of his subjects. Slatin Pasha, in his deeply interesting book,[1] gives an example of the arbitrary way in which this despot exercises his authority. Abu Anga, commander of the Black Troops (Jehadia), and his brother, Fandl Manla, were sons of a liberated slave-woman, their father being one of the Khalifa's relatives. Fandl Manla had a great friend and adviser, by name Ahmed Wad Yunes, of the Shaigia tribe. One day they appeared before the Khalifa, and the former asked permission for his friend Yunes to marry a certain girl and receive the prophet's blessing. Unfortunately, as it happened, the tyrant was in a bad humour on that day; the girl's father was at once sent for, and asked whether it was his wish to bestow the hand of his daughter on Yunes. Receiving a reply in the affirmative, the Khalifa, wishing to show his authority, said, "I have decided, and consider it to the girl's advantage, that she should marry Fandl Manla. Have

[1] "Fire and Sword in the Sudan," 1879–95, by R. C. Slatin Pasha. Translated by Major F. R. Wingate. London, 1896.

you any objection?" Needless to say the father assented, for he dared not refuse; and the Khalifa, turning to his attendants, ordered them to proceed at once to read the form of prayer and blessing used at marriages, which they did forthwith, and dates were partaken of by the bride and bridegroom. Then the Khalifa dismissed all those present, and "Fadl Manla departed, one wife to the good, whilst Yunes was one hope poorer; but what the girl said about the new arrangement I cannot tell." The Pasha was detained for seven years a prisoner in the Mahdi's camp, and is probably the best authority on the ways of these Sudanese Arabs; and he states that he knew men who, in the space of ten years, had been married forty or fifty times! Also that there are many women who, during the same period, have had fifteen or twenty husbands, and in their case the law enjoins that between each divorce they must wait at least three months.

The people of Abyssinia make a broad distinction between civil and religious marriages. The former are hardly considered binding, and so can be dissolved on some very slight pretext, while the latter constitute a solemn tie that cannot be broken. The consequence is that only those whose marriages turn out happily bind themselves together for the rest of their days. Most Abyssinians prefer a more temporary and experimental form of alliance.

The civil marriage takes place in a tent made of

wooden stakes and reeds, and there the feast is held. Certain places which we may call "the Seats of the Mighty" are reserved for distinguished people, but otherwise there is very great freedom. All are welcome without regard to age or rank, and feast to their heart's content. But those who have already done so must leave so as to make room for hungry mortals outside awaiting their turn, and sometimes a good deal of force is necessary to expel them. The bride is carried on a man's back and deposited on a stool. The bridegroom, probably in imitation of the ancient custom of carrying off wives by force, takes the bride in his arms and carries her either to his own house or round her own. The crowd of invited guests follow him and help to hold the orthodox nuptial canopy over her.

The men appear to be devoid of all sense of chivalry, and are very harsh and rough in their manner towards a wife. Should an angry husband box her ears, or strike her with a stick, the wife will bear her punishment with admirable fortitude. In some cases, if the man is not very much the stronger of the two, she may strike her husband back, but as a rule the injured woman replies with a torrent of abuse and stinging insults. Where the marriage tie is so loose it need not be wondered at that married women are often great flirts, and endeavour by means of languishing eyes to attract attention from those who happen to take their fancy.

When Abyssinians arrive at an advanced age they

Carrying off the Bride, Abyssinia. *From a Sketch by Frederick Villiers.*

very frequently become monks or nuns, whether they be rich or poor, married or unmarried. The rich then deliver over their possessions to their children.

The handsome and well-built people of Somaliland, some of whom a year ago were so much admired at the Crystal Palace, have a curious custom of shutting up the bride and bridegroom for seven days. Here follows the description of an eye-witness. "We were invited into a steaming mat-hut, and then formally presented to a youthful bridegroom who appeared as disconsolate as a fresh widower. This might have been due to the suffocating effect of the unadulterated incense which ascended from a small copper brazier placed on the floor, or to the sudden loss of a coy bride who, on our approach, had taken refuge in an adjoining compartment, which was sacred. As a prelude to the holy estate of matrimony, bridegroom and bride are confined during seven days in one of these stifling double-roomed dens, and are supposed to hold a daily *levée* open to all relatives and friends, who are licensed to chaff them to their hearts' content."[1]

The following description of a wedding which took place in Fezzan about fifty years ago will serve to show how marriages are celebrated by the Mohammedans of Tripoli. The Sultan had given two of his cast-off women in marriage to two of his own slaves: one of these was his secretary and barber, the other his

1 "The Unknown Horn of Africa," by F. L. James.

groom. For several days there were gay doings in the little square before the mosque. The first night the barber and secretary (who was the greatest man of the two) was seated in state on a carpet and mats placed on the ground, in the centre of the square, supported on each side by a friend, who, as well as himself, was covered with fine borrowed clothes, though the bridegroom of course showed most bright. He was very solemn and dignified, having a lighted candle and lamp placed on the ground before him. The men and women sung round him until near midnight, treating him with great respect. He held a fan in his hand, and occasionally bowed to the company. The bride was then brought from the castle, surrounded by a great concourse of women, who were vociferating in rapid succession their cries of joy. She held a lighted candle in her hand, and had on a profusion of silver and bead ornaments; she was quite black and very handsome, and had borne three children to the Sultan, all of whom had died. The bridegroom did not deign to look at her, but suffered the procession to pass along to his house; when, after waiting about half an hour, he rose in a stately manner, and leaning his hands on the friends who walked on each side of him (in the manner of the Bashaw of Tripoli and the Sultan of Fezzan) he slowly proceeded home, the dancers following him and singing songs of congratulation. The second night passed in much the same manner, and on the following day the bridegroom, who had been a few hours before glittering in scarlet and gold, was seen cleaning a horse in the street, with a ragged shirt on.

The people of Morocco, both men and women, take a great delight in weddings. Unfortunately, marriage with these people is far from being the sacred tie, or the life-long union of Christian men and women. Lightly made, it is lightly broken, and people are often married and divorced many times before they reach the age of thirty! The contracting parties have no opportunities for making each other's acquaintance before the wedding-day, consequently the first few months, or years, of their married life are sometimes very stormy. The youths in Morocco usually contrive to get a glimpse of their future brides by hiding in their mother's room when the young ladies come to pay their respects to her. As in most Eastern countries, marriages are "arranged," not, however, by a "match-maker," but very often by some friend of the young man. There is no hard-and-fast rule in these matters, and the search for a bride is often undertaken by the young man's mother, or some female relative. Moorish tribes are made up of *duars*, or clans, each one consisting of ten, fifteen, or even twenty families, all related to one another, and a man usually marries a girl belonging to his own *duar*. If a suitable young woman cannot be found in the town or village, a search will be made among those who inhabit the mountains. A visitor may be told that So-and-So is to be married at a certain time, but on inquiring the name of the bride they say, "that is not settled yet, but we shall be sure to hear of a girl somewhere!"

Generally, when a mother hears of some nice girl likely to prove a good wife to her son, she takes two other women with her and visits the young lady's mother, in order to see for herself whether what she has heard be true. Should she be satisfied she asks the mother for her on behalf of her son, and the mother replies, "Ask her father, and if he consents, I will give her." After that the young man must apply to the father, and, escorted by six or seven men, pays him a visit. In some villages the head man has a great deal to do with the arranging of marriages, acting the part of father to those who are orphans, and in any case assisting the father in his negotiation with the suitor. The formal engagement takes place in the head man's presence. The amount received by the father for his daughter varies greatly, and depends on the young man's position and means. It is never less than twenty dollars, and sometimes as much as six hundred or seven hundred. The bridegroom-elect provides an ox for the feast at the bride's house, and if he can afford it another to be killed at his own house. The people appear to attach some idea of sacrifice to the killing of an ox at these feasts. Among other things he must provide the *henna* for staining the bride's hands and feet, a kind of earth used in the bath, a considerable quantity of wheat, butter, charcoal, blankets, &c. The bride buys her trousseau partly out of the money received by her father. Girls love to make a good show at their weddings, and so lay by what they can from time to time for this purpose. Silver and gold bracelets she must have, and now she can afford to buy them. Bright, pretty robes she must also have, one of cloth and another of silk. But she also makes one or two garments for the bridegroom.

Feasting goes on day and night for seven days before the marriage takes place. Early on the first day native musicians arrive and play morning and evening for several days; their music and their chanting sound to our ears very dreary and monotonous, but the natives are delighted with it, young and old leaving their work to come and listen to the strains. As with the Jews of old and the Chinese of to-day (see pp. 40, 89) the bride is expected to make great lamentation at the prospect of leaving home, and to declare that she has no wish to be married, which, to say the least, is not sincere. Meanwhile, on the first day, a messenger is sent round to bid the guests "come to the marriage, for all things are now ready." Then the ox, or the two oxen, as the case may be, are led to the slaughter. In the afternoon the bride is taken by her girl friends to the bath, returning late in the evening. The feasting goes on merrily; guests, all arrayed in their best, remain with the bride all night, talking and laughing and making jokes, while she, poor thing, lies on the ground wrapped up in her blanket! On the next day also there is a great gathering of women and girls, the house and all its precincts being crowded with guests.

On the third day the final preparations are made, the bride again audibly bemoaning her fate. The lawyers draw up a marriage contract and make a complete list of all her worldly possessions. A married woman retains her own property, and if divorced, as is often the case, can claim everything that is written down on the list. An hour or two before sunset the bridegroom sends the box in which the bride is to be conducted on a mule to his house ; it has a pointed roof, and is only just big enough for her to squat in. A professional woman from the town is hired to dress the bride in simple white clothes. She paints her face, combs out her hair, and puts on her jewels for her. Then a little before sunset the bridegroom's men come with a mule (unless the distance to his house is very short) to fetch the bride. She squats in the little box and is borne in procession on the mule all round the town or village, the men dancing round her and firing off their matchlocks every few minutes, and a great crowd following. On her arrival the bridegroom, mounted on horseback, comes out a little way to meet her, with his cloak drawn over his head so far as to cover his face, and both together stop for a few minutes at the door of the mosque, while the *fakîh*, who is partly a minister, gives them his blessing and wishes them all happiness. At last they reach the bridegroom's house where the bride is received by women only. At about ten or eleven o'clock the women retire, and the husband and wife are left alone. Very early next morning the former goes forth, and if he is pleased with his wife there is more firing off of guns. This seems to correspond with the shout of delight given in Syria by the friends of the bridegroom, when they "hear his voice" (see p. 70). But the poor bride has to go through yet another ordeal; for on the day after the wedding she is obliged to sit on the bed, with a curtain before her, to be looked at. All day long the married women come to see the young wife while she is thus "on view" sitting patiently with her eyes shut! Each woman places a small gift in her hand and wishes her every blessing. The bridegroom, meanwhile, is spending a merry day with his friends, not at his own house, but perhaps at some neighbouring garden, and he also receives presents. On the fifth and sixth days the couple are left pretty much to themselves, being only visited by an old woman who brings their food, but on the seventh and last day, the husband goes out to the mosque (or perhaps to a *café*) while his bride is being adorned once more; and now she is allowed to sit on a cushion, or in a chair. Both resume their girdles, which are not worn during the festivities. For many weeks, or even months, the bride is not allowed to go out. After a long period of seclusion she goes to visit her mother for about a week. After that a good dea' more freedom is allowed her. It will be evident from the above account that weddings in Morocco are a source of great expense. We are sorry to be obliged to add that, although the Koran certainly does not encourage drinking it is by no means rare for one or more of the guests to get drunk. The owner of the house is not expected to provide wine, or strong drink, but very often some of the men bring wine with them. In the cases of widows, or divorced women, the marriage festivities are much curtailed.

In some parts of Algeria and Tunis a curious custom is still practised. When the bride enters her new home the bridegroom, walking backwards, holds a dagger in his hand, and she follows him, touching the point of the blade with the tips of her fingers. In accordance with another still stranger custom, the unfortunate bride is obliged to stand against a column in the public place, and under the gaze of the people, for two hours or more, her eyes closed, her arms hanging straight down, and her feet resting on the narrow base of the column. So trying is the ordeal that she sometimes faints.

A Kabyle wife leads a much happier and far more rational life than an Arab married woman ; no rival shares her husband's heart—she is his wife in the best sense of the word, treated with affection and respect. She takes her meals with the family, and is present even when there are guests in the house. In summer, when her household duties permit, she assists her husband in his work, taking part with him in the labours of the field. Kabyle women are decidedly more handsome than those of the Arabs, or of the Moors.

An artist,[1] who has travelled in Algeria and pub-

[1] Mr. Edgar Barclay. "Mountain Life in Algeria." London : Kegan, Paul & Co., 1892, p. 82.

lished a book illustrated by his own drawings, thus describes what he saw of a Kabyle wedding in the neighbourhood of Borj Boghni :—

"The bridegroom had gone to fetch his bride, and I waited with many others beside a stream that flowed at the foot of the village, for his return. Suddenly we heard the sound of pipes, and saw the marriage procession streaming from the summit of a neighbouring hill, and then lose itself among the trees ; a few minutes later it issued from the avenue near us and ascended a slope towards the bridegroom's house. First came the pipers, then the bride muffled up in a veil, riding a mule led by her lover. As well as I could judge, she was very young, almost a child. Then came a bevy of gorgeously dressed damsels, sparkling with silver ornaments, followed by a crowd of her friends, and Kabyle Dick and Harry. In front of the bridegroom's house the procession stopped ; the girl's friends lined both sides of the pathway and crowded about the door. The pipers marched off on one side, while the bridegroom lifted the girl from the mule and held her in his arms. The girl's friends thereupon threw earth at him, when he hurried forward and carried her over the threshold, those about the door beating him all the time with olive branches amid much laughter. This throwing of earth, this mock opposition and good-natured scourging appear to be a symbolised relic of marriage by capture, and a living explanation of the ancient Roman custom of carrying the bride over the threshold of her lover's house (see pp. 8, 14, 15). In the evening on such occasions the pipers and drummers are called in, and the women dance, two at a time facing each other ; nor does a couple desist until, panting and exhausted, they step aside to make room for another. The dance has great energy of movement, though the steps are small. . . . As leaves flutter before the gale so do they vibrate to the music ; they shake, they shiver, they tremble. . . . They also deride the men by clapping their hands to the music and singing verses."

In ancient Rome customs such as these were observed. The bride was brought home in procession, with singing and the music of the flute ; she was carried over the threshold, and in the evening there was a marriage feast. This habit of carrying the bride was variously accounted for. "Concerning the bride, they do not allow her to step over the threshold of the house, but people sent forward carry her over, perhaps because they in old time seized upon women and compelled them in this manner." [1] Another explanation suggested by Mr. Barclay is that the bride was carried in order to avoid the chance of tripping at the threshold, which would have been considered a very bad omen ! And he quotes a verse as follows :—

"Let the faithful threshold greet
With omens fair, those lovely feet,
Lightly lifted o'er:
Let the garlands wave and bow
From the lofty lintel's brow
That bedeck the door."

[1] See Becker's "Gallus."

Theocritus, in his "Epithalamium of Helen," describes the twelve first maidens of the city forming the dance in front of the newly painted nuptial chamber. "And they began to sing, I ween, all beating time to one melody with many twinkling feet, and the house was ringing round with a nuptial hymn."

CHAPTER VII

Equatorial Africa

AMONG the Ewe-speaking people of the Slave Coast of West Africa, a girl who is looking out for a husband pays visits to her relations and friends attired in her best garments, and adorned with the family jewelry. Should some suitor come forward, he declares his intentions by sending a man and woman to her father's house, who bring two large flasks of rum and deposit them on the floor, with the remark, "Our uncle wishes to marry one of the girls," and then retire as soon as they have informed the father of the name of the person whom they represent. Should the proposed union be regarded in a favourable light by the girl's parents they return the flasks, empty, to the suitor, which means to say that he is accepted. Soon after this he sends round two more flasks of rum, together with cowries and two pieces of cloth for the girl, and enters into negotiations with the parents with regard to purchase money. When the fair one accepts his presents of cowries and cloth she is betrothed to him. If he be poor, and if the parents demand a high price for their daughter, it may be a long time before the wedding takes place. When at last the day of marriage comes, the parents appear to show, or rather, we should say, are compelled by custom to show, the greatest possible reluctance to part with their daughter, and so a curious little bit of comedy takes place. Soon after day-break the bridegroom sends a messenger with a present of rum to ask for the bride. At this her parents affect great reluctance, and delay the messenger with various excuses until about noon. A second messenger then arrives with the same request, but still the bride fails to appear; and not until about sunset, when a third messenger arrives from the impatient bridegroom, do the parents consent to give their daughter away. The bride's family then escort her to the bridegroom's house, where a feast is held. Finally four matrons deliver the bride to her husband, saying, "Take her. If she pleases you and behaves well, treat her kindly. If she behaves ill, correct her." Next day, if all has gone well, the husband (as in India) sends presents to the parents; after a week the bride returns to her old home—probably with the idea of showing that there is no ill-feeling between the two families. Seven days later she sends her husband food cooked by herself, and finally takes up her abode with him. It is interesting to note that the Turcomans, as well as Hindus and other peoples, have somewhat similar customs, doubtless of ancient origin.

According to Miss Mary Kingsley,[1] marriage among

[1] "Travels in West Africa," by Mary H. Kingsley, London, 1897.

the Igalwa and M'pongwe people is not brought about by direct purchase, but a certain present, of fixed amount, is made to the mother and uncle of the girl. In case there is a divorce, which is frequently the case, these presents must be returned.

Miss Kingsley also speaks of matrimonial quarrels. "The Igalwa ladies," she says, "are spirited and devoted to personal adornment, and they are naggers at their husbands. Many times, when walking on Lembarene Island, have I seen a lady stand in the street and let her husband, who had taken shelter inside the house, know what she thought of him in a way that reminded me of some London slum scenes. When the husband loses his temper, as he surely does sooner or later, being a man, he whacks his wife, or wives, if they have been at him in a body. This crisis usually takes place at night; and when staying on board the *Moré*, or *Eclaireur*, moored alongside the landing-place at Lembarene Island, I have heard yells and squalls of a most dismal character. He may whack with impunity so long as he does not draw blood; if he does, be it never so little, his wife is off to her relations, the present he has given for her is returned, the marriage is annulled, and she can re-marry as soon as she is able to." But the parents retain certain propitiatory offerings, which are given by the husband independently of the other presents, and they are often glad to receive their daughter back again on account of the prospect of more presents from the next suitor, supposing that she is still young.

Older women, who appear to be more prudent, or else possess greater self-restraint, are not so much given to nagging, and usually they have children to support them. The fate of a childless woman in Africa is a very sad one. The custom of infant marriage appears to have been recently introduced among the Igalwa, who, according to Miss Kingsley, have a curious story accounting for it. They say that in the last generation a certain man, who is still remembered by some of the old people, was so ugly and deformed that he failed to get a wife, the women being great admirers of physical beauty and strength. The man was very cunning, and hit upon an original plan to attain his object, and this was to become betrothed to one before she could exercise her choice in the matter. And so, knowing a family where a birth was expected to take place, he made large presents in order to secure for himself the coming infant if it should be a girl. A girl it proved to be, and thus, they say, the custom of infant marriage arose among the Igalwa, although they do not themselves make their arrangements quite so early as this man did.

M. Paul B. du Chaillu assisted at the departure from home of a young woman at Mobana, in Western Equatorial Africa. She had been given in marriage to a man in a neighbouring village. Her father was about to take her there with all the marriage outfit, which was carried by several members of her family. It consisted of eight of the ordinary plates of the country, two large baskets for carrying plantains from the plantations, a number of calabashes (gourds), a large package of ground-nuts, a package of pumpkin seeds, two dried legs of antelope, her stool, and a few more items. The bride was gaily dressed, and her chignon had been elaborately prepared on the previous day. As she left the village people remarked to each other, "Her husband will see that the Mobana people do not send away their daughters with nothing!" The aged mother, who went as far as the end of the street, took a great pride in sending her daughter away with such an outfit! [1]

The people who inhabit the island of Fernando Po (Bubé tribe), immigrants from the opposite coast of Biafra in West Equatorial Africa, wear hardly any clothing, but on certain great occasions rub themselves with *tola* paste, *i.e.*, palm oil mixed with the leaves of a herb called *tola.* It has a powerful odour. The men generally cover their heads with large flat hats of wickerwork, covered with monkey skin, chiefly as a protection against tree-snakes. Yellow ochre adorns their hair. Some years ago an Englishman residing in the island (Dr. Hutchinson) witnessed the wedding of the King's daughter. Great preparations went on in his Majesty's kitchen. The happy bridegroom was seen standing outside the hut of the bride's mother and undergoing his toilet at the hands of his future wife's

[1] "A Journey to Ashango land," by Paul B. du Chaillu, London, 1867.

sister. The current coin of this little realm consists of small pieces of a certain shell, which are called *tshibbu*; strings of these were fastened round his body, legs, and arms. The lady, who smoked a short pipe during the operation, anointed the bridegroom with *tola* paste. Finally she pinned on his hat, made of plaited bamboo, after which he and a groomsman partook of a hearty meal of stewed flesh and palm oil. Then the bride was led forth by her own and the bridegroom's mother, each holding one of her hands, followed by professional singers and six bridesmaids. She presented a strange appearance, being heavily loaded with rings, wreaths of flowers, and a great deal of *tola* paste. But her toilet was as yet far from complete, so the women led her away to a place out of sight, where they plastered her whole body with *tola* paste, and covered her face and head with a large veil of *tshibbu* shells. A head-dress of cow-hide served for a hat. For more than an hour the patient bride stood in the broiling sun undergoing these operations, while the professional singers were employed in celebrating her praises. However, as the poor creature had been closely confined in a hut for the previous fifteen months, we may naturally suppose that standing in the sunlight would be by no means an unpleasant change. Bride and bridegroom now took up their positions side by side in front of the hut whence the two mothers had led out the bride after her long captivity. The bridesmaids, who were all of different ages, stood in a row, all wearing parrot's feathers in their hair.

And now the wedding ceremony began; the professional singers chanted their songs, while the bride's mother stood behind the happy pair and folded an arm of each round the other's body, and, with words which could not be heard, pronounced them to be man and wife. Each was exhorted to be faithful to the other, a pledge which was confirmed by passing round a goblet of palm-wine. Each took a sip therefrom: first the mother of the bridegroom, then her son, then the bride, and lastly the bride's mother. After this there was much dancing and singing, and the scene became very animated. Finally the newly-married pair proceeded to their hut, the old wives walking before them. Arrived at the door, they embraced, presents were given to the bride, the bridegroom placed four rings on her fingers, and after further exhortations from the mother-in-law to the bride, they were left to themselves.

Among some of the central African tribes, the Banyai, for instance, women are treated with great respect and deference. They possess land, and their husbands always consult them in any important matter of business; and not only so, but they frequently transact business on their own account, travelling for that purpose to distant towns. Here the girls are not bought with oxen or cows, as among the Kaffirs, but the young man comes and lives with his wife's parents, working for them and obeying them in all things. He must be a hewer of wood and a drawer of water, and if he gets tired of the service is free to leave the house, but the wife and children remain.

Among the people of Masai Land marriages take place at the calving season, since an abundance of milk is considered desirable. As soon as preliminaries have been arranged, the girl allows her hair to grow longer than usual, and places round her head a band of cowries, from which hang a number of strings forming a kind of bridal veil, somewhat like that of a Chinese bride, except that in the latter case the strings hold beads. When the wedding-day arrives both the bride and bridegroom dispose of their chain earrings, substituting for them double discs of copper wire arranged in a spiral fashion. The lady also changes her costume, replacing her suit of clothes all of one colour by two skins, one of which hangs from her shoulder, the other from the waist. Probably these warlike people are somewhat averse to their young men getting married, fearing lest they should thereby become effeminate (compare the Spartan custom referred to on p. 132), for they have a rule whereby the bridegroom is compelled for a whole month to wear the cast-off garments of the bride! This looks as if their object were to discourage matrimony. The author heard recently of another African tribe (at Lagos) who always shut up a bride and bridegroom together in a hut for a whole month, with the idea that the young man may by that time have repented of his folly!

The people of Uganda[1] are divided into clans, each distinguished by its crest, or *totem*, the figure of some animal which is sacred to the members of the family, and may not be eaten by them. Two persons of the same clan may not marry (compare China, p. 48). Marriage is simply a matter of bargain. As soon as the young man has paid the price of his bride to her father he is at liberty to take her to his hut. But the rich and powerful do not pay anything. Peasants are only too glad to give their daughters in marriage to the chief, who can take them by force if he wills. For ordinary people the usual way of proceeding is to buy a slave girl, who becomes the absolute property of her master. Such wives give less trouble, for they cannot return to their own people if harshly treated.

The late Mr. Joseph Thomson, who led a famous expedition across Africa, describes a curious domestic quarrel illustrative of the thoughts, manners, and customs of the people in the region of the Central African Lakes. He had officiated, at a place called Kwa-Muinyi Mtwanna, at the wedding of a certain porter and a freed woman. For three days all went well, and the young wife was well treated, but this happy state of things soon ended. One morning Mr. Thomson was aroused early by screams proceeding from the hut where these two had put up, and on

[1] The real name of this part of Africa is Buganda, which becomes Uganda on the coast. Muganda means a native of the country, of which the plural is Baganda; so we ought to speak of these people as Baganda.

Marriage by Capture, Equatorial Africa. *By* George Morrow.

inquiry was informed that Mrs. Kombo had dreamed during the night of her late husband, which of course she interpreted as a sign that his spirit was much troubled! After imparting the sad tidings to her present husband she implored him to use his best endeavours to give peace to the soul of his predecessor by making a great feast and sacrificing sheep and fowls. "Thereupon," in Mr. Thomson's words, "Mr. Kombo replied that 'if it had been her father, or her mother, or any of her relations, he would have cheerfully complied with her request that their souls might be comfortable; but to do so for her late husband—he would be hanged first! and the defunct spouse would remain long in purgatory before he would stir a finger to release him'"[1] At this the wife, not unnaturally, lost her temper, and became insulting. This being more than Kombo could endure, he forthwith proceeded to beat his wife so violently that the whole camp was aroused by her shrieks. Mr. Thomson, however, did not feel disposed to interfere in such a purely domestic concern.

According to Sir Harry H. Johnston,[2] British Commissioner for Central Africa, "marriage by capture" prevails among the Awa-nkonde, at the north end of Lake Nyassa. In fact this custom affords one of the chief inducements for indulging in war and

[1] "To the Central African Lakes and Back," by Joseph Thomson. London, 1881.

[2] "British Central Africa," by Sir Harry H. Johnston, K.C.B., Commissioner for British Central Africa. London, 1897.

slave-raiding. When the British authorities first began to wage war against the slave traders there, and were in want of native troops for the purpose, thousands came forward to volunteer for service on the understanding that they should be permitted to carry off the enemy's women! Needless to say the men could not be accepted on those terms; but the porters, though unarmed, gave a good deal of trouble on the march by helping themselves to wives. The women, as a rule, made very little resistance; perhaps they rather like a change. Such scenes have their comic aspect too. "It is almost like playing a game," says our Commissioner. The man waits his opportunity, and takes the woman by surprise on her way to the stream to get water, or as she passes by from the plantation where she works. It is only necessary for the man to show that he is determined or that there is no way of escape, and the woman submits to what, no doubt, to her mind appears to be "Fate." However, if the new partner treats her badly, she can generally find some means of escaping to her first husband—we cannot say "first love," for the people do not marry for sentimental reasons. But, as a rule, the women cheerfully accept these sudden changes. Perhaps they add a variety which otherwise might be wanting in their matrimonial experience.

CHAPTER VIII

South Africa

WHATEVER virtues may be ascribed to the dark races of Africa, it cannot be said that they possess a sense of chivalry to women; the gentler sex seem to do all the hard work. An Englishman once looked into the hut of a Kaffir and saw a stalwart man sitting there smoking his pipe, while the women were hard at work in the broiling sun, building huts, carrying timber, or performing other equally severe tasks. The Englishman, feeling indignant, as he naturally would, told the Kaffir to get up and set to work like a man. Now the Kaffir is naturally very polite, and as a rule carefully avoids saying anything which might appear rude to a stranger, but this individual was so amused at the suggestion that he replied with a laugh, "Women work, men sit in the house and smoke!" But, if the men are hard on the women, the latter are often hard on each other. For example, a favourite young wife is liable to be badly treated by the others, especially if she be good-looking. Their jealousy prompts them to beat her and scratch her face in order to diminish her charms. They know they will receive a beating at the hands of their husband when he finds out, but revenge is sweet, and so the wives take their punishment quietly and with a good grace, having had their way with the obnoxious rival.

With the Kaffirs, among whom we must include the Zulus, a wife is bought, but this implies no degradation. It is the way with most Eastern nations. The bigger the price, the more she is pleased, for her husband evidently valued her highly. A marriage is not valid unless the bride is purchased from her parents. On inquiring into the state of the matrimonial market we shall find when it is "firm," as city people say, that a man must pay as much as twelve or fifteen cows for a wife, while in some particular case the father may demand no less than fifty cows. If, on the other hand, wives are "down," a girl may go for only ten cows. A purchaser naturally wishes to get good "value" for his money, and in this case the "value" depends, first, on the young woman's personal qualifications, good looks, &c., and, secondly, on the rank held by her father. Part of the purchase money *must* be paid at once, as a guarantee of good faith; but if the bridegroom be not too well off, he may give a guarantee to pay the rest as time goes on. It is clear, then, that an impecunious man runs a considerable chance of remaining a bachelor, at least for some time. The word impecunious in this case is especially appropriate, for, as every schoolboy knows, the ancient Romans measured their wealth by cattle, as Kaffirs do now, and hence their word for money was *pecus*, from which the English word impecunious is derived. These preliminary matters having been settled, the young man must put in an appearance, in order to give his wife an opportunity of seeing him. In justice to the Kaffirs we ought to say that, although the bride is bought, yet she has a certain amount of liberty in choosing a husband. At all events, she has the power of veto, and that means a good deal. On this subject we will quote from Mr. Shooter, who has written on Kaffirland. He says, "When a husband has been selected for a girl, she may be delivered to him without any previous notice. But usually she is informed of her parents' intention a month, or sometimes longer, beforehand, in order, I imagine, that she may, if possible, be persuaded to think favourably of the man. Barbarians as they are, the Kaffirs are aware that it is better to reason with a woman than to beat her, and I am inclined to think that moral means are usually employed to induce a girl to adopt her parents' choice before physical arguments are resorted to. Sometimes very elaborate efforts are made to produce this result. The first step is to speak well of the man in her presence; the kraal conspire to praise him—all the admirers of his cattle praise him—he never was so praised before. Unless she is very resolute the girl may now perhaps be prevailed on to see him, and a messenger is dispatched to communicate the hopeful fact and summon him to the kraal. Without loss of time he prepares to show himself to the best advantage;

he goes down to the river and, having carefully washed his dark person, comes up again dripping and shining like a dusky Triton ; but the sun soon dries his skin, and now he shines again with grease. His dancing attire is put on, a vessel of water serving for a mirror, and then, clothed in his best, and carrying shield and assegai, he sets forth with beating heart and gallant step to do battle with the scornful belle. Having reached the kraal, he is received with a hearty welcome, and, squatting down in the family circle (which is here something more than a figure of speech), he awaits the lady's appearance. Presently she comes, and, sitting near the door, stares at him in silence. Then, having surveyed him sufficiently in his present attitude, she desires him, through her brother (for she will not speak to him), to stand up and exhibit his proportions. The modest man is embarrassed ; but the mother encourages him, and, while the young ones laugh and jeer, he rises before the damsel. She now scrutinises him in this position, and, having balanced the merits and defects of a front view, desires him (through the same medium) to turn and favour her with a different aspect." After this "mutual seeing," to use the Japanese expression, the girl retires, pursued by her family, who are greatly excited, wishing to know her decision. But she is not going to be bought too easily. The suitor must "call again" in the morning and show off his paces in the cattle-fold. His friends on that occasion praise him up to the skies, and, in the end, the girl usually gives her consent. Arrangements are then made for the betrothal. Perhaps in the majority of cases the girl accepts the suitor from fear of her parents, who may use both moral and physical arguments on behalf of the man; but there are evidently exceptions, and it is not every Kaffir who can win the fair one. The suitor may have plenty of wealth in the form of cows (*pecunia*), and yet she may refuse him. If a youth, in spite of all his wealth and ornaments, is faint-hearted and fears rejection, he buys a "charm" from some witch-doctor. If still she dislikes him, the maiden may seek refuge with another tribe, just as Arab girls flee to the mountains (p. 74). Great then is the excitement, all her relations setting out to try and discover her whereabouts.

Kaffir young women are not so submissive as their sisters in China or Japan, and sometimes make a brave fight for freedom, as the following story will show. A young Kaffir chief won the heart of a certain girl by his dancing. The two were total strangers to each other, but that was no obstacle to her, so she went to his kraal and threw herself at his feet. Unfortunately, the chief did not return her affection; therefore the only course open to him was to send for her brother to "take her away," which he did. Before long, however, she appeared again, which breach of Kaffir etiquette met with a severe beating, but to no purpose; a third time she presented herself, and then, at last, her brother suggested that it might save a good deal of trouble if the fascinating chief would be so obliging as to marry her, which he accordingly did, the brother having offered to pay a certain number of cows.

On the wedding-day, a Kaffir bride, arrayed in beads and other finery, is led in procession to the bridegroom's kraal. Before starting, her head is shaved with an assegai, all except a little tuft at the top. Oxen are given to the bride's mother, for the feast, and others to her father. There is much dancing on these occasions, and very violent dancing it is, such as barbarous people indulge in. Bride and bridegroom also dance to each other in turn. Some sing to the dancers, while others are either criticising or praising the bride, and this is done with very great freedom (which reminds us of what takes place in China. See p. 44). The husband's women friends and relations do not hesitate to tell the poor bride that she is not nearly worth the price he paid for her, while her own women cannot sufficiently express their admiration of her. To them she appears to be the belle of the whole tribe, and her husband ought to be very proud of her, and she was worth many more oxen than he gave. But all this is only "words, words, words," as Hamlet says, and means practically nothing; custom demands these formalities. Then comes an address by the father of the girl, who gives the bridegroom a great deal of good advice. If this is his first wife, he is told not to beat her too often, for wives can be ruled without violence, a doctrine which suggests the well-known saying of the late John Bright that "force is no remedy." When the bride dances before the bridegroom, she calls him names, and kicks dust in his face, just to let him know that he is not master yet. But it is her last and only opportunity of taking liberties with him, and so she delights in this open defiance. The ceremony is called "insulting the bridegroom."

Then "the ox of the girl" is presented by the bridegroom. The slaughter of this ox is an important ceremony, for it makes the contract binding. When the feasting is all over, the pair settle down to married life. A few days afterwards the bride's father sends round an ox, just by way of showing that he is satisfied with the alliance, and as a sort of pledge that when, after death, he joins the spirit-world, his ghost will not haunt his daughter's home, nor cause any evil to happen to it ; these simple people attribute all evils to the influence of bad or unhappy spirits.

Such practices as we have described appear to be common to the whole Zulu tribe, but on account of the influence of white men, are fast dying out, so that at the present day there is often very little ceremony at a wedding.

Like many other races, Kaffirs object to the presence of white men at their marriages, and are very reluctant to give information on the subject, hence there is some difficulty in getting true accounts of their proceedings.

These people have a very curious custom with regard to that most important person, the mother-in-law. After marriage the husband, if he wishes to converse with the mother of his wife, must do so at a considerable distance, and is obliged therefore to shout. He must not come near to her, or look upon her face. Should they be so unlucky as to meet, they pretend not to see each other. The woman generally takes advantage of any convenient shelter, such as a bush, while the man looks the other way, using his shield as a screen. Moreover neither is allowed to mention the name of the other, which is often rather awkward. In that part of the world names of people are often those of some familiar object, such as lion, or house, or some common implement, and so there are times when much circumlocution is used to avoid mentioning the name which is "taboo" to the husband.

The Kaffirs of Delagoa Bay have some peculiar customs of their own. The marriage ceremony takes place in the bride's kraal; here, on the appointed day, great preparations are made for the feast, towards which the bridegroom must contribute a black goat and the bride a white cock. Refreshments having been served, the bride is escorted by her maidens to a hut where they dress her up as gaily as possible for the occasion. The bridegroom also retires in order to attire himself in his best. During their absence a curious scene takes place, such as we have already described on p. 122. The bride's relations disparage the bridegroom as much as they can, while the other family make nasty and unkind remarks about the bride. She is not worth the money they paid for her. She is lazy, or not well-born, and so forth. However, there is a truce to these pretended quarrels when the bride comes forth from her kraal, covered with a long garment, reaching from head to foot. Her companions surround her so closely as to hide her from public view; in this fashion they move along very slowly, singing and chanting all the way. The bride, on arriving at her own kraal, still closely veiled, sits down and begins to manifest great grief by crying. Then her future husband leaves his hut, and having entered the kraal, sits down somewhere near her, but not so that they can see each other. It is customary to separate the men and women; so the girls take up their position by the side of the bride, and the men by the side of the bridegroom. When all are seated the black goat is led in, walking on his hind legs, and is slain by the master of the ceremonies, who plunges his assegai right into the victim's heart. With the same weapon he then beheads the white cock. The entrails of both creatures are immediately examined, in order to ascertain whether the fates are propitious, and little portions of the flesh are handed to both the bride and bridegroom, who are expected at least to taste them before they are cooked for the feast.

Much rum and native beer are consumed on these occasions. For two or three days, or more, according to the wealth of the bride's family, the feasting and jollity is kept up, with much singing and dancing.

Basuto betrothal and marriage customs are curious. If a man take a fancy to some native girl, he must not say a word to her on the subject of matrimony. Having found some old woman (or, it may be his mother), he confides to her his wishes to settle down and marry, and requests her to make all the arrangements. Accordingly his mother, or friend, arranges for an appointment with the mother or guardian of the girl, and the two ladies talk it over and discuss the important question of ways and means. Should no objections arise, everything is arranged between these two. Infant betrothal is common, especially in the higher ranks. The father of the prospective bridegroom sends an ox as a present to the father of the girl-child, and the family hold a feast. The child receives the skin of this ox as her marriage portion, and she keeps it for her use in after life. Her uncle provides a blanket, and sometimes a very handsome one. When the girl is old enough and her relations think that the right time has come to celebrate the marriage, they send a message to her betrothed to say that he has their leave to come and pay her a visit. The family receive him with every mark of attention, and all sit down (except the young ones) in a circle. At first silence reigns, and the betrothed couple only exchange glances. After some time the man stands up and says, "All hail" (*Eh! dumela*), which is the Basuto form of respectful salutation to the girl. She responds in the same terms, and he then takes his departure, to return in about a fortnight. On returning, he comes to her father's kraal and looks to see whether the skin of the ox presented by his father is displayed or not. If it is spread out he claims her as his wife without further ceremony. A great feast is held before the wedding. After marriage every ox killed for feasting by the bride and bridegroom belongs partly to the bride's father, who also keeps some of the cattle wherewith his daughter was purchased. This custom never alters among the Basutos, even after they become Christians the chiefs still compelling the young men to pay cattle for their wives. A mother will say, "It is the very least a man can do to recompense me a little for all the troubles, fatigue, and anxiety which I have gone through in bringing up his wife for him. It makes no difference in that respect to what religion she belongs, the trouble is the same." There is much rejoicing when a girl is born (which is quite the reverse of Chinese, Indian or Arab ideas); but the reason is purely a mercenary one, for girls, when grown up, will always command so many head of cattle.

Civilisation has had hardly any effect on those very primitive people, the Bushmen. There lingers among them a very ancient custom, which probably was once wide-spread, namely, that a man may not for a long time look his bride in the face, but must visit her after dark (see p. 132). He can divorce a wife at his pleasure; and should she take a fancy to some other man, he can challenge her husband to battle. The woman meekly follows the conqueror.

Dr. Emil Holub,[1] writing in an illustrated paper,

[1] "Africa Illustrated." New York, January, 1896, No. 85.

which was kindly sent to the present writer (in answer to inquiries) by Mr. H. M. Stanley, gives an account of the very cruel manner in which a princess, by name Mo-Rena Mo-Quai, forced a slave-girl to marry a certain man much against her own will. Dr. Holub had just arrived at a place called New Shesheke. About nine o'clock in the evening, having retired to rest earlier than usual, he heard a tumult, the sounds appearing to proceed from a lagoon about thirty paces distant. Narri, the servant, who had been sent to ascertain the cause of the disturbance, suddenly reappeared, almost out of breath after a sharp run, with the startling intelligence that the princess, who was really Queen of Ma-Bunda, had ordered her servant to be nearly drowned because, poor thing, she had been so bold as to refuse to take an ugly old slave for a husband in spite of the princess' command! The girl's wishes, of course, were not consulted; all she was expected to do, being only a slave, was to obey. When first the princess communicated her order, the slave crossed her hands over her breast in token of obedience, but burst into a violent fit of tears, on account of which she was immediately dismissed. The same day the princess summoned the girl to her presence again and repeated her command in a peremptory manner, when, to her astonishment, the slave firmly declined to do as she was told! This was more than her haughty royal highness could endure, and orders were given for the disobedient slave-girl to be held under water until nearly dead, then drawn out and brought to the hut of her future husband, where, on her recovery, she would be compelled to make the best of it and remain with the man who was royally elected to be her husband! Impelled by a natural desire to prevent this catastrophe if possible, Dr. Holub hastened at once to the lagoon. On the high bank of the river he found a frantic crowd, all gesticulating, some in low tones, others with loud and angry exclamations. But a little lower down was another group; descending as quickly as the darkness and the nature of the ground would permit, he saw a weird sight. Several men and women were standing on the edge of the calmly flowing stream, while between them crouched a weeping girl. Two figures were bending over an object which they seemed to be holding between them. As soon as the would-be rescuer stepped into the water the two persons in the water arose and approached the bank, dragging some object between them. It was the motionless and insensible body of the slave-girl, whether alive or dead it was hard to say. The men went off with their burden in the direction of the princess' house, the gallant American following. Then they placed the body down near one of the huts. One of the men remained by the side of it, and also the weeping girl, sister to the one lying helpless before her. The man was actually the man selected to marry this victim of royal tyranny, and had been appointed to carry out the sentence, possibly with the idea that he would naturally endeavour to prevent a fatal result. Be that as it may, the girl was not actually drowned, and a few hours afterwards, in the early morning, the natives were celebrating her wedding! The event was announced by sounds which disturbed the slumbers of Dr. Holub. "The friends and acquaintances, together with the heartless spectators, had gathered before the hut of the half-drowned bride to enjoy the wedding dance! Dressed in a *thariskin*, their ankles adorned with shells, they whirled in a circle, and were accompanied in the dance by the beating of drums and by singing, which was now and again interrupted by shouts. This dance continued two full days and nights without cessation, other dancers taking the places of those who became exhausted. As I was returning home the following day from my elephant hunt, passing the huts of Mo-Quai's servants, I saw the *Mosari* (the newly-married woman) seated on the floor before the entrance to her hut with one elbow on her knee, sustaining with her hand the weight of her head, with a tired and broken-down expression, her gloomy eyes staring into the grass which grew around her hut. It was not like the look of a newly-married wife, but the appealing glance of one in despair."

In Madagascar, where not a few Jewish customs are to be traced, very great respect is shown to the old people, reminding one of the precept, "Thou shalt rise up before the hoary head, and honour the face of the old man" (Lev. xix. 32). Many a passage from the Malagasy public speeches (the *Kabàrys*), which have been committed to writing, recalls to mind some passage in Holy Scripture, *e.g.*, "I am young, and ye are very old; wherefore I was afraid, and durst not show you my opinion" (Job xxxii. 6). Considerable respect is also shown by the young to their seniors, even when not old. With these people betrothal is a formal and binding ceremony, reminding us again of Jewish customs. The law of the Levirate also obtains here: that is, a man on the death of his elder brother is bound to marry the widow, and so preserve his name and the family possessions. Each tribe and family wishes to retain its property. As in India and elsewhere we find the custom prevails of betrothing children. The parents, however poor, always give a dowry with their daughter; and should there be a divorce this is returned.

In Madagascar the woman receives much honour and attention. She is always regarded as her husband's helpmeet; her position is one of honour, and her influence often very considerable.

We have already alluded to the strange custom of Kaffirs and some others of avoiding the mother-in-law; and a few examples, culled from diverse countries, of curious rules of etiquette and notions of modesty, very different from the ideas of Europeans, may conveniently be given here. To begin with the inhabitants of the Aleutian Islands;

these people, according to Dall, know nothing of what civilised nations call modesty, and yet a man blushes when he is obliged to speak to his wife, or to ask her for anything, in the presence of others. Etiquette demands that they shall assume the attitude of perfect strangers! The Hottentot woman must never enter her husband's room in the hut; and the husband, as among the Spartans of old, should never be seen anywhere near his wife. One cannot but wonder how such rules were ever invented. Among the Yoruba, an African tribe, a woman is forbidden to speak to her husband, and may not see him *coram populo*, if it can possibly be avoided. A similar notion appears to have prevailed among the early people who spoke Sanscrit, for, in the Story of Urvasi and Purânas, the wife says to her lord, "Never let me see thee without thy royal garments, for such is the manner of women." And when by accident this rule is broken, the husband must softly and suddenly vanish away.

A Circassian bridegroom must not live with his wife without the greatest secrecy. Fiji Islanders display the greatest distress of mind when adventurous missionaries suggest that there is really no harm in a man living under the same roof with his wife! In Fiji, neither brothers and sisters, nor first cousins of opposite sex, may eat together—much less speak to each other. The young Kaneka (also of Polynesia) bolts with a wild scream into the bush if you mention the name of his sister!

CHAPTER IX

Aborigines of North and South America

AMONG the Eskimo of Greenland we find "marriage by capture" in full force. Young men in this part of the world are not troubled with romantic views of matrimony, and so do not marry for love, but seek for a strong and healthy partner in life who will not shrink from the severe daily toil which is a necessary condition of life in these barren and cold regions. Having selected some young woman as his future wife, the youth goes straight to her house, or tent, seizes her by the hair, or catches hold of her garments, and drags her ignominiously to his own home. Young men are sometimes ashamed to do this for themselves, and so employ others to capture the young woman on their behalf. This, however, must not be taken to imply that "proposals" are never made. But in these cases the young woman is invariably expected to answer "no," however much in her own mind she may be willing to become the man's wife. To say "yes" all at once and without a good deal of pressing would be considered, according to Eskimo standards of good taste, to imply want of modesty on her part.

On the east coast of Greenland the simple method of capture above described is still the only one in vogue. This time-honoured custom is so much respected in those parts, that the bride's relations, so far from offering any resistance to the rough usage, remain passive spectators of the little comedy, and refuse to interfere on her behalf. Greenlanders have a strong objection to interfering in other people's affairs. After all, to a certain extent the young woman's fate depends on herself; for, should she entertain a strong dislike to her would-be husband, it is in her power to wear out his patience by continued and violent resistance, until the young man, thinking he is becoming an object of ridicule to the spectators of the scene, finally renounces all claim to her hand—we cannot say her heart—because, as we remarked above, Greenlanders do not marry for love. Unfortunately the standard of morals being very low, love affairs sometimes take place after marriage, and vigilance must be exercised by the husband to prevent his wife from running away to some other man whom she prefers. Graah, who led an expedition to the east coast in 1837, narrates a story which proves how difficult it is for others to know a young woman's real feeling when being carried off. An able-bodied young woman who rowed in his boat was one day seized by a Greenlander and carried to the mountains in spite of apparently genuine struggles on her part. Graah, not seeing through the farce, really believed that she had a strong dislike to the man, and was confirmed in his opinion by her friends. Consequently, like a gallant man, he went to the rescue and brought her back. After a few days Graah was about to proceed on his journey and the boat had already been launched, when suddenly the bride appeared again on the scene, and jumped into the boat, as if seeking refuge with her deliverer like a stowaway. Before they could get away from the shore the husband appeared, reinforced by his father, to enforce his claim. Once again a struggle took place, and the apparently unwilling wife was dragged forth from her hiding-place among the baggage in the boat. Whereupon, for the second time, the kind-hearted Graah rescued her from the husband, recommending him at the same time to make the best of a bad job and turn his attention to Black Dorothy, another of the rowing-women, who perhaps might be more inclined to lend a willing ear. The husband, apparently baffled and refusing to wed the other woman, went away in anger muttering revenge. The father had not, however, given up hope, but cheerfully lent a helping-hand in loading the boat. During these operations the young woman, watching her opportunity, contrived to give them the slip; for when the time came for starting she was nowhere to be found! Graah and his party searched for her in every direction but to no purpose, and eventually set off without her. It then dawned upon them, as doubtless the reader has already suspected, that her resistance was entirely feigned, and that after all she was anxious to rejoin her husband, which doubtless she did in due course.

The inhabitants of the wild prairies of North America, idealised so delightfully by Mr. Longfellow in his "Hiawatha," appear to be generally as unromantic in their marriages as other uncivilised races. A father sells his daughter just as a Kaffir does. Mr. Catlin, who wrote an important work on these people, describes how a clever young son of a chief obtained no less than four brides on the same day. The story runs somewhat as follows :—

The father, to start his son in life, gave him horses and other property of considerable value. The young man, rejoicing greatly in his newly acquired wealth, conceived a plan, by means of which he thought he could "break the record"—at least in matrimonial affairs ; and he succeeded. His first step was to go to one of the chiefs and ask his daughter in marriage ; the request was granted for the consideration of two horses, a gun, and several pounds of tobacco.

So the "happy day" was fixed between them, with the understanding that the engagement should be kept a profound secret. Being "on the war-path" for brides, one only would not content him. He must needs win three others. So the same tactics were repeated with three other chiefs, who all promised him their daughters, on the same terms, secrecy being promised in each case.

The appointed day having arrived, the artful young man gave it out to the tribe that he was to be married at a certain hour. His friends assembled at the rendezvous ; but no one knew who was to be the bride, while each of the four fathers stood by his daughter, ready to give her away with all due formality. The bridegroom then gave the two horses, gun, and tobacco to the father with whom he had first negotiated and claimed his bride. The other chiefs naturally were highly indignant, each declaring that *his* daughter was the "true bride." A scene of great uproar and confusion followed; the bridegroom coolly explained to his fellow-tribesmen how matters stood, and claimed the other three young women in the same way as he had already claimed the first. It was a case of "ready money," for horses and all were produced and given to the chiefs. No one was able to forbid the other alliances, since all was fair and honourable; and so in sight of an admiring crowd the enterprising young man led his four brides to his wigwam, two in each hand.

The "Medicine Men" were so struck with his boldness and originality that they enrolled him in their ranks, making him thereby equal with some of the greatest men in the tribe. In this way he rose, as it were from the ranks, to a position of great influence.

Mr. Catlin says: "I visited the wigwam of this young installed Medicine Man several times, and saw his four modest little wives seated round the fire, where all seemed to harmonise very well, and for aught I could discover were entering very happily on the duties of married life. I selected one of them for her portrait, and painted Mong-shong-shaw the 'bending willow' in a very pretty dress of deer skins, and covered with a young buffalo's robe, which was handsomely ornamented, and worn with much grace and pleasing effect."

The same author, who spent so much time with the Indians, sketching them and studying their manners and customs, bears strong testimony to the affection which, in spite of the hard work put upon women, exists between parents and their daughters. There are cases in which the wishes or decrees of parents are set at nought; but this is quite the exception. The Sioux have a bold projecting rock six or seven hundred feet high overlooking a lake, from which, it is said, a beautiful Indian girl, the daughter of a chief, threw herself in the presence of her tribe some seventy years ago, and was dashed to pieces, rather than become the wife of a man whom her father had selected for her husband.

Among the Sioux, if one of them contracts an alliance with the eldest daughter of a chief, he is thereby "married to the family," not only in name (as we should say in jest) but in fact, for he is then at liberty to claim any of the other daughters. With the Ojibways the young people are betrothed in "childhood's happy hour" by their parents, at least it is generally so. But if a young man is not so engaged he may send a present to the girl he fancies, the acceptance of which is equivalent to a promise of marriage. After a few months of courtship he is allowed to take her with him, not exactly for a "honeymoon," but on a little hunting trip. She steers his canoe for him, and on their return they offer whatever game they may have caught to the parents, who then acknowledge the match.

Betrothals are greatly respected, so that the engagement is seldom broken off, and in some cases children are betrothed. Although business-like and practical in all matrimonial arrangements, these people are not entirely devoid of sentiment. Their songs are often about love, and English travellers are sometimes the bearers of love-messages to girls of distant tribes; elopements frequently take place. Wives are generally well treated.

Among some tribes a young man goes courting in the following fashion. Every morning he rises early and makes straight for the wigwam where the girl lives who has taken his fancy. Hour after hour the faithful swain sits outside on the ground, wrapped up in a blanket. After a while the people in the lodge, or tent, begin to stir, going in and out on their several errands; no one, however, takes any notice of him, they all know what he has come for; but it is not etiquette to say anything, at least for the present. After some days, it may be a week, the patient lover is invited to enter, and if the parents entertain a good opinion of him (for they doubtless are acquainted with his family), they offer him food. Should they wish to show their esteem for him, the father cooks the fish, or whatever food is offered himself, and then the lover knows that all is well, and the fair one will soon be his wife. Later on, friends come forward on his behalf to negotiate with the father as to the amount of the purchase money; for purchase it is in reality, although an Indian, if you asked him, would deny this, and say that the gifts of the husband were of a more complimentary nature.

The Indians inhabiting the western shores of Vancouver's Island have a curious way of arranging marriages, which is, in some respects, unlike anything else we have come across. The suitor is escorted by a great number of his friends, in some thirty or forty canoes. Nobody speaks for about ten minutes, for these "children of Nature" are very reserved indeed. At last the visitors are requested to say where they come from, and what is their object in coming. Thereupon some man gets up in his canoe and harangues the natives on shore at the very top of his voice, and a very loud voice it is. His business is to laud the would-be husband in every possible way; and this he does by giving his name, his titles and history, stating also the number of his friends and connections, hoping thereby to obtain a considerable reduction in the purchase money. Then, by way of a first bid, the canoe is paddled to the shore and a number of blankets thrown out. This very small offer is received with derision and roars of laughter from the bride's friends. They are not going to let her go quite so cheap as that; he must offer a great deal more. The answer given is more or less equivalent to our slang expression, "Get along with you." Then arises an orator from the shore

Demanding a Bride, Vancouver's Island. *By* George Morrow.

who speaks up right gallantly for the bride, praising her virtues and describing her in the most glowing terms with many a flowery epithet, until the original offer is considerably increased. All this oratory and bartering occupies a good many hours, until at last the bride is handed over with nothing on but her under garment, so greedy are her relatives. The first present she herself receives is a blanket.

Fathers are sometimes very particular in their choice of a son-in-law. In the same island, in the front of the house of the chief of Clayoquet, lies a large stone, and any young Indian applying for the hand of one of his daughters is politely requested to prove his strength by lifting it up. If he fails, it is hopeless; he must try his luck elsewhere.

On "The Plains," extending from Missouri on the east to the Rocky Mountains on the west, a boy begins to look out for a wife as soon as he has passed through the painful ordeal imposed upon him, and become a warrior. Having seen a maiden who takes his fancy, he lingers about near her lodge, showing by his looks that he is in love. A little later on, supposing that he meets with no rebuffs, the young man takes to serenading, with some wretched substitute for a flute. His doleful strains drive all the neighbouring dogs and old women nearly frantic! Becoming now a little more hopeful, he lies in wait each evening, watching anxiously for the fair one to appear, but carefully concealing himself, lest any other person should see him. If the girl ventures out after dark he promptly seizes her in his arms, with the object of carrying her to some convenient shelter, where they can hold sweet converse together unseen. This is the test of her real feelings; for if his attentions are unwelcome, she screams and struggles, so that he is obliged let her go. But should she offer no resistance he knows that she may be won ; and so they go off and sit down together under the cover of a large blanket, which almost entirely hides them.

It happens from time to time that two or three youthful aspirants are all paying court to one damsel. In such cases they all apply this same test. Coming near her lodge at night they conceal themselves, and when she appears on the scene one seizes her, and if she resists must give up all claim and let her go, whereupon the next one does the same. Perhaps he also is equally uncared for, and so lets her go for the third one to try his luck. Should this prove to be the favoured swain, the others promptly retire, and leave the happy lover to do his courting unmolested, as described above. We will suppose that the girl is now won. But what about her father ? He, of course, must have a voice in the matter. A curious scene ensues between the lover and the parent, which may be described as follows :—

"I think of taking your daughter for my wife," says the lover. "She is an ugly thing, lazy as a bear, does not know how to cook or to work, and is of no worth ; but, as I am sure you must want to get rid of her, I came to tell you that as a favour to you I will take her off your hands."

"Oh," answers the father, "we want my darling girl, the best and most loving daughter man ever had, the best cook and dresser of buffalo skins, the finest bread-maker, the hardest and most willing worker in the whole tribe. I cannot spare my darling. I will not part with her to any one, much less to *you*, who are young, who have taken only one scalp, who have stolen not more than two ponies. You indeed! No, you cannot have my daughter unless you give me twenty ponies for her."

"Twenty ponies!" cries the astonished lover with great contempt; "twenty ponies for an ugly girl not worth one buffalo robe; I can buy a dozen better at the price."

And so the haggling goes on, often with bitter and cutting personal remarks, the father praising and the lover disparaging the girl. Both parties often become very violent; but at last the father sees it is of no use asking too much, and so in the end the lover gets his sweetheart for one or two or three ponies. The ponies having been duly delivered, the young couple live in the house of the bride's father until her husband is rich enough to provide a lodge for himself.

A wife is the husband's absolute property. But she has this hold over him; he knows that if he ill-treats her she will probably elope with some one else. In that case matters are reported to the chief, and the man who stole her pays a fine, but the woman will not go back to her first husband.

The Cherokee Indians have invented a marriage

ceremony which may be said to be both simple and poetic, as well as original, so far as the present writer is aware. The youth, having wooed and won the maiden of his choice, as soon as the usual presents have been made to the father, takes her to a small stream, where the two solemnly join hands over the running water. It is not quite easy to see how this custom arose, but with all old races water appears to possess some special virtue and symbolic meaning, as we see from Brahmin, Russian, and other customs. However, the poetic side of the picture will be obvious to all. We speak of "the river of life," and doubtless the Indian and his bride wish that the course of their lives may run smoothly and harmoniously, and that neither in life nor in death may they be divided.

The father's regret when his daughter leaves him is pathetically told in Longfellow's well-known lines :—

> "From the wigwam he departed,
> Leading with him Laughing Water ;
> Hand in hand they went together,
> Through the woodland and the meadow,
> Left the old man standing lonely
> At the doorway of his wigwam,
> Heard the falls of Minnehaha
> Calling to them from the distance,
> Crying to them from afar off,
> 'Fare thee well, O Minnehaha !'
> And the ancient Arrow-maker
> Turned again unto his labor,
> Sat down by his sunny doorway,
> Murmuring to himself and saying :
> 'Thus it is our daughters leave us,
> Those we love, and those who love us !

Just when they have learned to help us,
When we are old and lean upon them,
Comes a youth with flaunting feathers,
With his flute of reeds, a stranger
Wanders piping through the village,
Beckons to the fairest maiden,
And she follows where he leads her,
Leaving all things for the stranger!'"

The very primitive and degraded specimens of the human race who inhabit that part of South America known as Araucania, exhibit in their marriage customs unmistakable survivals of "marriage by capture"; more so, in fact, than Arabs or Thibetans. The bride is carried off to the woods on horseback, though not without her consent. The young man is supposed to steal his bride and take her away by force, but in reality the affair is all "arranged" in a business-like manner with her parents, who are liberally requited for their loss. Araucanians, like Papuans, negroes, and others, are very fond of the Jew's harp, and it is with this not very melodious instrument that a young man woos the girl of his choice. If his affectionate glances are favourably received he knows he may proceed to business and arrange matters with her parents. If not well endowed with worldly goods, he borrows oxen or horses from his friends.

When the purchase has been effected his male friends proceed on horseback to the home of the girl and ask her parents' consent to the match. Some of the best speakers amongst them expatiate on the young man's merits, and draw a glowing picture of the happiness in store for the daughter of the house, to whom the father replies in a formal speech.

But all this palaver is mere ceremony and waste of words, for in the meantime the would-be bridegroom is searching for his intended. When found she is expected to show the greatest possible reluctance, and this she does by shrieking and screaming at the top of her voice, thus reminding one of the Greek custom where the bride says, "Drive on, never mind these tears" (see p. 181). Her cries are the signal for a fierce mock combat. All the women take up sticks or stones, or "anything that's handy" (as Mr. C. S. Calverley says), and rush to her aid. The men do the same, and often get rather severe blows. Finally the bridegroom makes a dash for the bride, and drags her to his horse by the hair or heels, leaps on his horse, pulls her up, and gallops away to the forest. Her friends give chase, but are warded off by his companions, until finally they get tired of all this sham fighting.

On the second day the bride and bridegroom are allowed to emerge from the wood, and the marriage is recognised. If "the wrong man" should endeavour to run away with the girl he is pretty sure to be beaten off.

After a few days friends call, offer their good wishes, and bring wedding presents. But the mother-in-law—for the sake of appearances, we presume—is not so easily appeased. In fact, as is the case among Kaffirs, she may not speak to her son-in-law. At the feast which concludes the ceremonies the bride must speak to the husband for her mother, and asks him if he is hungry.

Among the Patagonians "marriage by capture" is unknown; there is no ceremony, only an exchange of presents on either side, those given by the woman being in value equal to those she receives from the man. Should they separate after a time her property is restored to her. The bride is escorted to the bridegroom's hut amidst the cheering of his friends and the singing of women. They slaughter a mare for the occasion, and take great care not to le the dogs touch any of the meat or offal, which would be considered unlucky. Its head, tail, backbone, heart, and liver are taken to the top of a neighbouring hill as an offering to the evil spirit.

Judging from the description given of them by Darwin in his famous Journal, the inhabitants of Tierra del Fuego (the land of fire, a highly volcanic region) are the most miserable and degraded specimens of the human race. Here, as might be expected, we find "marriage by capture" in force. As soon as a youth is able to maintain a wife by his own exertions as a fisherman and hunter, he obtains the consent of the girl's parents, builds or steals a canoe, and waits for a chance to carry off the particular girl he fancies. She, of course, is aware of his intentions, and, if unwilling to become his wife, seeks shelter in the woods until he is tired of searching for her, but in practice this seldom happens.

CHAPTER X

Australasia

AMONG the the wild aborigines of South Australia and other parts of the continent there are no marriage rites at all, and a wife is obtained either by purchase from her father or brother, or else carried off by main force. As in China, men and women having the same family name are not allowed to marry. In accordance with customs not yet fully understood, girls are betrothed to certain men as soon as they are born. This engagement is considered so binding that a woman breaking it is killed (and often eaten); while a man who offends in the same way is punished by being severely wounded with a spear. A married woman is the mere slave of her husband; it is her duty to provide him with an ample supply of roots and other kinds of vegetable food. Hers is indeed a hard lot; when game forms part of her lord's dinner, she receives nothing but bones and refuse. When ill, or seriously injured, she is left to die without the smallest compunction, and, on the slightest pretext, is liable at any time to be cruelly beaten or speared. Few women are free from frightful scars on the head or marks of spear wounds on the body, while some are completely covered with marks and ugly gashes! One would think that such degraded creatures as these men are would be quite incapable of appreciating female beauty, but that is not the case. Good-looking girls are much admired, and consequently frequently stolen away. A young woman at all celebrated for her beauty usually undergoes a series of captivities to different masters, and meets with cruel treatment. She never stays long with one man because others endeavour to steal her away. It is her sad fate to be a wanderer amongst strange families, where the other women are jealous of her, and to be the cause of many a fight, and to receive many severe wounds. Those of the men who are in a position to maintain more than one wife do so. If in any particular tribe there is a scarcity of women, they make a raid on some neighbouring tribe and carry off as many women as they can (see the Author's "Primeval Scenes," Scene xv.—Methuen & Co.).

In New Zealand the Maoris sometimes betroth children at an early age, but that is exceptional. A little girl thus pledged to some man is as strictly bound as if she were actually married. They seldom have more than one wife, who always expects to be consulted by her husband in every important matter. Hence Maori women are treated with more respect and consideration than in many other countries. Marriages take place when the bridegroom is about seventeen, and the bride rather younger. As soon as a young man considers that he is in a position to support a wife, he begins to look around, if he has not already done so, for a suitable partner. We find no "match-makers" here; the young people prefer to choose for themselves, though, we are sorry to say, there is usually not much liberty of choice for the girls. They can, and frequently do, refuse offers of marriage from men who do not take their fancy; but for all that, the young man generally gets the girl he wishes for in the end, however much she or her friends may object to the marriage. Occasionally, it happens that a maiden is courted at the same time by two men, whose claims are pretty nearly equal. In such a case the father, refusing to arbitrate between the rivals, leaves them to fight it out between themselves and his daughter. They do not, however, actually come to blows; but each one taking her arm, endeavours forcibly to persuade her to come and live with him. So severely do they handle the object of their affections, that her arms are often dislocated, and always so severely strained as to be useless for some time. In old times, according to several travellers, actual combats took place between the men, and these sometimes had a fatal result. A young man whose offer has been refused sets to work and contrives somehow to capture the girl who has taken his fancy. Her relations and friends make preparations against a sudden attack; and when, sooner or later the "raid" is planned, a severe struggle takes place, in which clubs and other weapons are freely used. Instances are known of the girl being killed in spite by one of the losing side!

The island of New Guinea is inhabited by three races —Malays, from the Malay Peninsula, Polynesians, from neighbouring islands, and Papuans. The latter people received their name from the Malays, who called them "frizzly-haired" (*Pua Pua*, or *Papuas*).

Among the Papuans, when a young man is "grown-up," that is to say, when he is about twenty years of age, he looks out for a wife. But there are difficulties in the way of marriage; and when the future partner has been selected, the would-be husband may have to wait a long time. Wives cannot be got for nothing, and so the lover must make the best use he can of his time and get together no small amount of worldly goods wherewith to buy his wife from her parents, or, if they are dead, from her relatives. The payment usually consists of pigs, food, ornaments, pearl-shells, calico, and beads, or other European articles of manufacture if such have found their way to his village. But there is a great variety in the presents received by a bride from her husband, as the following account will prove: "Among other curious sights, we were shown the price, or dowry, of a wife, heaped upon the platform[1] of one of the houses. It consisted of a quantity of all kinds of New Guinea goods and chattels, pots, earthenware, wooden weapons, bird-of-paradise plumes, baskets of yams, bunches of bananas and other produce. Among the articles were two pigs tied up

[1] These platforms are at some height above the ground. See the large framed photographs in the British Museum, Ethnological Gallery.

underneath the house. The bride herself sat, all smiles, on the verandah above, over her earthly treasures, with as much pride as any white sister might feel on exhibiting her trousseau."[1]

The pig, or pigs, must on no account be omitted. As a rule, a woman, on her marriage, is deprived of all her hair and ornaments. But at Maiva the bride retains her pretty hair and the ornaments. As a sign to all that she is now married her face is tattooed; young girls are tattooed all over the body, their faces only excepted. On the day of the wedding a great feast is held, at which the company devours yams, bananas, betel nut, *and* the fatted pig. Presents are brought by the invited guests, and these consist chiefly of contributions such as can be eaten. Bride and bridegroom are dressed in all their best garments and decked out in feathers, shells, and bright leaves of plants. No priest is called in to tie the knot, and, as soon as the feasting is over, the young couple settle down to married life. Some of the Papuans, not content with one, marry three or four wives, buying each in the usual way. The marriage tie is not considered very binding, and it is no uncommon occurrence for a woman to leave her husband three or four times during their married life. Under these circumstances domestic life can hardly be said to present a pleasing picture! Often it is the other way, and the husband is the offender. These unfortunate affairs lead to frequent conflicts.

[1] "Picturesque New Guinea," by J. W. Lindt, F.R.G.S., London, 1887. Illustrated by a series of admirable photographs.

Revenge takes the malicious form of destroying cocoanut trees and vegetable gardens. Some of the people live in little huts constructed near the tops of trees, like so many birdsnests ; one wonders what the result is when husband and wife "fall out !" Possibly the situation has its advantages ; for the woman, being the weaker, might be afraid of seeking a quarrel, as a fall to the ground would certainly prove fatal.

Among the Nufoor Papuans, *i.e.*, the people who inhabit Long Island, which is not far from New Guinea, the woman is little more than the slave of her husband. A wife must cook the food, draw water, make pottery and fibre baskets, and submit to much ill-usage. Children are betrothed at an early age ; and as soon as the marriage has been agreed to, the parents of the future husband pay the other family a part of the price stipulated, or, to put it in very modern English, pay so much "on account." A childless wife is dismissed. According to a curious custom, the bride-elect and her near relations are compelled to keep out of the way of the boy to whom she is betrothed, and all his people, until the marriage takes place. It is difficult to see any reason for a custom so inconvenient and unnatural. It may, however, be a case of "taboo." Such betrothals are not binding, consequently the boy, when he becomes a man, may refuse to fulfil the contract. In some other islands it is exactly the other way, and the bargain must be carried out.

The bridegroom, on the day of his marriage, goes to the bride's house preceded by a crowd of women, each carrying in her hand a small present. A room is set apart for the ceremony; the young couple are placed back to back, the guests meanwhile taking up their position around them—men on one side and women on the other. The oldest relation is chosen to perform the simple but curious ceremony. Joining the right hands of the bride and bridegroom, he spurts a mouthful of water over them, with these words—"May no enemy kill you, and no evil spirit affect you with sickness!" Sago is brought, of which both partake, and afterwards the guests.

After marriage certain remarkable customs are observed. The husband and wife must sit up all night; should they appear for a moment to fall asleep, their friends, who sit up with them, immediately arouse them. These attentions, however, are well-meant, for the people have a firm belief that only in this way can a long and happy life be ensured! It is sometimes easy to suggest explanations of savage customs, but always unsafe. Maybe they hope thus to drive away evil spirits, but who can say? This sitting up continues for four nights. Sleep is permitted by day to the bride, while her husband stays away. On the fifth day they are allowed to meet alone, and then only by night.

There is little or no ceremony when widows are married. The chief thing appears to be to make sure of driving away the ghost of the "late lamented" husband. With this important object in view, the bride and bridegroom walk into the jungle or forest, attended by some widow, or married woman, who breaks twigs off the trees to pelt the bride. A small present is given to the woman who renders this valuable service, and the widow, now once more a wife, changes her old garment for a new one.

Among Papuans, the men, being warriors, look down upon their women-folk, whom they regard as labourers—at least to a certain extent. The wives, however, are not, as a rule, badly treated, and are by no means mere slaves. They contrive to have a voice in the management of affairs, both domestic and public. As in Europe in the time of Julius Cæsar, so here, it is often the women who incite the men to war, or perhaps to deeds of murder and plunder. They have been known to arouse the fighting instinct in men by rushing wildly into their midst and addressing them in terms such as these : "What, you are afraid to do this ; and yet you call yourselves men and warriors ! Out upon you ! you have not the hearts of men ; you are more like a pack of old women ! You ought to put on the grass petticoat, stay at home and do the cooking !" Taunts such as these, it is almost needless to say, usually have the desired effect. On the whole these people appear to travellers to be a bright and merry race, for Nature supplies nearly all their wants.

The people of New Britain, east of New Guinea, have

somewhat different customs. A young man contemplating matrimony confides the secret to his parents, or if he is an orphan, to the chief of the tribe he belongs to, informing them at the same time who is the maiden that has won his heart. The would-be husband is then sent off into the bush, in order, we may suppose, to be out of the way while his father, or the chief, as the case may be, goes to the girl's relations to arrange about the dowry, or purchase money, over which there is much haggling On the wedding-day a feast is held at the bridegroom's house, with the usual accompaniments of music and dancing. The bride does a good deal of dancing herself. Meanwhile the unfortunate husband is still in the bush. The parents at last send some one to bring him in. The person deputed for this purpose may have greatly difficulty in finding him, for young men, on these interesting occasions, frequently wander away for many a mile—with the idea of escaping from the power of departed spirits, who are supposed at such times to exercise an evil influence! These excursions into the "forest primeval" are not unattended with danger; for there is the risk of the bridegroom being killed by some hostile tribe on the war-path.

As in some other places marriages are even arranged for women before their birth. Thus, should a chief desire to be allied by marriage to some particular family, he buys a child beforehand. Should it prove a boy, the money is returned; if a girl, she becomes absolutely his property, although living with her parents until old enough to become the chief's wife. When married, there is no limit to the power of her lord and master. He can even take her life. There is a horrible story of a chief who lived on the shore of Blanche Bay. This man's unfortunate young wife used to cry and beg to be allowed to return to her own people ; moreover, what was worse in the eyes of her brutal husband, she refused to do any work. This he could not endure, and flying into a furious passion, told her that, since she was of no use as a wife, he would make use of her in another way. Seizing a spear, this inhuman monster killed his wife on the spot, cooked her body, and called his friends together for a feast.

On another occasion a man and his wife were taken by surprise in the bush, and made prisoners. The chief who captured them gave orders for the man to be killed ; this was done, and the wife became his property forthwith. So little do they regard a woman's feelings that at the marriage-feast the new wife saw the body of her late husband served up.

CHAPTER XI

Melanesia and Polynesia.

IN the Solomon Isles (Melanesia), a girl is not sought in marriage until her charms have been enhanced by the tattooer's art. The painful and tedious operation is performed by a medicine man, whose services are handsomely rewarded. It is considered necessary to employ musicians as well ; so he first engages a company of professional singers. The concert begins at sunset, and is kept up vigorously throughout the night. The poor child is kept awake by her friends in order to hear it all. At sunrise the man begins the operation, using only a sharp bamboo knife (bamboo is very hard, and frequently used for knives). Thus he makes curious and artistic network patterns on her face and chest. It is a painful process, but she suffers without a murmur, for all primitive races train up their young people to bear pain silently.

Next day all is forgotten in the joyful thought that she is now an eligible young woman ! From this time her parents keep a watchful eye over their daughter, and check any levity on her part.

Proposals follow before long, and her friends who

have subscribed towards the expense of tattooing look forward to repayment when she is married. The higher her rank, the more her parents demand of the suitor ; consequently, needy young men often have to wait a long time for a wife. But if a swain is known to have "expectations," he may pay down a part of the purchase-money, and claim a girl as his *fiancée*, in which case she will not be given in marriage to another. The daughters of chiefs seldom marry early on account of the unreasonable demands of their fathers. A young man who dares to propose to the daughter of a chief and cannot pay the amount is liable to be heavily fined for his presumption !

Occasionally it happens that a chief's daughter remains in single blessedness until the death of her father, in which case she may be bought "for an old song," as the saying is, by some middle-aged widower, or an impecunious person who has been waiting many years for a partner.

When a young girl is betrothed, and her future husband has paid the amount in full, she goes and lives with his mother until the time arrives when she may become his wife. Soon after the purchase has been made her parents give a feast to those who subscribed towards the tattooing ; this is followed by another feast given by the bridegroom's parents, and there are no other ceremonies, either at betrothals or marriages.

Somewhat different customs prevail in one of the Solomon Isles known as Florida. Here the usual tattooing takes place, but there may be a delay of several months, or even years, before the young man's father pays down the full amount of the purchase-money. In order to transact this business, he pays a visit to the girl's home, and even when the payment has been made, and the visit has been prolonged for two days, the parents make a great fuss about giving up their daughter, interposing many imaginary difficulties. When at last the time of parting comes they demand further payment. This is called "the money to break the post near the door (used to take hold of in going in and out of the house), to finish her going in and out of the old home." This payment is made to the bride's female relations, who take her by the hand and give her up. The act of giving away the bride is rather curious; she is lifted off the ground and carried out of the house on the back of one of the women, who delivers her to the bridegroom's father. For two or three months after this the bride stays in her father-in-law's house, until the necessary presents of pigs and food arrive. Not till then can the wedding be celebrated. And here we meet with a curious custom, rather suggestive of the "ransom" paid in the Tyrol and elsewhere. During the morning of the feast, the boys of the village harass the bride's relations by playfully shooting arrows at them. So skilful is the youths' practice that they can safely send arrows whizzing past the ears of a guest, over his head, between his legs, or even through his hair! These delicate attentions, however, become a positive nuisance; and after many forcible expressions of disgust, the men gladly purchase immunity by paying ransom.

At Saa, in the large neighbouring island of Malanta, when children have been betrothed, the little girl, bringing food with her, comes on a visit to the home of her future father-in-law. In this way the young people get to know each other, for they have frequent opportunities of playing and conversing together. From time to time the visit is renewed, and at intervals the boy's father pays part of the purchase money, porpoise teeth being used as money. One advantage of the arrangement is that when the betrothed girl is grown up and her wedding-day has come, she shows none of the usual reluctance, either real or affected, to enter the bridegroom's house, or rather that of his father, where she feels already quite at home. Hence there is no necessity for carrying her away or lifting her over the doorstep.

At the Santa Cruz islands, also known as Queen Charlotte islands, we find the same custom of infant betrothal. The father seeks a bride for his son without telling him. Some time elapses before the boy is told that a girl is engaged for him. His parents do not say who it is, but only warn him that he must not go near a certain house—for it is not allowed for betrothed ones to meet. This is equivalent to informing him that his *fiancée* lives there. Sometimes youths show great reluctance to marry the brides thus chosen for them.

In various parts of Western Melanesia marriages are performed with religious ceremonies. Thus at Dorey, on Geelvink Bay, the couple join hands sitting before an ancestral image, and eat sago together, amid the exhortations and congratulations of their friends. The wife offers her partner tobacco, while he gives her betel nut. They must sit up all night while the relations partake of a solemn meal.

In the Northern New Hebrides it is only chiefs or other great people who betroth their children in youth. As in Malanta the betrothed child lives in the same house with her future husband, who very often is taught to regard the little playmate as his sister. Sometimes the boy, on growing up to manhood's estate, is quite shy on learning the relation in which they stand. Girls assume the petticoat when they arrive at a marriageable age. On the wedding-day guests arrive in large numbers to enjoy the good things provided for them. The bridegroom fixes a branch of a tree, or shrub, in the ground, and brings forward his gifts of pigs, food, and mats. The bride's father, or some special friend of the family, makes a speech—which is unusual for these parts—and exhorts the bridegroom to feed his wife properly and to treat her kindly. With such and similar admonitions he hands over, or "gives away," the blushing bride, gaily attired and wearing her new petticoat. At the feast which follows the bridegroom is saved the trying ordeal of a speech; he merely strokes his father-in-law to show his gratitude and affection.

This is followed by a scene such as might be witnessed at an Arab wedding. A sham fight takes place, in which it sometimes happens that men are wounded. On the one side are ranged the bride's kinsmen, on the other those of the bridegroom. Should a brother of the latter be injured, "compensation," in the form of a present, is required. When the bride's family consider they have made enough show of resistance to prove how highly they value their daughter's services, they allow her to be taken away. Accordingly she is dragged off by female friends to the bridegroom's house—sometimes with much reluctance, even to tears. It sometimes happens that a bride who is unhappy seeks the earliest opportunity of running away from her husband, and seeking a home with some man she likes better. In such cases, if her parents perceive that nothing will induce her to return to the injured husband, they offer him a pig, as *solatium*, to soothe his wounded feelings; and there the matter ends.

In the Gilbert Islands a man can demand his wife's sisters in marriage; he is also expected to take his brother's widows. Widows in New Ireland and New Britain are considered to belong to no one in particular. But if a widower wishes to marry again, the idea is at first opposed by all the ladies of his late wife's family; at first sportively, by using every possible form of annoyance to make the man keep at a distance, and then in real earnest (if he carries out his intention), by destroying his house and all his goods!

In the Fiji Islands, when a young man wishes to marry a certain girl, he must obtain her father's permission. This having been granted, he makes her a small present. Shortly after he sends to her house some food prepared by himself; this is the ceremony known as "Warming." For four days the girl enjoys a brief holiday, sitting at home arrayed in her best, and painted with turmeric and oil; she is then taken to the sea by some married women, and all set to work to catch fish. As soon as the cooking of what they have caught is finished the young man is sent for, and the betrothed ones take a meal together. Some little interval follows, during which her future husband is busily occupied in building the new home, while the girl is being tattooed—a painful operation. On the completion of the house a great feast takes place, after which the bride and bridegroom settle down to married life. On her departure from home her friends and relatives make a great fuss, all showing their affection by kissing her.

The following account of the presentation of a bride in former days is interesting.

"She was brought in at the principal entrance by the king's aunt and a few matrons, and then, led only by the aunt, approached the king. She was an interesting girl of fifteen, glistening with oil, and wearing a new *liku* (waistband), and a necklace of curved ivory points, radiating from her neck and turning upwards. The king received from his aunt the girl, with two whale's teeth which she carried in her hand. When she was seated at his feet his Majesty repeated a list of their gods, and finished by praying that the girl might live and bring forth male children. To her friends, two men who had come in at the back door, he gave a musket, begging them not to think hardly of his having taken their child, as the step was connected with the good of the land, in which their interests, as well as his own, were involved. The musket, which was equivalent to the necklace, the men received with bent heads, muttering a short prayer. Tuikilakila then took off the girl's necklace and kissed her. The gayest moment of her life, as far as dress was concerned, was past; and I felt that the untying of that polished ornament from her neck was the first downward step to a dreary future. Perhaps her forebodings were like mine, for she wept, and the tears which glanced off her bosom and rested in distinct drops on her oily legs were seen by the king, who said, 'Do not weep. Are you going to leave your own land? You are but going a voyage soon to return. Do not think it a hardship to go to Mbau. Here you will have to work hard; there you will rest. Here you fare indifferently; there you will eat the best of food. Only do not weep to spoil yourself!' As he thus spoke he played with her curly locks, complimenting her on her face and figure. She reminded him of a sister of hers who had been taken to Mbau in years past."

The daughter of a chief is usually betrothed early in life. Should her intended husband refuse to carry out the contract, it is considered a great insult, and becomes the cause of a serious quarrel, sometimes leading to blows. Should the young man die before the girl is grown up (which is not unlikely, for he may fall in battle), then his next brother takes his place, and the child is betrothed to him.

Among chiefs and their families, or, as we should say, in "high life," marriages are often the result of mutual attachment, being preceded by courtships and the exchange of presents. Young people may even be seen "walking out" arm-in-arm, as in England. But freedom of choice is not always allowed, even to a chief's daughter. A forced alliance sometimes leads to suicide. Some American travellers, a good many years ago, were told the story of the daughter of the chief of Ovolan, who jumped over a precipice because she had been married against her will. But among the lower classes of natives we find no such scruples. The usual price of a bride is a whale's tooth or a musket, and when this has once been paid she becomes the absolute property of her husband, and her life is in his hands. Until purchased, young women nominally belong to the chief, who may dispose of them as he thinks best. Elopements are not unknown. As in some other countries, when two young people have made up their minds to marry, and from difference of rank or other cause are forbidden to do so, they seek refuge in flight. Some neighbouring chief of a kindly disposition takes pity on them, and uses his best endeavours to effect a reconciliation with the parents.

In the Samoa, or Navigator Islands, now famous as the abode of the late Mr. Robert Louis Stevenson, marriage transactions may be said to be merely speculations in fine mats, of which a bride's dowry consists. These are handed over to the husband's principal friend and supporter ("best man"), who arranges the match and provides the feast. Widows follow the law of the Levirate, and marry the husband's next brother. Each bride brings with her one or two handmaids, who may become secondary wives.

A young man must be tattooed before he can marry. Having made his choice from among the girls of the island, he sends his "best man" to negotiate and make all the arrangements. The young woman usually has no choice, but is obliged to submit to the decision of her parents. They, on their part, must obtain the chief's consent. For a long time before the wedding takes place all the bride's relations help in getting in her dowry of fine mats and native cloths. The family of the bridegroom are likewise actively engaged in collecting property for him, such as cloth, pigs, canoes, &c. When the contracting parties are of high rank, the ceremony takes place in an open place of public assembly, surrounded by bread-fruit trees. Here the guests seat themselves in a circle cross-legged, glistening with oil and bedecked with plenty of beads and flowers. At first the bride remains seated in a house somewhere near, from which extends a carpet of native cloth reaching to the place of assembly. There the expectant bridegroom is seated at the further end of the long carpet. And now, all being ready, the bride comes forth. Needless to say, she is gaily bedecked with beads, flowers, and shells, and also girt round the waist with fine mats, some of which form a flowing train behind. Her maidens follow, all bearing mats. These they spread out before the bridegroom, and return to the house for more. This is repeated a good many times, until, in some cases, the number reaches two or three hundred. All these constitute the dowry collected by her relations. The bride takes her seat by the side of the bridegroom, and presently stands up to receive the applause of her assembled guests. It is now time for the husband to show his wealth, which he does with considerable display. The disposal of all these worldly goods is arranged by the parents (or brothers) on both sides.

It was stated above that Samoan girls usually are compelled to submit to the arrangements made by their parents, but elopements are not altogether unknown. If the young man whose offer was refused by the parents should be a chief, his companions (in order to show their resentment as well as his) gather together in the evening, and walk through the settlement singing his praises and coupling his name with that of the young woman who ran away with him. Should the course of their love run smooth, the chances are that a reconciliation will take place with the parents sooner or later, and then the event is celebrated by feasting and exchange of presents.

The people who inhabit the Hervey or Cook Islands (between Samoa and the Society Islands) have a remarkable custom. Here they are not content with mats where-

BRIDEGROOM WALKING OVER HIS BRIDE'S TRIBESMEN, HERVEY ISLANDS. *By* GEORGE MORROW.

with to make a pathway for the bride to walk along. But should she be the eldest girl, the members of her husband's tribe lie down flat on the ground, while she walks lightly over on their backs. This "street of human bodies," called in the native tongue *ara tangata*, extends from the bride's house to that of the bride-groom; and should the distance be so great that enough people cannot be found to make the pathway, then those on whom the bride has already stepped get up and quickly run on ahead, so as to lie down again and fill up the rest of the path. A curious custom certainly, but one may perhaps safely argue thereupon that women (and especially brides) are held in greater honour than in many other parts of the world, such as China. This ceremony takes place a few days after the wedding. The husband, on the day of his marriage, goes through a similar ceremony, walking on the backs of the people of the tribe to which his wife belongs. On that occasion the bridegroom's friends walk on each side of the human pathway, clapping their hands, and singing songs in his praise, not omitting to mention his ancestors.

Marriage customs in these islands may also be illustrated by the following story, which a traveller heard from the natives. There was war between certain tribes, and Uriitepitokura, one of the defeated tribesmen, remained in hiding. This enterprising young man occupied his time in making fish nets and valuable dresses, the latter being composed chiefly of the feathers of birds which he contrived to catch. There was a pathway running down to the sea, and looking through a little hole in the rock he could see the people going down to the shore. In this way he one day saw a young woman of some rank who had escaped the watchful eye of her grandmother. Akamârama was her name, and to her he made himself known, entreating the damsel to afford him her protection and to become in time his wife. Of course he did not forget to mention those treasures which he had so skilfully made with his own hands. He was handsome and young, but that alone would not have enabled him to win the fair one's hand and heart. The nets and dresses were the chief cause of his conquest. She henceforth rejected all offers of marriage, and refused to undergo the fattening process which is customary in those islands. Her parents, suspecting some previous attachment, inquired of her if there were any man whom she would be inclined to marry, whereupon she revealed her secret. Next day they arranged matters with the young man, who bestowed his feather garments and nets on the father and uncle of the bride, and some more nets on the chief, so as to ensure his protection. On the wedding-day Akamârama wore a splendid head-dress of feathers made by the bridegroom, and sat by her husband on a white cloth to receive the presents of their relations. They then partook of food together, and entered forthwith into the married state.

In Tahiti and others of the small Polynesian Islands

wives do *not* appear to be purchased. That is one way in which their marriage customs differ; but here is another, and a curious one too. The young girl who has been betrothed, as she grows up is zealously guarded from contact with the outer world, and this is effected by keeping her railed up on a high platform in the home. Food is brought, and nearly everything is done for her. Only very occasionally is she allowed to go out, and then she must be accompanied by one of her parents.

On the wedding-day an altar is set up in the house, on which are displayed the relics of her ancestors—their weapons, skulls, and bones. The presents she receives are usually pieces of white cloth. If bride and bridegroom are related to the reigning family, the party repair to the temple of two chief idols of the country in order to procure their blessings. If not so related, prayers can be offered up at home. In the former case bride and bridegroom put on wedding garments, which become sacred ever after, and when they have taken places assigned to them the bridegroom is asked the following question—"Wilt thou cast away thy wife?" The bride is addressed in a similar manner, and both answer "No." They receive a blessing, and prayers are offered up for them. Then the relatives spread out a piece of white cloth on the floor; the bride and bridegroom step on to it, and take each other by the hand. Sometimes the skulls of ancestors are here brought out, no doubt in order to represent their spirits, with the idea that they may take part in such an important affair of the family. This reminds us of the Chinese custom of informing the ancestors and worshipping their tablets. The bride's relatives then take a piece of sugar-cane, wrap it up in the branch of a certain sacred tree, and place it on the head of the bridegroom, and then lay it down between the now wedded pair who are still holding each other by the hand. The relatives on both sides consider that the two families are now for ever united. Finally, another cloth is produced and thrown over bride and bridegroom by the relatives. This cloth, as well as the wedding garments, is considered sacred. The day ends in much feasting. A good deal of dancing takes place on the day before the wedding.

Mr. William Ellis, a missionary, who wrote on Polynesia,[1] describes the arrangements made for a marriage in the island of Huahine, one of the Society Isles, where he was stationed at the time, in the year 1822. The bridegroom was Pomare, the young chief of Tahaa, and the bride was Amiata, the only daughter of the late king of Tahiti, not far off. They met at Huahine, which was midway between the islands to which the respective families belonged. More than a week before his intended bride arrived from Tahiti, Pomare sailed from Tahaa and landed in Huahine, where he was entertained with due regard to his rank by the chiefs of the island. It was not, however,

[1] "Polynesian Researches," 4 vols., 1831.

supposed at the time that his consort would become queen of Tahiti, because her brother was then living, and Amiata arrived on a brig belonging to the king, and was introduced to her future husband, who wore an English beaver hat, but otherwise was dressed in full native costume. He took his seat and awaited with gravity the appearance of Amiata. Presently she and her friends arrived and took their seats near the young chief. But Pomare continued motionless, neither rising to welcome his guests nor taking off his hat. The princess, who sat by the side of her mother, occasionally glanced at her future husband, who sat like a statue before her.

The interview was a singular one, considering that the two had never met before. Not a single word was exchanged between them. After about twenty minutes the queen and her daughter and companions rose and went off to the house prepared for them, while Pomare and his friends returned to their encampment. Shortly after this meeting they were publicly married with Christian rites and afterwards removed to Tahiti. The bride was sixteen years of age, and her husband not much older.

Occasionally real courtship takes place, and there are instances of brides being only won after a great deal of wooing. There was a case of this in the same island, according to Mr. Ellis. It was a young chief, tall and powerfully built, with pleasant manners, who fell in love with the niece of another chief, and tendered proposals of marriage. Her family had no objection, but the young lady refused to accept his oft-repeated offers, although no means to gain her consent were left untried. The unhappy young man gave up his ordinary occupations and took up his abode in the house where the object of his affections lived, in order to devote himself to her constant service, which he did with great zeal, although subject to the deepest melancholy. Kind friends interested themselves on his behalf, and his sad fate became for a time the topic of general conversation. But in time the fair one relented, the two were married and lived together very happily.

After this a case of the opposite kind occurred. A party of five or six men arrived at the island of Huahine in a canoe from Tahiti, and remained there some time, the guests of a certain chief. A good-looking girl, one of the belles of the island, who belonged to the house where the men were being entertained, fell deeply in love with one of them. It was soon intimated to him that she would have no objection to becoming his wife ; but, alas ! there was no love on his side, although the unhappy girl endeavoured in every possible way to obtain his affection. She followed him about everywhere. Things went on like this for some time, until the enamoured one, becoming very unhappy, declared that, if he continued indifferent to her, she would either strangle or drown herself. In the end, however, the young man relented, and married her. In this case the marriage proved an unhappy one, for the wife before long took a violent dislike to her husband.

CHAPTER XII

Greece

FROM the ancient civilisations of the East, and from the customs of primitive races, we now turn to modern Europe.

The unfortunate Greeks having so long been under the yoke of Turkey it is not surprising to find that some of their marriage customs resemble those of the Turks. But the reader who follows this account will very soon perceive other ceremonies similar to those observed in China, India, Russia, and among the gypsies; while here and there we shall note some relics of classical times. Hence the marriage rites of these people—to whom England has always been friendly—possess more than ordinary interest.

Parents in seeking husbands for their daughters require the aid of a professional match-maker. When the amount of the dowry has been satisfactorily arranged, the first betrothal takes place (an exchange of rings, called *arravon*) and the future husband declares in the presence of witnesses that he is satisfied with the amount. Notice that this is a reversal of the custom of Hindoos and other peoples who demand a sum of money from the suitor.

He may now visit the girl at her home. Friends call to offer their good wishes, and are received by the bride-elect standing with much affected humility and downcast eyes. Hence the Greek saying, "As affected as a bride." As in Turkey, so here, the girl kisses the hands of the friends of her future lord. They present her with sweet basil and gold coins.

Marriages take place at all seasons, except in the month of May; as a rule late in the autumn after the olives have been gathered in. The day is usually a Sunday, and by preference the next one after the full moon. There is considerable variety in the customs observed in rural districts, and even in the larger towns. Weddings are attended with a good deal of ceremonial. The marriage takes place some time after the betrothal, and the interval may be a long or short one.

We will first take Southern Macedonia, where the customs are especially interesting. For instance at Vodhena, the ancient Macedonian capital Edessa, the festivities last a week. On the Sunday a copy of the marriage contract it sent to the bridegroom, who in return sends his *fiancée* a few trifling presents, such as sweetmeats, henna, rouge, &c., and a jar of wine for her parents.

During the next four days, *i.e.* from Monday to Thursday, the ceremonies observed are all connected with the wedding cake and unlike anything to be met with in those countries of which, so far, we have spoken. On the Monday and Tuesday the grain for the cake is sifted and carried to the mill by the bride and her girl companions. On Wednesday they bring it home, and the friends come to the house to help to knead the dough. The kneading is done in a trough at one end of which sits a boy girt with a sword, while at the other end a little girl pretends to help, but in reality is endeavouring to avoid being seen while she hides in the dough some coins and the wedding ring. No children who have lost any relatives may perform the ceremony, otherwise it would be a bad omen. It is easy to see the drift of this symbolism. The boy with the sword stands for the husband, whose duty is to guard and defend; the little girl is a reminder of a wife's domestic cares. The cake is made, and on the Thursday portions of the dough are given to the company. Of course each one hopes to find the wedding ring, just as English children still expect to find one in a birthday cake. The lucky one who gets the ring surrenders it to the bridegroom in exchange for a present. In the afternoon of the same day the wedding cake is placed over a bowl of water, and the youths and maidens dance three times round it singing "the song of the wedding cake." After this they break up the cake and throw the pieces over the happy pair, together with figs and fruit—emblems of plenty and fruitfulness.

On the next day (Friday) the presents given by

the men are carried in procession through the streets, as in China. They are mostly articles such as a young couple starting in life would require. On the Saturday evening (the day before the wedding) a feast is held, and on this day the bride is prepared for the morrow by her maidens (as in Turkey and elsewhere), who sing to her while attending to her toilet.

At all Greek weddings an important part is played by the *koumbáros*, as he is called, an influential friend or relative, who, among the poorer people, provides the entertainment, and is saddled with a number of other responsibilities should the wife and children be left destitute. The same name is applied to godfathers by their godchildren, and reciprocally to the godchildren by godfathers, and is intended to apply to all the members of families between which such a tie exists. Thus an important relationship is created, and one which is most solemnly regarded, so that a man of influence may be a kind of protector and counsellor to all the young people of the country side. The head bridesmaid too plays her part as a kind of godmother, and is called *koumbára*.

Now Sunday has come, and the actual wedding ceremonies begin. First of all the bridegroom and his friends leave the house; as he departs his mother pours water out of a jar before him, and lays down a girdle in his path, over which he steps. A procession starts from the house of the *koumbáros*, and from there go to the bride's house, his friends singing as they walk along. Arrived there the priest receives them, and presents the marriage contract to the parents of the two parties, after which the second exchange of rings takes place. Sweet basil is presented by the bride's father to the father, or nearest relative of the bridegroom, on a plate, with these words thrice repeated, "Accept the betrothal of my daughter to your son," and a similar ceremony is performed on behalf of the bridegroom, in accordance with the custom in ancient Greece (compare the Brahmin custom, p. 2). Then a glass of wine, a ring-shaped cake, and a spoon, are given to the bridegroom, who, after he has drunk the wine, drops coins into the glass, and gives the spoon, together with half the cake, to the best man, who keeps them, but gives the half cake next morning to the bride. The bride's shoes, given by the bridegroom, are put on her feet by the best man, and as she leaves the threshold, her mother pours out a libation of water for her to step over (which custom may perhaps be another form of the Arab sacrifice of a sheep and the bride stepping over its blood before entering her new home). At the church door the mother says three times, "Bride, hast thou thy shoes?" On entering the church the bridal pair proceed to the altar carrying decorated tapers. (In many parts of Greece a priest performs the ceremony at the bride's house.) Then takes place the third exchange of rings, or third *arravon*, presided over by the priest, who reads a portion of the ritual, then makes the sign of the cross with the rings, three times over the heads of the bride and bridegroom and places them on their hands, saying, "Give thy troth, servant of God (adding the man's name) to the servant of God (adding the woman's name) in the name of the Father, the Son, and the Holy Ghost." They are then formally betrothed : the actual marriage ceremony is as follows :—Both bride and bridegroom are crowned with wreaths of flowers (orange blossom) by the priest, who places them on their heads with these words, "Crown thyself, servant of God (name) in the name of the Father, the Son, and the Holy Ghost." Three times the sentence is repeated while the best man changes the crowns three times. After bridegroom and best man have drunk the consecrated wine, the pair are led three times round the altar, the best man following. The priest removes the crowns and gives his blessing. The pair are now duly married. Kissing and congratulations follow, the best man having the bride's first kiss. On arrival at the bride's house her mother welcomes them both, placing a loaf of bread on their heads, while the rest of the company throw sweets at them. Then the feasting begins, and healths are drunk, the glasses being thrown over the left shoulder ; and it is unlucky if they remain unbroken.

The bride on quitting her home takes away with her half a loaf, the other half being kept by the parents. Then the party adjourn to the village green, where there is much dancing and music. They have, of course, no honeymoon, and the pair presently leave for the husband's home. Next day that important person, the best man, appears again, bringing with him the half cake and the spoon, delivered into his care on the previous day. The bride eats the cake and then takes the first mouthful of food with the spoon. After breakfast she and her friends pay a visit to the well, in order to observe a custom that prevailed with the ancient Greeks, the object of which is to propitiate the Water-deity, the "Naiad of the Spring." A coin is dropped into the well from the lips of the bride, who then draws water and fills her pitcher. On arriving at the home she pours some of this water over her husband's hands, and he gives a small present in return. The rest of the day is spent in feasting and dancing. After a few days the newly-married pair return to the house of the bride's father, where they remain for a whole day and night; and the visit is repeated a few days later. Judging from a somewhat similar custom in parts of India, we should say the object of the visits is to show that there is no ill-feeling, as there might have been in earlier days when brides were captured. And speaking of capture, it may be mentioned here that among shepherds in the mountainous parts of Greece, there still remains a survival of that ancient way of marriage. A large armed party come to fetch the bride; her friends pretend resistance, and a mock combat takes place, as with Arabs, Druses, Turcomans, and others. The bride, who knows her own mind, allows herself to be carried off by the friends of the bridegroom, whence the Greek proverb, "Drive on, and never mind my tears."

Greek parents are very anxious to see their daughters married. The girls all work at the loom and spinning-wheel, and help to make a trousseau for their eldest sister, who is a favoured person, and inherits the family dwelling. She does not, however, take all their work, but from each piece of finished stuff reserves some lengths for the younger ones. On the father's death the brothers, or eldest male relatives, are expected to support the daughters and provide the dowry when one of them marries. Nor may the brothers marry until their sisters are provided for. This custom is said to have begun after the conquest of Mytilene by the Turks, when nearly all the men were slain, and husbands consequently very scarce.

Some of the curious local customs of this country may now claim our attention. The peasants, instead of throwing sweetmeats at the newly-married pair, smear the lintel of a bride's door with honey. In Northern Greece, and in Epirus, an engaged couple must not be seen together until after the betrothal. On this occasion the *fiancée* is introduced to her future husband at the priest's house, veiled, and attended by her parents. The priest, after giving his blessing, bids them not to meet again or converse until the wedding-day. On that day the bride takes leave of her parents and starts on foot, or on horseback, or on a mule, for the house of the bridegroom. After two or three days they are both led to the village fountain, where the bride throws sweatmeats (not a coin) into the water, and fills a new jar. In the district of Mount Pelion, the loaves for the wedding are publicly kneaded on the Thursday (the wedding being on a Sunday, as before). A young man chosen from among the bridegroom's friends does the kneading, while the others stand round and throw money into the trough.

In the Morea, the mother of the bridegroom, standing at the door of the house, gives the bride a glass of honey and water to drink, in the hope that "her lips may become as sweet as honey," and the lintel of the door is smeared with what remains, "that strife may never enter in." One of the company breaks a pomegranate on the threshold. Solon, in his laws, prescribed that the newly-married couple should eat a quince together, so that their converse might for ever be sweet. In Rhodes we find the same idea, only with a somewhat different ceremony. There the husband (after the wedding) dips his fingers in a cup of honey and traces a cross over the door, while the friends cry out, "Be good and sweet as this honey is," a piece of advice apparently intended only for the wife. The husband then crushes a pomegranate with his foot as he passes the threshold, and the guests throw corn, cotton seeds and orange-flower water on the bride, just as we in England throw rice.

In Cyprus the village girls and women assemble at the riverside some days before the wedding to wash the fabric of the bed. The filling up of the mattress is also done in public, and friends put in pieces of money, which remain there until the end of the first year, when the money may be taken out and spent. In some parts of China a somewhat similar custom prevails. Here in Cyprus, if the bridegroom hails from a distant village, he arrives on horseback. The young men meet him and endeavour to dismount him, while his friends come to the rescue to prevent this, and it is considered a triumph if he manages to ride all the way to his bride's house. Should the young men succeed in their object, the friends of the bridegroom must make a chair for him with their hands. Then follows a sacrifice, reminding us of Arab customs ; a fowl is held up, which the bridegroom kills by cutting off its head with an axe before entering the house.

The Albanians of the Orthodox creed have a curious custom connected with the kneading of the dough. One of the girls of the village is allowed to put on clothes belonging to the bridegroom, as well as his weapons, and thus attired chases him about, with the object of smearing his face with some of the dough from the trough. His friends throw in money, which the girl keeps, instead of the bridegroom, or his best man, as in Macedonia (see p. 177). Another of their customs is for the bride's mother to sprinkle the bridegroom with water, when he arrives at her house ; and she also places a handkerchief on his left shoulder. The bridegroom's man (the *vlam*) puts both her shoes and girdle on the bride ; and is also obliged to steal two spoons, or other articles (compare Tyrol). On the day after the wedding the newly-married couple sprinkle each other with water. (For a cognate Russian custom, see p. 201). Brahmins also use water in a similar way.

CHAPTER XIII

The Danubian Principalities.

AS might be expected, the peasants of Bulgaria retain many very old marriage customs, although the upper classes are gradually assimilating those of the modern Greeks. Marriages are arranged either by the young man's parents or by professional match-makers, who fix the sum to be paid by him, which must be at least £50, together with a smaller sum (head money) paid to the girl's mother. Our present description applies to marriages among the peasants only.

Betrothals are, as a rule, celebrated on a Wednesday or a Thursday evening with much feasting and rejoicing. On these occasions documents are produced stating that the bridegroom elect promises to pay the amount previously arranged by his parents or the "match-maker," while his future father-in-law declares his willingness to furnish his daughter with a trousseau.

The contracting parties exchange rings and a priest gives them his blessing. At the feast the elder guests arrange themselves around a cloth spread out on the floor: and there is a great variety of dishes all flavoured with garlic. The young people's banquet is served in a separate room, and they afterwards dance outside the house, singing songs every now and then. The wine flows freely. At this feast the young man produces his presents to the bride, such as slippers, bracelets, earrings, a head-dress of gold and silver coins and a silver girdle. At first her father expresses dissatisfaction, and so the would-be husband goes on adding one coin at a time to the head-dress until the former is satisfied. These presents are collected in a wooden dish, such as the people use for making bread, and then the feasting continues as before. Some of the guests are pretty sure to drink to excess before daylight appears. Next day the betrothed young woman dons her pretty jewelry and coins, and then her engagement is recognised.

It would be incorrect to say that love-matches are unknown among the peasants of Bulgaria, but they occur very rarely. It must be confessed that the husband chooses and buys his wife much in the same way as he would purchase a yoke of oxen or buffaloes. His object is to find a strong, healthy partner for life, who will be willing to work, and, he hopes, become the mother of strong lads to help him in the hard labour of working his farm. Beauty, therefore, does not count for much ; strength commands a higher price in the markets.

If a young man fails to fulfil his promise of marriage he is fined somewhat heavily by the aggrieved parents. The interval between betrothal and marriage is not less than six months, and may be as much as two or three years. The bridegroom has time, therefore, to change his mind should he be in some way disappointed, but it is quite exceptional for engagements to be broken off. There is much for him to do before the marriage takes place ; he builds a house with his own hands and furnishes it, buying at the same time cattle to stock his little farm or peasant's holding.

The bride's father and mother also contribute towards the furnishing of their daughter's new home. When all is prepared the young man sends his parents, or it may be some friend, to announce that he wishes the wedding to take place shortly. Marriages take place on Sundays and at a time of the year when there is little outdoor work going on, as might be expected among peasants.

The village girls dance in front of the bride's house and the young men before the bridegroom's. As in Sicily, and some other parts, the bride's trousseau is on view at her home a day or two before the wedding ; the neighbours, at least the women, take a curious delight in the inspection. This takes place on the Friday ; next day the bride's girl friends (as in Turkey, Greece, &c.) assist her at the bath and braid her hair. She never takes a bath again, and never had one before. The girls present flowers and sweets, and then cheer their friend with songs and dances. Her parents make cakes and send them round to their friends : this little courtesy is equivalent to an invitation to the wedding feast. The marriage generally takes place at the church, but sometimes at the house of the bridegroom.

According to Mrs. Blunt,[1] marriages take place in a store-house, or granary, for the sake of safety. She says the custom of marrying in some retired part of the house is due to a dread of Turks, who might fall on the bridal party and rob them. This lady, writing in 1878, tells a tale of events of "some months ago," which took place in a certain village in Macedonia. The dreaded Turks suddenly appeared on the scene, and after robbing and beating all the company, stripped the poor bride of all her belongings, and behaved with fiendish brutality. We need not mention details. When the ceremony has been performed at church the whole party go in procession to the bride's house, where the feast is held. Corn is sprinkled over the newly-wedded couple, and the young girls dance. The bride is veiled and kisses the hands of the married women present, each of whom gives her a fig. These wedding feasts, like those given at betrothals are very festive occasions, frequently marred by excessive drinking.

The following custom reminds us of what happens in some parts of Africa, for the unfortunate bride and bridegroom are shut up in their house for a week, during which time no visitors are allowed. At the conclusion of this term of imprisonment, married women come and conduct the bride to the village fountain, or spring, as in Greece, round which she walks three times. Then she kisses their hands and they give her figs. After which, let us hope, the

[1] "The People of Turkey."

water-nymphs will be good to her! Nothing more is then required of the young wife but to visit her mother.

The Bulgarians of Macedonia have certain peculiar customs in connection with the home-coming of a bride. When the husband's house is situated at some distance from that of his father-in-law, the party that conducts the bride is led by one of the guests carrying a standard on which is placed an apple—symbol of love and maternity. All are mounted on horseback and gaily decked out with garlands of flowers. Thus she is led with much singing and laughter to her new home, and we seem to see here a faint reflection of some old Greek procession in honour of Bacchus. On arriving at the village they are met by the "best man" and others with cakes, baskets of fruit, and flasks of wine. The *nuncio* (best man) leads a goat with gilded horns and carries the bridal crowns. Arrived at the house, the bride alights in the courtyard, where the standard has been placed. The father helps his daughter to dismount; she kisses her horse on the forehead, and is led by her parent, each holding one end of a handkerchief, to the granary down below. Here is displayed the wedding cake, which rests on a barrel of wine. The priest, arrayed in gorgeous robes, marries the couple at this Bacchanalian altar; they drink consecrated wine from a glass, and walk three times round the wine-barrel, while the company amuse themselves by throwing showers of sweets and fruit at them. There is the usual Greek ceremony of propitiating the water-nymphs at the well, in company with married women and girls. This is done by throwing in coins. It is interesting to find here the custom of throwing over the bride water from the well which she has herself drawn from it. In Russia the peasants throw water over both bride and bridegroom. Finally the bride kisses the hands of her women friends, and receives from each a fig, which is, of course, a symbolical act.

In Roumania, as in Bosnia and elsewhere, girls of a marriageable age wear coins and pearls on their heads as a sign to all that they have no objection to a husband. They begin at an early age to make garments for the trousseau. An Englishman once saw a little girl, six years old, knitting stockings for that purpose. The mothers are very anxious to let the young men know the extent of their daughter's trousseau, and allow them the privilege of inspecting the chest containing the necessary garments. Consequently the village bachelors become very mercenary, and if not satisfied with what they see, will look elsewhere for a wife. In a certain village the mothers anxious for a son-in-law seize the opportunity of carnival time to display the trousseau, by hanging out the various articles on a wall, or otherwise.

Fathers spend so much in providing for their daughters that the sons must look out for themselves, and seek well-endowed partners. The young lady must select her husband from a list of candidates—even when she has not the honour of their acquaintance. But the list informs her of their means and qualifications.

Some of their customs appear to be thoroughly Keltic: thus, in certain districts, on the wedding-day, when the bridegroom arrives at the house of his future wife, they make a pretence of being unwilling to give up their daughter, first of all bringing forward an old woman, as in the Tyrol, Brittany, and Switzerland.

An old custom, now dying out, is the "Maiden Market," somewhat akin to the Bride-show of Russia. On the Festival of St. Peter and St. Paul (June 29), the girls assembled on the top of a high mountain called Gaina. Trousseaux, packed in chests, were laboriously brought up in carts drawn by horses or oxen; and, in order to make a fair show, articles were sometimes borrowed. Each family stayed in a tent. Then came the young men with their parents, and a strange sight it must have been. But there was more sense in this plan than might appear at first sight; for in old days, the shepherds, who lived on the mountain sides, had very few opportunities of coming down into the valleys. And so, if the shepherds could not come to see the lassies, the lassies came up to them. Shepherds who had thus found wives went off with them, and the fathers and mothers down below were deserted. A girl betrothed at this fair would go to the village and offer a kiss to every decent man and woman she met. That was the way they bade farewell to their friends.

Bride and bridegroom frequently meet for the first time at the altar. It is on record that once a betrothed young man failed to appear at the church—perhaps having changed his mind. The situation was embarrassing, to say the least, for he could nowhere be found, though diligent search was made by messengers sent out for the purpose. Then a happy thought occurred to one of the party. The intended but missing bridegroom had a brother; "would he not do quite as well—or better?" So messengers were sent off in hot haste to ask if *he* would be so obliging as to marry the young lady his brother had so basely deserted? This invitation was accepted, and the bride married after all, which was better than coming away from the church unwedded! The remedy was simple; but one would think that the future relations between those two brothers must have been somewhat strained. It is to be hoped that the defaulter at least kept out of the way of his brother's wife.

Jilted suitors have a spiteful way of showing their disgust; they go out at night and cut down all the hemp and flax in the field from which the girl was about to spin the material for her clothes.

Marriages, among the upper classes, are celebrated late in the day; among poor people somewhat early. The ceremony does not always take place at church. Coins are thrown on to a carpet, on which the bride and bridegroom stand. Crowns are placed on their heads by the officiating priest. Sweets, or nuts (in country districts), are showered upon them — thus recalling the words of Virgil, "*Nuces sparge, marite.*" The day ends with dancing and feasting.

In Bosnia the married Mohammedan women go about closely veiled, like Turkish ladies, whereas girls are allowed more freedom in this respect. Hence the Turks have a proverb—"Go to Bosnia if you wish to see your betrothed." Although marriages are arranged by parents, the young people are not denied opportunities of converse before the wedding, consequently love-matches sometimes take place, and young men find their way to the fair one's window to whisper words of love ; but, by a curious restriction, only on Mondays and Fridays. Acccording to a well-known story a Bosnian young lady committed suicide because her lover was slain in battle. Omer Pasha, in narrating the story, remarks : "It all comes of not wearing the veil, and letting affianced couples see each other. If she had always kept her *yasmak* on her face, she might have married another man, for there would have been no great love in the matter."

Amongst the Morlacci of Dalmatia, the suitor approaches the family of his young lady through an intermediary. On being accepted by the fair one, he sends her certain presents, such as shoes, a mirror, a ring, a comb, a red silk ribbon for tying the hair, and an apple, stuck all over with gold and silver coins. His family also sends her gifts, such as shoes ; for unmarried girls usually wear only sandals. The bride-elect herself works stockings and garters for presents to the men of her future husband's family ; for the women, aprons, &c.

A good many official persons take part in the wedding ; for instance, there are the master of the ceremonies (*stari-svat*) ; the bridegroom's man (*compáré*) ; the flag-bearer (*bérakdár*), who carries a silk flag with an apple fixed to its spear-head—a symbol used by Bulgarians ; the two bridegroom's brothers (*divari*), who attend on the bride, carrying the umbrella over her ; the beadle (*cháiis*), who clears the way for the wedding procession. A woman accompanies the bride to the nave of the church. There the bridegroom and his *compáré* kneel before the altar awaiting the bride. When the service is over the two brothers of the bridegroom conduct the bride back to her home, where the marriage feast is held. And here we find an Armenian custom cropping up, for the bride, on approaching the door of her husband's house, takes in her arms a child. She then kneels down and kisses the threshold of the door. Her mother-in-law hands her a sieve containing dried fruits, which she scatters among the guests, thus symbolising the abundance she hopes will come to her new home. The husband, at dinner time, leaves her in charge of his two brothers, with whom she sits in a separate room—why we cannot say. During the meal he must not use a knife—that would bring unhappiness, and so his best man cuts up his food for him. Next day, all go to church again, and another feast is given by the husband at his own house, and the bride gives presents to the guests.

In certain parts, where the girls wear red caps, the cap is replaced at the church door by a veil. The unmarried girls wear many coins on their caps as well as on the front of the bodice. This gives the young men a chance of seeing at a glance how much they are worth, and resembles the Russian "Bride-show" described in the next chapter.

A Servian bride, before entering the bridegroom's house, must walk, or ride, three times round her mother-in-law, who holds a sieve of wheat in her hand. Then, on entering the house, she must walk three times round the hearth. A jester (the *çans*) throws the logs about the hearth, and the bride takes them up and sets them down properly.

CHAPTER XIV

Russia

THAT Russians do not esteem women highly is clearly shown by their proverbs. "There is only one soul," they say, "between ten women." A husband declares, "I love thee as my soul, and I beat thee as my cloak." In country districts they marry early, but the sons do not quit their father's house. This arrangement is found to be very profitable, for the daughters-in-law not only all work, and so increase the wealth produced by the family, but also bring a portion of land with them as dowry. Boys are now forbidden to marry until they attain the age of seventeen, but it is not very long ago that grown-up women were to be seen carrying about boys of six to whom they had been betrothed.

Kovalevsky has well shown that many of the marriage customs of this country are survivals from a primitive and prehistoric age when the woman ruled the household and had more than one husband. The tie between brother and sister is very strong, the brother being her guardian and protector. He plays a very important part at the wedding. Thus, in accordance with old custom, when the bridegroom has arrived at the bride's house her brother sits down by her side with a naked sword, or a stick in his hand, and, on being requested by the bridegroom to surrender his seat, replies that he is there to keep ward over his sister, and will not move unless he is paid for it.

"Dear brother, don't give me away for nothing; ask a hundred roubles for me, and for the veil which covers my head a thousand roubles. Ask for my beauty, God alone knows how much." Such is the tenor of the songs composed for the occasion. This shows that brothers had the power of selling their sisters in marriage, and it all points to a distant age when the matriarchal system prevailed, and the brother was his sister's guardian. In Little Russia the brother's sword is decked with the red berries of the rowan tree, red being the emblem of maidenhood.

The "Bride-show," another ancient custom, is no longer kept up. Youths and maidens of the trading class used to assemble in great numbers, some to admire, others to be admired. The girls stood in a row, arrayed in their best dresses, their mothers keeping guard behind. Speaking of one of these shows, an English traveller relates that one of the mothers, being at a loss to think of any fresh charm for her daughter, made a necklace of six dozen silver-gilt spoons, a girdle of an equal number of tablespoons, and fastened a couple of silver ladles behind in the form of a cross. The young men walked up and down like inspecting officers, but were not allowed to express their admiration. If a youth found a maiden to his fancy, he could arrange for the betrothal through a match-maker. The embassy or party which, among the peasants, goes to the girl's house always starts at night, and tries to avoid meeting any person, for that would be a bad omen. Having knocked at the cottage door and asked permission to enter, they are politely received and requested to take seats, which they refuse to do until the purport of their visit has been declared. "We have a brave youth," they say, "you have a fair maiden. Might not the two be brought together?" The parents of the girl acknowledge the compliment, and then all sit down to a meal. When this is over the embassy ask for a final answer, and the parents, having first pleaded for delay, give their consent. Then follows the "hand-striking," or first ceremony, before the betrothal, which cannot be broken. A candle is lighted and placed before the holy picture; the youth and the maiden utter a prayer and strike hands over the bargain. As with the Chinese, the Jews of old, and other peoples, so here the girl must bewail the change that is in store for her, and continue to do so up to the time of the actual marriage. Her companions, on the day before the wedding, express her feelings in many poetic forms, while she undoes her long single plait of hair, the badge of maidenhood, and distributes the ribbons and flowers thereon.

In old days a betrothed maiden, by way of expressing complete submission to her lord, presented him on the wedding-day with a whip made by herself, and he went through the ceremony of giving her a gentle stroke on the shoulders, to show that he intended to be master. Another custom, now changed, had the like significance; after the marriage ceremony the bride used to knock her head on her husband's shoe in token of obedience, and he cast the lap of his gown over her in token of his duty to protect and cherish her (compare Ruth iii. 9). But at the present day the bride need only make a show of prostrating herself at his feet.

The betrothal is a ceremony performed with the rites of the Eastern Church, and takes place eight days before the marriage. During the interval between betrothal and marriage the bride's girl friends endeavour to amuse her and keep up her spirits (for she is supposed to be in a state of lamentation and grief) by singing to her, and their songs tell of the happiness of married life. On the day before the wedding they conduct her to the bath (as among Arabs and others), where much time is spent in dressing her hair, while she listens to their songs.

Russian marriages are attended by a great deal of ceremony. In middle-class life there are a great many "assistants" to be invited. These are the "witnesses" to the register, being the nearest relatives of the pair; the "ladies of honour" who accompany them to church; the "bridesmen" acting as stewards; and the *boyárin*,[1] who carry the sacred pictures. Among

[1] Large landed proprietors, who used to attend the reigning princes.

nobles the wedding takes place in the evening. Both bride and bridegroom receive a solemn blessing from their parents before leaving their houses, and even the wedding garments are blessed by the priest. The *boyárin* carry the sacred picture in procession before the couple to the church, where a lighted wax taper is given to each, and the belief is that the one whose light goes out first will be the first to die.

The marriage service is divided into three parts, once celebrated at different times, but now all taken together. The first is the office of Espousals, in which gold rings are exchanged. Secondly, the office of Matrimonial Coronation, in which bride and bridegroom are crowned with crowns of silver filagree (or garlands). Thirdly, the office of the Dissolution of the Crowns. It has been well pointed out that all these ceremonials are so exactly like those of the old Roman nuptials that they would appear to have been derived therefrom. Roman poets and historians allude to them all.

The giving of wine mingled with water is an allusion to the marriage of Cana, and takes place after the last of the above ceremonies. Then the pair, following the priest, walk three times round the small movable altar on which the cross and the Gospels are placed, listen to exhortation, kiss one another three times, and receive his benediction. They also kiss the holy pictures.

One of the many superstitions still prevailing among the peasant population of Russia is that, on the occasion of a marriage, the happiness of the newly-married couple is not assured unless the parents of the contracting parties are soaked with water from head to foot. When a marriage takes place in summer this is easily accomplished by ducking the fathers and mothers in the nearest river, but in winter they are laid on the ground and rolled in the snow. According to the Moscow correspondent of *The Daily Mail*, the observance of this curious custom has recently caused the death of a bride's father in the village of Sysertsky, in the Upha province. In this case the wedding guests were all drunk, as is usual on these occasions, and, instead of simply rolling the man in the snow, they brought water out of the house in a bucket and threw it over him. Now the temperature was far below the freezing point, and consequently it is not surprising to read that the unfortunate man took a severe chill from which he never recovered.

The following account of a marriage in middle-class life is chiefly derived from a detailed description, given many years ago by Dr. Granville in his book on St. Petersburg. At the appointed time a large number of friends of the parties, having previously assembled in the church, attended by a deacon, proceeded down the church from the altar to the door, where he received the candidates for matrimony. After he had delivered to each a lighted taper, and made the sign of the cross three times on their foreheads, he conducted them to the upper part of the nave. The bride was attended by young ladies in splendid dresses, and incense was scattered before them as they advanced. The priest, as he went, recited a litany in which the choristers assisted, and, at its conclusion, halted before a table, on which the rings were deposited; then, turning towards the altar with the bride and bridegroom behind him, he repeated a very short and impressive prayer, or invocation. After this he turned round to the couple and blessed them; and then, taking the rings from the table, gave one to each, proclaiming in a loud voice that they were married to each other "now and for ever, even unto ages of ages." This declaration he repeated three times, the bride and bridegroom exchanging rings at each declaration. The rings were then again surrendered to the priest, who, after having crossed the foreheads of the young couple with them, placed them on the forefinger of the right hand of each. He then again turned towards the altar and read another impressive part of the service, in which allusion is made to all the passages of the Bible in which a ring is mentioned as the symbol of union, honour, and power.

After this, the priest took the young couple by the hand and led them towards a silken carpet which lay spread on the ground. This is to the mass of spectators a moment of great interest; for it is firmly believed that the one who first steps upon the carpet will have the mastery of the other throughout life. "In the present instance," says Dr. Granville, "the bride secured possession of this prospective advantage with modest forwardness."

A BOYAR BRIDAL FEAST, RUSSIA. *By* K. E. MAKOWSKI.

By Permission of Friedrich Bruckmann, Munich.

Two silver imperial crowns were then produced by a layman, and received by the priest, who, after blessing the bridegroom, placed one of these ornaments on his head ; the other was merely held over the bride's head in order that the superstructure raised by a fashionable hairdresser of St. Petersburg might not be deranged. After the crowning, a cup was brought to the priest, who after drinking from it himself, gave it to the bridegroom, who took three sips, and then delivered it to the bride, by whom the same ceremony was repeated. After a short pause other prayers were recited, and, these being concluded, the priest took the pair by the hand, and walked three times round the desk, reciting some sentences. Then, taking off the bridegroom's crown, he said, "Be thou magnified, O bridegroom, as Abraham! Be thou blessed as Isaac, and multiplied as Jacob, walking in peace, and performing the commandments of God in righteousness." In removing the bride's crown he said, "And be thou magnified, O bride, as Sarah! Be thou joyful as Rebecca, and multiplied as Rachel ; delighting in thine own husband, and observing the bounds of the law, according to the good pleasure of God."

After this the tapers were extinguished, and taken from the bride and bridegroom, who were then dismissed by the priest with his blessing, and received the congratulations of the company, and saluted each other. Dancing and feasting continue for three days after the wedding, and on the eighth day, the parties again repair to the church, when the priest performs the ceremony of "Dissolving the Crowns" with appropriate prayers. Things have changed since Dr. Granville saw this wedding, and now the "dissolving of the crowns" is part of the actual marriage service.

Marriages sometimes take place among the poor convicts in Siberian prisons. According to law, the woman must follow her husband, and therefore the wives and *fiancées* of the condemned must ask and obtain permission to follow them into exile. When husband and wife are both prisoners, the man being condemned to exile in Western Siberia, while the woman must go to Eastern Siberia, the position is reversed and the husband follows the wife. How sad and strange are these marriages, performed by consent of the Minister of the Interior, before a temporary altar in the Director's office, or in one of the cells, all wearing grey cloaks and sometimes chains! The unhappy pair cannot live together until after arrival at their destination.

Among the Koraks of Siberia a young man seeks for a maiden with considerable dowry in the form of reindeer which are the most valuable kind of property in these parts. As in all eastern countries, the marriage is arranged with the young woman's parents. Should they be satisfied with his position and prospects in life, the would-be husband is allowed to propose matrimony to the girl herself. On being accepted, the lover takes up his abode in the home of his future wife, but he must not be afraid of hard work; for a young man in this position is expected to be a hewer of wood and a drawer of water, and generally to contribute to the interests of the family who have adopted him. These people have an interesting survival of the ancient institution of marriage by capture. The game, as played by the lover and the betrothed, somewhat resembles the well-known "hide-and-seek" so popular with children in all countries. It appears to be the chief ceremony at a wedding, and doubtless affords endless amusement to the assembled guests. The family dwelling-place is a large tent, with many compartments, separated off by hanging curtains of reindeer skins. Some contain as many as twenty-six compartments; all arranged in a circle around the open space in the centre. Here the assembled guests are crowded together to witness an amusing and highly exciting scene. Points of matrimonial etiquette are keenly discussed as they stand round the fire that lights up the tent, or regale themselves with the good things served up for the feast. Much hot tea is drunk on these occasions. There is plenty of noise too; for a drummer is employed who vigorously beats a native drum. Soon a tall, elderly Korak enters, bearing under his arm a bundle of willow-shoots, which he distributes throughout the tent, leaving one in each compartment. We shall see presently how these are used. The drummer now adds to the noise and excitement by singing a loud and barbarous chant. Then the bride and bridegroom are brought forth in the company of an old man. The music grows louder and louder, and the excitement is intense, as the venerable relative suddenly gives a signal to the bride to begin the game of "hide-and-seek!" Quick as thought she darts away into the first compartment, the bridegroom following with no less rapid steps. Both are now hidden from view by the first curtain of reindeer skins, and by that time the bride has doubtless escaped into the second division of the tent. Not so, however, the luckless bridegroom! His progress is considerably impeded by the women who have taken up their stations in each compartment, and endeavour to prevent him from catching his bride by beating him with the willow rods, as he rushes along in hot pursuit. Some try to trip him up; others endeavour to entangle him in the reindeer skins, which they quickly throw over his head. But he rushes on, overcoming all obstacles, at least if he is determined, like a man, not to fail in his object. The women beat him unmercifully, but still it is all a great joke; and what does a little pain count when there is a chance of catching a wife? In a few moments the bride has reached the last compartment, and perhaps it is hardly necessary to say that the bridegroom, in most cases, catches her there. Should he fail to do so, it may be taken to mean that the girl does not wish to become his wife. Perhaps she hardly knows her own mind. In that case he must serve another two years, and try his luck again. But as a rule all ends happily, the bride waiting for her lover in the last compartment. May-be she pities him, and "pity is akin to love." The guests, of course, are greatly delighted when the young people come forth hand in hand. There can no longer be any doubt that the fair one is willing to become a bride, and so the two receive the congratulations and good wishes of the assembled guests. Henceforth they are man and wife. We seem to see here traces of certain customs observed in India, and perhaps of Mongolian origin, as, for instance, the pelting of the bridegroom with balls of boiled rice.

CHAPTER XV

Scandinavia and Polana

IN Sweden if a youth and maiden eat of the same piece of bread people say they are sure to fall in love with one another. This is not an indispensable preliminary—at least in the province of Bohus and in Finland. In those parts a matrimonial go-between is often employed to carry the youth's offer to the fair lady, whom perhaps her suitor has never seen. Should the proposal find favour with the maiden and her parents, the ambassador presents his client to the family on the following Sunday. The young people do not at this stage converse with one another ; the girl, ignoring her suitor's presence, devotes herself to knitting ; but the youth, having no resource of the kind, is often reduced to the last stage of self-conscious misery.

In the neighbourhood of Torna (Scania) the maid's acceptance of her lover's offer is celebrated by a feast called *Ja-öl*, or "yes-ale," and the suitor gives his mistress a *Ja-gofva*, or "yes-gift," a silver goblet containing coins wrapped in paper. At the betrothal they exchange rings and present gifts to each other—on the maiden's side a trifle of her own handiwork; from the lover a prayer-book, on the cover of which is engraved a heart and some Scripture texts. In Rackeby (Western Götland) the girl's present to her lover, a shirt of the finest material, which is worn on the wedding-day, but *never* afterwards. On his death he is buried in it. No one should make presents without due reflection; if a youth offer his intended bride a knife it will cut the love between them; shoes, and she will leave him for another; a pocket-handkerchief, and it will wipe away her affection for him.

Sometimes years may elapse between the betrothal and the wedding. Great preparations are made as the day approaches, and invitations are sent to a great number of guests. These do not, as in the Tyrol and elsewhere, pay their share towards expenses incurred at an inn, but they lighten the cost of entertainment by bringing with them to the bridal house a large supply of provisions. As long as these last the festivities continue. In Norway it was usual for the rejoicings to be spread over a fortnight, but nowadays people are content with a day or two of merriment. A pretty custom obtains in Bohus and Finland. Two spruce pine-trees, divested of their lower branches and bark, are placed one on each side of the entrance door of the bridal house, not, say some, to be removed until the bride becomes a mother. The wedding-day in Scandinavia begins with a repast at the house of the parents of one or other of the bridal pair. In the south of Sweden (Götland) the guests each take away with them a ring of wheaten bread and a flask of brandy, so that, as was the custom of old time in Scotland, they may be able to treat any friend they meet with on the way. Already the bride has been dressed by her tire-woman (*Drott-säta*), the wife of the pastor of the village. She wears a black dress, with much display of artificial flowers and parti-coloured ribbons ; a girdle clasps her waist ; round her neck hang pearls ; while her crown is either a myrtle-wreath, a circlet of spangled paper, or a gorgeous one of silver—a loan from the church. The shoes, which in some places are put on by two members of the bridegroom's party, form an important part of her apparel. There must be no buckles or ties in them, as she hopes for easy child-bearing, and in each a silver coin is placed so that money may never be lacking in her new life. Shod in these she sallies forth to the cowhouse, where, if she milks one cow, milk will never be lacking in her new home. While in England we welcome the appearance of the sun on the bridal day, the Swedes are glad to see a gentle rain ; she will be a rich woman, they say, on whose crown the rain falls.

During the ceremony the bridesmaids hold a canopy of shawls over the bride. When the service is over the Warend woman stands to distribute alms in the church-yard, no doubt, like her German sister, to "take away misfortune."

In some districts of West Götland, on the return home the mother meets her daughter on the threshold and puts a lump of sugar or a coffee bean in her mouth.

A HARDANGER BRIDE, NORWAY. *From a Photograph by M. Selmer.*

Is this a means of securing future plenty, or does it serve as a reminder of the necessity of preserving a sweet temper through married life? In the olden time an offering was made to the "trolls" or "fairies" by placing under the charmed tree of the homestead a plate of delicacies coming from the feast. Traces of the reverence paid to these "little people" still remain; the bride puts something of every dish of which she partakes during the wedding meal on a plate, and it is given in alms to some dependent of the family.

The dowry in Lapland consists of reindeer, so many head of cattle according to the state of the parental finances. The Lapp is above all things careful to "go where money is." "How many reindeer has she?" is always a bachelor's first question when he thinks of entering upon a marriage treaty. As he gives a goodly supply of presents, plate and jewelry, at the conclusion of the bargain, the Lapp may in a sense be said to buy his wife.

An American tourist once joined, out of curiosity, a wedding party of Lapps. He was invited to partake of their meal of boiled sheep. After drinking the bride's health, he watched the guests take their meat from a common dish, cut it with the knives they wear at the waist into small pieces, and swallow it at a gulp. He noticed that the bride was older than the bridegroom, and learned later that it was the usual thing in Lapland—a money match, in fact.

In Norway, where old customs are rapidly falling into disuse, it is not uncommon for a wedding feast to take place at a popular restaurant in the nearest town. A bridal party may sometimes be seen rowing in a boat across a fjord, as in our illustration.

When the guests have eaten and drunk to their heart's content, dancing is the order of the day. In many districts the bride "dances off her crown" with much ceremony. She stands blindfolded in the centre of a ring of dancing maidens, and puts her crown haphazard on the head of any one of them within reach. The maiden thus distinguished is looked on by the company as the next bride, and becomes in her turn the centre of the ring; so the crown goes from one to the other throughout the party. Lastly the young wife, lifted high on a chair, drinks to the speedy marriage of all the maidens present. She then takes her place among the married women.

The bridegroom takes leave of the ranks of his bachelor "associates" in a similar fashion. He dances with each in turn, and is then hoisted on their shoulders. A scuffle ensues for the possession of his person between the married and single men, and he is often severely handled in the struggle. At the conclusion of this ceremony the pair are sometimes called by the quaint title of "young father" and "young mother," and retiring, they take off their bridal clothing and reappear in simple garments befitting staid married folk.

The mirth and jollity continues far into the night, when in the Torna district the pastor conducts the wife and then the husband to the bridal chamber, where

A Norwegian Wedding Party going to Church. *From a Photograph by Valentine & Sons.*

he delivers a suitable exhortation. The guests presently throng in to utter their good wishes, whereupon the bridegroom hands every man a glass of brandy, and the bride gives to every woman one filled with wine. Next day, in Bohus and Finland, the bride hides away and a search ensues for the missing one. After she has been discovered, brought home in state, and installed as mistress of the house, she celebrates the occasion in the usual manner by filling glasses; and these are refilled when the friends make their offering to the young couple, each one placing a coin on the wedding cake. Perhaps these potations are less liberal now than they were a generation ago. The return home after these festivities must have been attended with some danger to those who had done honour to the host's cellar, and forests and mountains have witnessed strange sights.

Danish weddings are mostly celebrated in July, or about Christmas time. With regard to days, Thursday is considered favourable, but Danes are frequently married on a Saturday or a Sunday. Invitations are given through a friend of the bridegroom, who rides on a horse with gay trappings. Should the good people be not at home, this envoy goes in search of them. Hat in hand, he delivers his message in a formal set speech, which is written out legibly and placed in the hat, in case he should forget any part of it. "You must not put the messenger to shame," he says in conclusion, and rides away to the next house where friends or relations of the bridegroom may be dwelling.

The bride, on her way to church, must never once look back, such an act would augur ill for her future happiness. Musicians head the procession, bridesmaids come next, then the bride ; the bridegroom and his men follow in their own separate procession.

The feast takes place at the bridegroom's house ; a few speeches are delivered, and the company begin to dance. After about two hours the husband must take his bride's crown from off her head.

In West Jutland guests and relatives assemble at the bride's house in the morning, to help in preparing the feast, as in Lower Brittany. They bring contributions of butter, eggs, or poultry.

The bride, who has been attired by the clergyman's wife, heads the procession to the church ; she is accompanied by two "bride-women" (of whom one is the lady who attired her), and her own bridesmaids. All walk in twos, and after the ceremony (among Roman Catholics) the guests attend Mass.

The feasting is on a liberal scale, and the bride and bridegroom lead the dancing with a reel. When the girls are tired of dancing they play games until supper is served, about three o'clock in the morning. Each guest takes away a present in return for his contribution to the feast.

The following account of a Polish wedding in high life nearly a century ago, shows that the nobles of the country married their daughters with a splendour and magnificence which was almost royal. Its accuracy can be relied upon, for the facts are all taken from a diary kept by the sister of the bride herself. The ceremony of betrothal was briefly as follows :—

The family lived in a castle, and one day at the dinner, which took place at noon, the mother put into the hands of her daughter Barbara an entangled skein of silk, upon which she blushed and appeared unable to raise her eyes. Her future husband had been invited to the meal—all eyes were fixed on the bride elect. The family jester made many sly jokes to amuse the company. After dinner the girl sat in a recess of one of the large windows, and began to unravel the skein of silk, upon which her future husband approached with these words, "Am I to understand, madam, that you do not oppose yourself to my happiness?" Barbara's way of saying "yes" was, "My parents' wishes have ever been sacred to me." The young man was conducted by his father and the priest, to a sofa on which the noble lord and lady of the castle were seated. Then the father, addressing the latter, assured them that his heart was filled with sentiments of the sincerest affection and of profound esteem for the illustrious family of ——, and that he had long desired this coming alliance. Their daughter was a model of virtue and grace, and his son was to his father a source of pride and consolation. He then took from one of his own fingers a diamond ring and, placing it on a salver held by the priest, said, "This ring I received from my parents and placed upon the finger of my lamented wife upon the day of our betrothal. Permit my son now to place it on your daughter's hand, as a pledge of his unalterable love and true devotion."

This was followed by an address from the priest, after which the bride's father replied that he willingly consented to the union, that he now gave up all rights over her. The mother then placed a valuable ring on the salver with these words, "I concur in what my husband had said, and present my daughter with this ring, the most precious jewel of our house. My father received it from the hands of Augustus II. when he concluded the Treaty of Karlowitz. . . . It was with this ring, the memory of which is so dear, that I was betrothed. I bestow it now upon my child, in the fervent hope that she may be as happy in her marriage as I have been in mine." The priest having pronounced a blessing, one of the rings was given to the daughter, the other to her betrothed husband, who placed the one she received on the little finger of her left hand, fastening it down with a kiss. This finger is called the "heart finger." She, however, did not keep the ring, but presented it to her future husband with trembling hands. He again kissed her hands and, throwing himself at the feet of her parents, swore to do all in his power to make their daughter happy. While her father was filling a large goblet with old Hungarian wine, many pretty compliments were paid to his daughter. The health of the betrothed couple was then drunk—first by the father, who completely drained the goblet, and then by all the gentlemen present, so that it was refilled many times. Thus ended the first day. On the following day a consultation was held over the trousseau, the result of which was that the lord of the castle put down one thousand Dutch ducats with orders to prepare all that was necessary.

Chamberlains carried the news to all parts of Poland. The eldest of these chamberlains, all gentlemen of noble birth, attended by a groom splendidly equipped, was entrusted with letters for the king, the princes, the lord archbishops, and the chief senators, begging their blessings, and saying how greatly he would be honoured by their presence at the wedding.

The bridegroom, it goes almost without saying, gave costly presents to all members of the bride's family. One day the whole of the court at the castle went hunting, according to an old custom which is supposed to bring good luck to the betrothed. They came back in the evening with the spoils of the chase. The wild boar laid at the bride's feet had been killed by her betrothed.

For several days the ladies of the house were busily occupied in making useful gifts for the bride, the mother being naturally very busy with the trousseau. The skein of silk so successfully unravelled by the daughter (by which she fully proved her fitness for matrimony) was made into a purse for her husband. The latter then left the castle to return later on for the wedding. During his visit he confined his attentions not, as an Englishman would, to the young lady, but to the parents of his *fiancée*. This was the strict etiquette then, the idea being that the true way to win the lady's affection would be by pleasing her family. There is certainly something to be said for this custom—if only by way of rebuke to those engaged young couples in our own country, who constantly go and sit in a room by themselves, regardless of their relations and friends.

Time passed quickly, and noble guests arriving at the castle were received with discharges of musketry and troops presenting arms. Bands played at intervals.

The marriage deed was drawn up in the presence of all the assembled guests. At last the wedding-day arrived. Early in the morning the bride and bridegroom went to church to confess and receive the Holy Sacrament. The priest gave his blessing as they knelt before the altar. Breakfast was served at the castle, after which the bride was attired in a rich white dress, with Brabant lace worked in silver. In the bouquet worn at her waist there had been put a golden coin, struck on the day of her birth, a piece of bread, and a little salt; when this custom is observed they say the married pair will never be in want of food or funds. A morsel of sugar was added to give sweetness to their lives.

Then the folding doors were thrown wide open and the bride appeared supported by two ladies. She was in tears, and advanced with trembling steps striving hard to restrain her sobs. The bridegroom came forward, took her hand, and led her to his father and mother-in-law, before whom both knelt down together to receive a blessing. On rising from their knees, the bride and bridegroom walked all round the room, while each person present wished them happiness. Then all proceeded to the private chapel attached to the castle, where the priest stood before the altar on which an immense number of candles were burning. A rich cloth covered the altar steps. The bride and bridegroom knelt, while bridesmaids, groomsmen, and parents behind stood at one side. The *Veni Creator* was chanted, and the priest gave a long discourse in Latin. Rings having been exchanged, the newly-married couple threw themselves at the feet of the bride's parents to receive their blessing. At a signal from the master of the ceremonies, an Italian vocalist, sent expressly from Warsaw, began singing, accompanied by a band of musicians. Outside the dragoons kept up a continued discharge of musketry, and at intervals cannon were fired off. At length when the noise had ceased, the bride's father made a speech which so affected his daughter that she could make no reply.

Dinner was served in the great hall. The wedding cake, an edifice of sugar four feet high, represented the Temple of Hymen adorned with allegorical figures and surmounted by the arms of the two families now allied by marriage, surrounded by French inscriptions. This cake was the product of a fortnight's work on the part of the confectioner. The table bore many other beautiful things, such as china figures, gold and silver baskets, and toast after toast was drunk with great enthusiasm, and a tun of Hungarian wine was emptied during the dinner! The company drank to the newly-married couple, to the State, the king, the princes, the archbishop, the clergy, and lastly, to the host and hostess. After each toast glasses were broken and cannon fired, and a blast was blown on the trumpet. When dessert was ended there followed a silence, during which the father called for the master of the household, and in a low tone of voice gave him orders to fetch something. This proved to be a morocco leather box containing a golden cup in the form of a crow, studded with precious stones; showing it to the company he told them that it had descended to him from a long line of ancestors. He then filled it with very old wine, and drank to the health and prosperity of the bride and bridegroom. The toast was received with great enthusiasm, the music became louder than ever, and all the guns thundered at once. Before all had drunk from this beautiful old goblet, a hundred bottles of wine had passed out of it. In the evening there was a grand ball. The king's representative danced with the bride by way of "opening the ball." First a polonaise was danced, then came minuets, quadrilles, mazurkas, and other more lively dances.

In the middle of all this dancing a curious ceremony took place. A chair having been placed in the centre of the room, the bride sat in it while the twelve bridesmaids unfastened her coiffure, singing all the while in the most melancholy tone, "Barbara, it is all over, then—

you are lost to us ; you belong to us no more ! " Her mother took the rosemary from her hair, and a little matron's cap of lace was placed on her head. The dancing then recommenced, and each of the gentlemen had the privilege of a short dance with the bride, her last partner being her father, who gave her up to his son-in-law for ever. The married ladies conducted her to the bridal chamber with tears.

CHAPTER XVI

Germany.

THE Thuringian youths do their love making on the way home from a village dance, or fair ; and a swain puts the momentous question in its boldest form. "Will you have me ?" he says. "I should like to marry you." And, like Mr. Barrie's Thrums lassie, the Thuringian girl rarely dares to refuse the first man who asks her. So they walk home happily together, and look upon the matter as settled.

Should, however, a Schellroda girl (or her parents) wish to say "no," they do not give utterance to that disagreeable little word, but when the youth comes to make his offer, they put a sausage on the table during the meal, of which their guest partakes. Whenever this favourite dish appears, the lover knows that his is a hopeless suit. He must either seek a wife elsewhere or be condemned to bachelorhood.

Among Bavarian peasants the bride's fine eyes are often of less importance than the "fine eyes of her casket," for there the wooer's ambition is to have a wife with three thousand gulden. But to obtain this he must himself be in prosperous circumstances. When the matrimonial agent has laid the proposal before the eligible lady's parents, her father pays the youth a visit, during which he inspects the house from garret to cellar, as well as the stables, cattle and entire farmstead. If the inspection has produced a favourable impression, the suitor is informed of the fact, not there and then, but in a few days, and they enter upon the preliminaries of marriage.

Among the people of Saxe-Altenburg (a duchy to the north of Saxony), suitability of rank is one of the first considerations. The good folk are nothing if not exclusive, the peasantry being divided into three classes, according to the nature or amount of property they possess. The patrician class consists of proprietors who have at least two horses, and is further sub-divided according to the number—whether two, three, four or five—of these useful animals which a man's stable contains. Members of the second class are often not inferior to the first in wealth, but their stock consists of cows only; while day-labourers, artisans, and the rank and file, who merely possess or rent a house and garden, come last. It is not an unheard-of thing, but it is rare, for a member of one class to marry into another. The proud possessors of horses do not willingly link their fortunes with those who have only cows grazing in their fields; and it would be a distinct *mésalliance* for either to choose a partner from the ranks of those who have no cattle or fields at all.

A young man in the Upper Palatinate (Bavaria) gives to the lady of his choice an uneven number of coins, which he has obtained by exchanging them for some of his own money, but not with a woman; neither must he allow any of the fair sex to see them while they are in his possession.

A young Thuringian, after the betrothal, which is usually celebrated in the family circle, gives the bride-elect a finely bound prayer-book with name and date on the cover; and the Altenburger orders two rings to be ready by the time of the feast.

Like the Tyrolese Procurator the bearer of invitations is in many parts of Germany one of the most conspicuous of the wedding guests; and in Saxe-Altenburg this office, requiring such a happy combination of tact, fluency and activity, descends from father to son. When this person, decked out in ribbons and wreaths, arrives with his message of invitation to friend or relative of bride or bridegroom, he is sure to receive refreshment and a welcome. In some parts of Thuringia he appears a week before the joyful day, and in Niedergrundstedt, as a sign that his message has been duly delivered, he leaves on the courtyard door a chalk drawing of two hearts, inside which are the initials of both bride and bridegroom.

The condition of a betrothed maiden in the Upper Palatinate is so critical, and such dire consequences are supposed by these superstitious people to follow on her simplest action, that we wonder any young lady in those parts ever dares to contemplate marriage! She must particularly avoid contact with the dead and dying, and never, upon any consideration, lift up anything she finds in her path. A young girl by bringing into the house two horse-shoes she happened to find was believed to have caused the death of a horse!

Much difference of opinion prevails on the favourableness of certain times and seasons for the celebration of a wedding. In some parts of the Mark country (Prussia and Prussian Saxony) Thursday is a favourite day; in others Tuesday, for people say when there is a marriage on Thursday (*Donnerstag*), there will be thunder in the marriage, "*so donnert's in der Ehe*," or, as a sailor might put it, the pair must "look out for squalls." It is a pity that on such an important point as this there is not a clearer agreement. Wednesdays or Fridays are, in different districts, selected for the marriage of widows and widowers. When, however, Innocents' Day falls on a Tuesday, that day is, in the Upper Palatinate, avoided the whole year through. In Thuringia weddings usually take place in the beginning or at the close of the year, and a good deal of attention is paid to the signs of the Zodiac; people who are so foolhardy as to marry under Cancer, Scorpio, Pisces or Libra must expect misfortune. The like happens in all parts when a couple weds when the moon is on the wane, while, on the other hand, a waxing moon betokens increase.

In the Upper Palatinate, where a bridal pair appear to live in an atmosphere of superstitious terror, there are quite a catalogue of rules to be observed in conveying the dowry-cart to the husband's house. The bride may be observed following it, weeping as she goes, in order that she may not be forced to shed tears afterwards in her married life. It is true she has taken all manner of precautions to ensure happiness. She has sewn five crosses on the bed-cover, so that the witches may not cast their spells over her ; she looked to the spinning-wheel, and saw that it was properly placed in the cart with the distaff side towards the horses, so that she need not be afraid of dying in child-birth. And should she be a Neukirchen maiden, the first thing she carries into the new home will be a crucifix, or the pair will have nothing but crosses during their married life.

On his side the bridegroom is equally anxious to avert misfortune. At Tiefenbach, while he is helping to unload the cart, he marks with consecrated chalk every article of the bride's household goods, making on it three crosses, and sprinkling it with holy water. In the parts of Bohemia near the Tyrolese frontier he must be liberal with his money on this day, for while the cart is being driven to his home the village lads bar the way with poles or ropes, and ere they will let the horses pass, a toll of one or two florins is exacted from him. Here the priest enters to bless the house and all the bride's recently transported belongings, according to the old Roman ritual, "*Benedictio thori et thalami.*" Nor in the midst of this season of rejoicing do the young folk forget those who can no longer take part in their gladness. After the bridal furniture has been housed and arranged the pair go to the church-yard, and kneel down to pray at the graves of their

THE RANSOM. *By* C. A. PABST. *From a Photograph by Braun, Clement & Cie.*

relations. They have already engaged the priest to say a mass for the repose of these good people's souls.

A curious custom connected with the *Polterabend*, or wedding-eve, obtains in Hanover, Prussia, Thuringia, and other parts. The village children fling old crockery against the door of the bride's house, and the higher the heap of broken pieces, the more happiness will be enjoyed by the wedded pair. A friend of the present writer, once a wedding guest at a house in the old city of Hildesheim, well remembers how the ancient entrance door shook and rattled as each fresh crock broke against its panels, and the glee with which the youthful hopes of the Fatherland disported themselves amidst fragments of jars and dishes in the streets.

The Thuringian lads and lasses have a pretty custom of putting pine trees before the door of the bride's house, and decorating them with wreaths and ribbons on the night before the wedding day. The custom of preventing misfortune by distribution of alms, &c., is very prevalent. In some parts of Thuringia the poorest person in the village receives a slice of cake from the bride's hand at the house-door on the day preceding the marriage. The young couple are always mindful how frail are their chances of happiness. Do they think with the Greeks of old that felicity excites the envy of the gods? On the wedding-day the bridegroom of Kalbar-Werder, an island in the Havel, near Potsdam, sends a cart and six horses to fetch the bride from her father's house. Other guests, her relations and parents, are content to ride behind four, or merely a pair of horses in the procession ; but she drives up at noon into her future husband's courtyard, as she proudly says, "in a cart with six horses." Could a princess have more ?

The Thuringian bride is clothed in black, with a gorgeous display of coins and chains. On her head she wears a tall, tower-like scarlet covering, round which circles a wreath of myrtle or rosemary. In her pocket the Mark girl has dill and salt, as a protection against the evil one ; in her shoes she puts hairs of every kind of cattle in the farmstead, a practice which they say causes the flocks and herds belonging to the young couple to increase and flourish. So important is this matter that a bridal pair coming from the Altmark, a district of Prussian Saxony, eat ere they go to church a soup made of all kinds of fodder for the live stock of the farmyard ; this must be an unsavoury concoction, but the eating of it is a small price to pay for good luck, year in year out, with the lambs and pigs.

The bride of the Upper Palatinate guards against future poverty by putting in her pocket a pinch of salt and a piece of bread, while her husband hopes for plentiful harvests because he carries in his coat pocket specimens of all kinds of grain. And the women of Rauen, in the Mark country, believe that in tucking inside their gloves a broken twig of a besom, they have a sure charm against marital ill-treatment.

There is usually a breakfast at the house of the parents of one or other of the happy pair, before the procession starts for church amid the scraping of fiddle-strings and the blare of wind instruments. The Thuringian bride and bridegroom eat soup together from the same plate; but in doing so watch each other with careful eyes, for whoever eats the last spoonful will be the first to die. This idea of future widow- or widower-hood, one would think, must afflict the young couple like a nightmare during the wedding-day. On the way to church the bridegroom of the Upper Palatinate never looks behind, or the old wives will say he is seeking a second partner in life. If the procession meets with a funeral or a priest on the way to administer the last Sacrament to the dying, it is an infallible sign that one of the happy, or rather unhappy, pair will soon die. If a light on the altar goes out before the Elevation of the Host, the bridegroom must first prepare for death; if this happens after that part of the ceremony, it is the bride who will be cut off. Whereas, if the priest should unfortunately sneeze during the service, neither of the couple can survive a year. A cold in the head thus becomes ominous to the last degree.

Now is the time for spiteful folk or rivals to do an ill turn to the bridal pair. No wonder the bride with beating heart presses up close to her husband during the service so that there may be no room for the Prince of Darkness between them. The friends often form a serried rank behind so that neither of the couple may be "overlooked," for great is the power of the "evil eye" at moments of supreme happiness. Many are the ways of doing mischief. Take one of the bride's hairs, plucked from her head as she entered church, wrap it round a palm twig, and she will certainly go mad. There are manifold spells that the simplest actions on your part will throw over her, causing her, among other things, to be childless.

In the midst of these foreshadowings of evil the bride, if she wishes to secure her position for the future, must be careful not to lose her presence of mind. Can she contrive to lay her hand over that of the bridegroom while the blessing is being pronounced, she will be the ruler, he the ruled, in their married life. After the ceremony is over she may by various little ruses secure for herself matrimonial supremacy. A Tiefenbach woman of the Upper Palatinate has only to enter her husband's house, when the feast is held there, before her lord and master, and she is sure to have the upper hand.

The host who welcomes the bridal party to his house or inn for the wedding meal hands a glass of wine by way of greeting to the bridegroom. The glass goes the round, first of the male, then of the female, guests, and comes at last to the bride, who, when she has tasted, throws it away. This custom of first drinking from and then breaking a vessel is widely spread. Occasionally the bride throws it over her shoulder; sometimes it is tossed over the house-roof.

In Bavaria the so-called "bride's race" takes place before the inn where the feast is to be held. The goal is represented by two bundles of straw, which the winner carries to the bride. The prize of this race,

THE CIVIL MARRIAGE, BLACK FOREST. *By* BENJAMIN VAUTIER.

By Permission of the Berlin Photographic Company.

common to all Germanic peoples, was in olden times the key of the bridal chamber; this has now been replaced by a wooden key. In the Upper Palatinate time has somewhat obscured the origin of this race. There the best man's hat is the goal, and the fleetest runner obtains merely a money present from the bridegroom, and his share free of cost of the wedding meal.

At the wedding feast in Thuringia the bridegroom waits on the guests, but his young partner does not leave him to hunger while he attends to others' needs, but reaches him a dainty morsel now and then. She herself must scarcely touch food, such is local etiquette. The bridegroom opens the ceremony of "pledging the crowns" by toasting the bride's wreath; the other men follow suit, and, each receiving the tinsel crown of the maiden he has toasted, puts it round his cap. Another interlude lightens this lengthy meal. In Bavaria the girls escape from table and buy love-favours, which they pin on the hats of their respective swains. Whoever finds a girl's favour on his hat is bound to toast and treat her, and act as her "chevalier" during the evening.

In Altenburg during the dance the bride loosens her mantle, so that it may fall from her and be carried away. In Bavaria the wreath is the symbol of maiden honour, and the bride parts with hers during the "wreath dance," the principal one of the evening. When the time comes she pairs off with the best man, and the husband dances with the chief woman guest,

Ehrenmutter, who is always an ancient dame. The guests line the room and make jokes at the dancers' expense. Old slips of the bridegroom made long since, scandals he has half-forgotten, are raked up against him, and comments, not always of the most flattering description, pass from mouth to mouth. The *Ehrenmutter*, as his partner, comes in for some of the raillery. Inquiries whether he would not like to change partners with the best man, and other witticisms, not of the highest order, resound on all sides. At last the welcome change is effected, the bride passes back to her husband, and amid universal laughter the luckless old lady is trundled off in a wheelbarrow. The bride is then divested of her wreath, and a sprig of rosemary on a platter is handed to the young husband with a good wish.

The presentation of gifts to the bridal pair, which in a general way takes place on the day following the wedding, is, in the parts of Bavaria adjoining the Tyrol, a feature of the bridal night. The procurator, or master of the ceremonies, who has kept the whole gathering alive with his mirth, now stands forth in the middle of the room, and relates at great length in verse how a sad accident has befallen the crockery of the young couple. A hen, he says, and thirty chickens, flew into the kitchen, and in chasing them out every pot, cup, and saucer has been broken. And now comes the moral of the story. "Will the kind guests," he asks, "who have eaten and drunk of the best, contribute something towards the needs of their young friends, who are just entering upon life?" Such appeals are seldom in vain, and forthwith the guests all rise, and going to the table, where the *Ehrenmutter* sits awaiting them, one by one hand her a gift of two or more florins wrapped in paper. This donation forms a useful little nest-egg for the bridal pair.

But now others clamour to share in the liberality of the joyful night. The musicians gather round the young couple and begin a serenade. Suddenly all the instruments go out of tune, and there is a woeful discord. The husband gives them a small coin; still the scraping and squeaking continues, until at last the clinking of some florins purchases silence. The inn servants then bring in broken crockery and old rags, and the bridegroom finds that he is expected to repair these miscellaneous articles with a *douceur*. When this is over, after much merriment and jokes which might shock our sensitive ears, the bride and bridegroom leave the dance, and go out into the night towards their home.

CHAPTER XVII

Bohemia, Austria and Hungary

BEFORE a marriage takes place in Bohemia the two families about to become allied together hold a meeting in order to discuss the terms of the bargain. They sit down at two tables, either in the house of the future bride or some mutual friend, and at last, after much haggling over details, the matter is arranged more or less to the satisfaction of both parties. On these occasions the procurator plays a leading part. It is he who invites most of the relations on each side to the above meeting. On arrival at the bride's house before the meeting, this courteous person craves from the "well-beloved mistress of the house" permission for the "industrious bachelor," *i.e.*, the bridegroom, to enter. His mode of addressing a person is as follows: "Honourable, industrious, kind, well-beloved Brother-in-law, Neighbour, Godfather, Master of the house, or Good Friend," as the case may be. The meeting is attended by the bride and bridegroom, but only as silent listeners. The latter is accompanied by his father and godfather. The bride usually prefers to be out of sight, and hides away behind the stove.

When matters have been arranged the procurator begins, "Well-beloved brother-in-law, neighbour, &c., the bridegroom has too little. He has not seen the bride. If she is anywhere near, or in the house, I will go and fetch her." But even after this summons the shy betrothed one remains in her hiding-place, while a curious ceremony is performed, somewhat similar to the Tyrolese custom. A woman is brought forward who is not the bride; for her to answer the summons so quickly would hardly be considered modest. And so some servant appears, who declares, falsely, that the young man has deceived her, giving her gifts and promising marriage. This person is known as the "old bride," and the rather compromising accusations which she makes against the bridegroom are made partly with the object of getting a present from him, partly also with the idea of taking away as she departs all ill-luck from the house. One wonders whether she may represent a fairy, or perhaps a witch? When this little comedy, which doubtless affords amusement to the guests and young people, is over, the true bride is allowed to come forward, and the bridegroom takes her hand. After this there is much feasting and dancing.

Among the customary presents given by a youth to his betrothed are such articles as the following—a rosary, prayer-book, silver wedding-ring, a girdle with three keys, a fur cap. A little before the wedding it is usual for the bride to send her future husband a shirt sewn with gold thread and coloured silk, and a wedding ring. Friends come and inspect the bridal outfit. Invitations to the wedding are given by the procurator. The wedding breakfast takes place at the bride's house, each guest receiving a handkerchief. It is now getting near the time for starting off to the church, and so the procurator comes in and formally asks for the bride. The father, or godfather of the girl as the case may be, is expected to show great reluctance to part with her. When the request is first made he replies that he must "think it over"; being asked a second time, he says that he has been dissuaded from the step. But when the same request has been made a third time he gives way and answers, "All in God's name." The bride at last comes forward, very bashfully, and kneels down on the threshold to receive her father's, or godfather's blessing, before she goes in procession to the church. First come the inevitable musicians, then the bridegroom (in a fur cap, which is *de rigueur*). At a little distance follows the bride, carrying her prayer-book and rosary. She is expected to shed tears of grief at leaving the old home. The bride wears—if old customs have not quite died out—a kind of crown made of silver wire, and round her forehead a strip of black velvet, from which hang little bells. Pink ribbons adorn the back of her hair. The bridegroom wears a tinsel crown. Before the service begins the groomsman places the bride's mantle on the bridegroom's back, so that his body is quite covered by it. This curious little custom is evidently of ancient origin, for the act is performed for superstitious motives: it is to prevent a "marriage-devil" from creeping in and dividing two hearts which should be united. The bride on her return from church does not enter the house until her mother-in-law has come out to welcome her and offer a cup of coffee or wine. Having emptied the cup or wine-glass, she throws it over her shoulder to see whether it breaks. Should it not do so, the company take it as a good omen for her future happiness. The festivities are kept up till near midnight. Two slices of bread, cut from two loaves, are given to the newly-married pair, one to each. These they keep, and the first time the young wife bakes in her new home she puts some of this bread into the dough-tub, that she may never want bread. There is an idea also that so long as these slices, or part of them, are kept in the house, no bread ever baked there will ever turn sour. After a time they must inevitably grow mouldy, and the one whose slice first does so will be the first to die. On the second day there is more feasting. On this occasion the bridegroom himself waits on the guests; his brother lends a helping hand. The inevitable procurator makes a speech, in which he solemnly offers thanks to Almighty God for allowing the bride and bridegroom to be spared to see "this honourable day." In the bridegroom's name he returns thanks to the bride's parents for kindly lending their house; to the women who have brought round in a cart the bride's trousseau. Nor does he forget the bride's mother, who "carried the maiden under her heart, bore her with pain, and brought her up as a Christian." A curious game is then played. They take a hen, place it on the floor under some kind of pot or vessel, blindfold the boys, and tell them to try and hit it. The one who is so lucky as to do so takes the hen. The bringing in of the dowry-cart on the wedding-day is rather an important ceremony. Four chamber-women sit in it, spinning as they go along. Spindles are given to bride and bridegroom to unwind, and whichever gets the shorter thread will be the one to die first. The bridegroom is asked to lift a basket of crockery out of the cart. Every one watches to see whether he does it neatly or awkwardly. Should he be so clumsy as to drop it there is much merrymaking at his expense. When everything has been taken out of the cart the bridesmaids ask the husband if he is content. "Yes," he says, "if you will get me the best thing, *i.e.*, the bride." This happens late in the day, after the ceremony at church.

The people living at the foot of the Bohemian Erzgebirge have a custom peculiar to themselves. On the morning after the wedding two little girls enter the bridal chamber and put on the bride's cap. Three times they set it crooked on her head, and each time she puts it off. Then the old frau comes in and put it straight. At breakfast-time the groomsman conducts the bride downstairs to the assembled guests. All are expected to praise her, and the groomsman has the honour of dancing with her, the bridegroom looking on. Then follows a mock ceremony, which may perhaps be regarded as a survival from ancient days ; the company pretend to put up the bride for sale. The husband offers a few gulden for her and is allowed to claim the fair one as his wife. Then it is his turn to dance with her. She must dance clumsily, pretending to be lame, so that the company may tease him by saying he has made but a poor bargain.

The Czechs have certain customs which may be mentioned here. On the wedding-eve the bridesmaids and certain girl friends of the bride meet to bind the rosemary twigs for her wreath. The bridegroom is admitted as a special privilege, but probably because the girls find some amusement in teasing him. To other men it is a case of "No admittance." The eldest bridesmaid takes a twig, binds it, and passes it on to the next one, who adds another and then passes it on, and so the wreath passes round till quite finished.

In some places the newly-married couple receive their presents on the day after the wedding, *i.e.*, the day on which the bride goes to her husband's house. The ceremony of receiving presents somewhat resembles the taking of a collection. The young wife sits in a corner of the room, with the women around her. The groomsman, placing a dish on the table, makes a short speech, asking the guests to give according to their means. Each male guest comes up in turn, puts a coin down on the plate, and refreshes himself with a draught of beer from a mug standing on the table. Then the women come forward with their gifts of flax. Amongst other presents the bride finally receives a cow, a sheep, and a goose. She then takes a child in her arms, kisses it, and gives it a coin from the plate.

In the neighbourhood of the Riesengebirge the maidens come in the evening before the wedding to make the bridal wreaths. The youngest bridesmaid makes the bride's wreath, the eldest that of the bridegroom. The others are allowed to make wreaths for their favourites among the youths invited to the wedding, a delicate attention which is doubtless appreciated. The girls sing as they make the wreaths, and their songs are of love, of youth, of beauty and marriage. The master of the ceremonies, however, takes a different and more cynical view of life, and so speaks in praise of a bachelor's happy days. During the meal which follows, he places three dishes before the bride: first, wheat, symbol of fruitfulness; secondly, ashes, with a little millet for her to pick out, to see how patient she is; the third dish is a covered one, and when the bride lifts up the cover a sparrow flies in her face. Is this symbolical of anything, or only a joke? Instead of rice, people throw peas at the husband and wife.

The last custom we mention here recalls the origin of the practice of giving presents to the bridesmaids. It is, as already pointed out, of the nature of ransom, and has been handed down from the days when a man carried off his bride in spite of a brave defence on the part of her maidens. When the dancing is all over, and it is time to deliver the bride over to her husband, the girls first lead him up to a figure hidden in a white drapery. This is not the bride, but some old woman of the house. A second veiled woman is then brought forward; but again the husband is deceived, for she is only another woman of the house, rather less old than the first. At last they bring the real bride, and for this service her grateful but impatient husband rewards them handsomely.

In Croatia the bride wears no wreath, but a string of pearls, which her father places on her head, giving her at the same time a little slap on the cheek; but the bridegroom is allowed to inflict a box on the ear, and rather a loud one too, as a sign that he means henceforth to be master. The bride's mother-in-law stands on the doorstep of her own house to receive the bridal party, holding in her hand a cup. "Mother," says the bridegroom, "what is in the cup?" to which she replies, "Son, my honey and thy goodwill." Coins having been thrown in, the mother, bride, and bridegroom all drink of its contents, and the money goes to the bridegroom. The bride then throws an apple over the roof of the house; having entered the house, she is led three times round the hearth, on which a fire is burning, each time bending down over the fire. The mother-in-law sits down by the hearth and the bride pushes the burning logs towards her. They then go to the well, walk three times round it, and throw in apples. Here again is the Greek custom of going to the well to propitiate the water-nymphs.

The romantic marriage of the late Archduke John of Austria with a daughter of the people was much talked of at the time. The Archduke was a keen sportsman, and on his way to Styrian chamois grounds frequently passed a certain posting-station on one of the Alpine passes. Here lived the pretty Anna Plochel, who made him an excellent wife, and became the foundress of the still-flourishing race of sportsmen, the Counts of Meran. It is said that he first saw her on the occasion of one of his frequent winter journeys across the Alps, when she, dressed up as a postboy, rode one of the leaders of his carriage, which otherwise could not have proceeded on its journey over a snowed-up pass ; and he was much struck with the courage she displayed.

Among the gipsies of Transylvania a man selects the girl who happens to please him best, and leads her before the judge or *gako*, in whose presence she breaks a jar, or dish, at the feet of the man to whom she has pledged herself. Each of the contracting parties collects a portion of the broken pieces and carefully preserves them. Should these pieces be lost, either by accident or by design, both are free, and can only be re-united by the breaking of another vessel in a similiar manner.

The Saxons in a part of North Transylvania have several peculiar marriage customs. First, with regard to courtship, a young peasant woman, at the time of harvesting the oats, shows her preference for some particular young man by going in his cart to help him to carry in the oats. One may sometimes see quite a procession of gaily-decorated carts all going to the field, a willing maid seated in each.

A Wedding Procession in Austrian Poland. *By* A. Wiernsz Kowalski.

From a Photograph by Franz Hanfstängl.

The happy swains ride like postilions, on the left hand horse of each cart, and are dressed for the occasion in their gayest suits. After this the young man must send an intimate friend to demand the girl's hand in marriage, which is done with much formality and making of set speeches. Her acceptance of the offer is celebrated by a feast, and four weeks later another banquet takes place at which the betrothed ones formally exchange rings.

St. Catherine's day is a favourite one for a wedding, and a good many couples are united on that day. Half a dozen young men go round on the Sunday before the wedding to collect contributions of butter, eggs, milk, &c., for those houses wherein wedding feasts will take place. There is a good deal of mutual co-operation; the women of both the families of bride and bridegroom meet together in order to bake the cakes, while some of the young men go to the forest to collect firewood. On their return, a curious and playful custom is observed. While the men are away gathering sticks the women close the courtyard, or stretch a rope across to bar the way, from which rope bundles of straw are now hanging. A mock fight takes place in which the men are victorious, each as he enters the courtyard seizing one of the straw bundles. These they open and examine, some find cakes or apples inside, others only egg-shells or bits of crockery.

Early on the day of her marriage, the bride receives from her future husband, through his "best man" (*wortmann*) the "morning gift" (*morgen-gabe*) consisting of shoes, handkerchiefs, and other useful articles. She, on her part, presents the bridegroom with a shirt entirely made by herself; this he wears on the wedding-day, and then lays aside, as being too precious for daily use. It is kept till he dies, and he is buried in it.

In some villages it is usual for a bride and bridegroom to step over the threshold of the new home with their hands tied together; they also partake together of bread and wine before entering, the bridegroom throwing the glass over the roof of the house. At the feast, all the guests come forward in procession with their gifts, the father of the bridegroom laying on the table a ploughshare, as a reminder that his son must work, and doubtless a useful present too. His mother contributes a pillow adorned with ribbons, the bride's father presents a copper cauldron or kettle, and her mother another pillow decorated like the former one. About midnight the bride "dances off the crown," the symbol of maidenhood, This is done with certain curious ceremonies which doubtless are of ancient origin. The married women, joining hands, form a wide circle round the bride, and dance until somehow the circle is broken up, when they all run away into the courtyard. Then one of the bridegroom's men, who has been lying in ambush, rushes forward and endeavours to rob the bride of her crown; she is defended by two brothers, or other male relations, but the young man always succeeds in getting the crown. Then two of her own women step forward and put a matron's cap on her head. Next morning a cake is brought to the house, of which both must eat, although it contains certain unsavoury things, such as cow-hairs, swine-bristles, egg-shells, &c., but the act is supposed to ensure the welfare of their cattle and poultry. And here we have the custom of "Ransom" turning up once more. The day after her marriage the young wife goes to the church to be blessed, the husband meanwhile waiting outside. Directly she appears outside the church door, the newly-married couple are surrounded by a crowd of young men wearing masks, who separate them, if they can, and a hand-to-hand fight ensues—probably half in jest. But, however that may be, the husband, if he cannot win her back otherwise, must pay a ransom for her. A dance takes place near the church door.

Each wedding party—and there are generally several on the same day—has its own band of musicians, consequently the discordant noise is terrible. "This is nothing at all," said a pastor to a lady who was looking on at the dancing of three wedding parties. "Sometimes we have eight or ten weddings, each with its own fiddlers—that is something worth hearing indeed!"

Among the Austrian settlers (*Ländlers*) in Transylvania, the men have a novel way of proposing marriage; watching his opportunity at a dance, the lover slips into the hand of the maiden who has stolen his heart a new silver coin, wound up in bright

such occasions by these go-betweens, who name the suitor, and, if the parents have no objection, return to him with the good news. In a few hours he is on his way to the house accompanied by a friend who acts as his spokesman, and knows the speeches proper to such occasions. This important personage bears in his hand the loving-cup, and wears a badge of the national colours. His stick is ornamented with ribbons and silver bells. Followed by the would-be bridegroom, he enters the cottage and addresses the girl's parents somewhat in the following manner, only in verse. "It is known to you through our *envoyées* the reason why we pay a visit to your respected roof. It is God who has initiated holy union, when He said to Adam 'It is not good to be alone,' and created Eve as his partner. This gentleman, having considered his fate, wishes to take a wife unto himself, in obedience to the wishes and the laws of our Lord. We have heard the fame of your daughter, and if the Almighty has pleased to tie in a knot the hearts of these two, it would be a sin for us mortals to untie it. Therefore we ask you humbly to give permission for your daughter to enter."

Then the girl comes into the room dressed in her holiday attire; the "loving-cup" is handed to the man, who drinks therefrom and then gives it to the maiden of his choice. But the young people may not yet consider themselves engaged. "There is many a slip 'twixt the cup and the lip"; or in this case, between the ceremony of the "loving-cup" and the "kissing-feast" to be presently described. These simple Magyar peasants appear to take a more serious view of marriage than some people do in countries where divorce is easily obtained. And so three days' grace is allowed in case the parents, or either of the lovers, should change their minds. The youth must send his *envoyées* on the third day to ascertain if all is well. If not, and the parents have thought the match undesirable, a message is sent through the *envoyées*, couched in some such terms as these: "We have thought the matter over, and find that the young man is going in the wrong direction, and not in the way pointed out by the Lord, so you had better turn your steps to other paths." This may not imply that they have any misgivings about the character of the lover, but probably only that the girl has changed her mind. If, on the other hand, his suit prospers, the messengers return to him with the good news that he may call at the house and see the family. He does so accompanied by his spokesman, and certain set speeches in verse are made. The young people are now practically engaged, and towards evening go to the priest to receive his benediction. On their return, a feast called the "hand-taking" is made. The man must then make a present of money and a betrothal ring to his *fiancée*, who gives him in return a silk handkerchief embroidered by herself and another ring.

For two successive Sundays the banns are asked in church, after which follows the "Kissing-Feast." After supper the engaged couple are allowed for the first time to converse alone, in a separate room, where they seal their vows with a kiss—probably more than one. The wedding takes place after the banns have been put up for the third time.

Nearly every one in the village is invited to the wedding feast; and, as in the case of the "Penny Wedding" of Scotland, now abolished, each guest contributes something, it may be eggs, flour, or wine.

The bridegroom's spokesman has now retired, having played his part; his place is taken by the best man, who goes round to each house and conveys his invitation in verse, in the following manner: "Most humbly do I implore forgiveness for my intrusion, and ask you to listen to me. I am deputed by So-and-so and his wife to ask you politely with all your family to partake of a dish, and to drink a glass of wine, to be followed by an entertainment on the occasion of their daughter's wedding. Bring with you knives, forks, and plates." In the original the expression used is not "wedding" but "the feast of the seed grown beneath their wings."

These people seem to have a taste for speech-making, and more speeches are made the day before the wedding, when the best man comes, with several carriages, to take away the bride's dowry of household effects to her future home.

The next morning the same personage comes to ask permission, on behalf of the bridegroom, to take away from the parents their daughter. Once more he makes a speech in verse. A touching scene follows, as the girl bids farewell to her home and the old people. It is a gay procession which then goes to the church—not on foot, but in carriages, and to the strains of music. But the final leave-taking is not yet. When the ceremony at the church is over, and the happy couple are at last united, the bridegroom must go straight home to see that the feast at his house is prepared, whilst his best man accompanies the bride to her old home. She does not stay there long; in a short time the bridegroom presents himself and asks permission of the parents to conduct his bride to his own house. Then the final adieu takes place, and she is led with much ceremony to the wedding feast. Some one is found to propose the health of the bride in verse, usually the composition of a peasant. Here is a specimen in prose: "I wish your two hearts, which have been tied together, every happiness. May holy love in lasting bonds encircle you, so that God may feel delight in you. May your union blossom into fruit as the trees burst into bloom. May the Almighty surround you with so much happiness that it may weigh upon you as a burden. Finally, when life departs from its seat and your bodies rest in the soil, may your souls joyfully look back upon the past, and be received with greeting in eternal paradise."

A curious old custom, which even now has not quite died out, may here be mentioned. The wedding procession is headed by a cock guarded by two men with drawn swords. As soon as the ceremony is over a mock trial is held, and the poor bird having been found guilty of bigamy is solemnly sentenced to death and executed by two men with swords. Apparently this is intended as a warning to the bride and bridegroom to be faithful to one another; but perhaps some students of ethnology may be inclined to regard the ceremony as a relic from heathen times when animals were sacrificed on such occasions.

At the conclusion of the feast, when the bride has laid aside her wreath and changed her dress, yet another opportunity is found for a little speech. On approaching the large tent, where dancing is about to take place, the best man steps forward and addresses the newly-made wife somewhat as follows: "May the Almighty crown this head with every happiness in place of the wreath which has been removed. May Nature's bloom rest on this face. May no care or burden draw sighs from these lips. May she live in peace and happiness with her husband. May the light of their life last for long, and may its flame be extinguished amidst happiness and peace." Then the best man is kissed by the bride who takes him for her first partner in the dance.

Long after the bridal pair have retired, the village young men and maidens keep on dancing vigorously. Needless to say there is much merry-making, and the long day or night having come to an end, one might conclude that the wedding ceremonies were all over, but such is not the case. These Magyars are so fond of festivities, that on the following Sunday the wedding is celebrated over again at the bride's old home. After that the young couple settle down to the routine of ordinary life.

A fuller account is to be found in "Hungary and its People," by Louis Felbemann, from which the facts narrated above are taken.

CHAPTER XVIII

The Tyrol and Switzerland

VARIOUS are the ways in which maidens silently reveal their preference for some particular swain.

In the Tyrol, if a girl presents her lover with a bottle of spirits, it is equivalent to saying that he has found favour in her eyes, and henceforth is at liberty to visit her at home. If her parents look upon the young man with disfavour, she may contrive to lower the precious bottle at night from her chamber window.

In the frontier valleys of Upper Styria (part of the Eastern Tyrol) invitations to a wedding come through the "best man," or "wedding-inviter" (*Hochzeitslader*), about a fortnight before the event. His position is in some respects rather a delicate one. He goes round the village inviting the people in each house. If they offer him food it may be taken as an acceptance. Should they deny him that courtesy, the probability is that they will not attend the celebration. All who come to the feast are expected to contribute towards the expenses; the result of which rule is often a good many refusals. It is no easy matter, however, in spite of this understanding, to tell of some people whether or no they intend coming; and in the neighbouring Bavarian Highlands, professional "best men" are employed on this errand, and they very rarely fail to arrive at a correct conclusion. On the wedding morn a curious little comedy takes place. The groomsmen call at the bride's house with a request to let them see "a maiden whom they bade pick rosemary and darn torn linen," which description is presumed to apply to the bride. However, instead of her an ugly old peasant woman, bearing a bunch of nettles and a basketful of torn linen, is brought forward. Needless to say, "she will not do!" Presently the old crone, having been rewarded by a little present of money, departs; a second appeal is made, and this time the real bride appears, led by her father, and carrying a bunch of rosemary in one hand and a shirt (for the "best man") in the other. The feast is held at an inn, and as the bridal party approach the church where they are to be married, the hostess steps forward, seizes the bride, and conducts her to the kitchen, in order that she may "salt the *kraut*" (a kind of cabbage). As she throws a handful of salt into the pot containing the *kraut*, one of the bystanders repeats a verse bidding her to "salt well the *kraut*, but not her husband's life." The party then proceeds on its way to the church. After the priest has given his blessing and made the two man and wife, a great feast is held at the inn. Late in the evening husband and wife depart for home, where, on arrival, they find the entrance blocked by a small tree; this the man must himself remove. It is called the *Wiegenholz*, because the custom is to keep it for the purpose of making the first cradle.

In the Unter Innthal, the lover, on his first visit (having previously received permission to come), presents his fair one with a glass of wine from a bottle he has brought with him ; thus reversing the custom prevailing in other parts of the Tyrol. Acceptance is equivalent to a promise on her part to become his wife—a custom which once more illustrates the importance attached in many countries to the act of eating or drinking together. Should she refuse, the girl means to confess she has only been playing with him. One who has not yet made up her mind, puts the young man off with excuses. Should the wine unfortunately be spilt, or the glass broken, it is considered a bad omen for the future happiness of the lovers. So much so that the peasants say of an unhappy couple who do not suit each other, "They have spilt the wine between them."

As in Switzerland, so here, the bride is frequently stolen away after the wedding! This is done for a joke by some smart lads, who contrive to divert the bridegroom's attention during the festivities. Sometimes they even take her as far as the next village ; and if the man to whom she has been married is unpopular, they take his bride to some inn and there entertain her, and themselves, until quite a big bill has been run up, which the unfortunate bridegroom, who is sure to arrive before long, must pay out of his own purse!

In these parts, widowers who marry again, if they

are known to have treated their first wives badly, are tormented on the wedding night by hideous noises in the street, old kettles, wooden trumpets, &c., being used for this purpose by a band of young men.

In the South Tyrol (Ampezzo) weddings take place about a fortnight after the betrothal. During this interval the bride is jealously guarded by a chaperon, who is known as "the growling bear" (*Brontola*). When the lover comes to visit his mistress, any love-making the young people may indulge in takes place under the eye of a *Brontola*; and it is even said that she inflicts a fine of several florins on a too ardent lover who dares to kiss his *fiancée*.

On the Saturday before the banns are put up for the first time, the priest examines the bride in the Creed, the Ten Commandments, and the prayers of the Roman Catholic Church. Here again we meet with the curious little comedy of running off with the bride, only in a different form. Some of the bridegroom's friends carrying her away, return with her to the church, where she is compelled to walk three times round the central aisle; after which they take her to the inn where a feast is prepared, for which the bridegroom pays. Nor do they surrender to him their fair captive until a handsome sum has been paid by way of ransom! It is difficult to account for such a custom except as a survival from very early days when the institution of marriage was not in existence.

In the village of Pergine, about thirty years ago, several other curious customs were still in vogue. For instance, on the wedding-day as the party proceeded on its way to the parish church, it was accompanied by several of the bridegroom's friends, one of whom held in his hand a stick, to which was attached a live hen; while the other held a spinning wheel, the distaff being wound round with flax. These were symbols: the hen signifying a good mother, the spinning wheel and distaff referring to the duties of a careful housewife. Also when the service was over, and the newly-married couple arrived at the bridegroom's house, the door was slammed in their faces, whereupon a quaint dialogue took place between the bride and her mother-in-law. The former began by uttering certain words in an unknown language, the meaning of which had been entirely lost. These words had been transmitted orally from one generation to another, and it was at last discovered by some antiquarian that they were like those recited by Roman brides on these occasions. The mother-in-law replied by asking the meaning of the bride's speech. Whereupon the newly-wedded one would reply that she was the lawful wife of the man by whose side she was standing, and that the church had confirmed their union, adding further that she would revere the parents of her husband, was pious, diligent, and accustomed to hardships. Then the relenting mother-in-law threw open the door and welcomed the young couple. These Pergine customs, being known to be survivals from heathen times, have of late been suppressed by the clergy.

In the West Tyrol, adjoining the Bavarian highlands,

before a betrothal actually takes place the parents on either side formally inspect each other's houses, with the object of ascertaining how much property the family may possess. This visit is called *Auf B'schau gehen*, and the young woman's fate depends very much on the conclusion arrived at by her lover's parents. Of course it is not in the nature of "a surprise visit." To give no notice would be considered impolite. So the young man's father and mother send word some weeks beforehand to say that they are coming on such and such a day. After this a great deal of scrubbing and cleaning takes place. When the inspection has come off, the lovers' parents retire to the living room and hold a consultation about the dowry. Etiquette forbids them to say whether they consider the sum mentioned sufficient. Should they arrive at an adverse decision, the young woman's părents will hear no more of the matter, and the proposed match will be "off." If, however, they are satisfied both with the dowry and their inspection of the house, the parents allow their son to visit his sweetheart on some Sunday. On this occasion he comes in his best clothes and clenches the bargain by presenting her with a sum of money, according to his means. The youth and maiden then partake of a pancake together.

Invitations to the wedding are given by the "best man" and the girl's brother, who accompany each other.

Entering the house of the future bride the "best man" (procurator) who in this case is a professional, exclaims: "Methinks I smell a bride." A search takes place and at last, with many blushes, she comes forth to listen to the set speech in which the best man conveys his invitation. In some parts this important functionary passes the night in the house of his friend's mistress; but until the time comes for him to deliver his message he says not a word about the nature of his business. It sometimes happens that the first person invited is the bride herself.

In visiting other houses the brother of the bride is allowed, if he can do so unobserved, to steal a hen while his friend the procurator delivers the invitation. Hence the nickname of "hen-prigger" applied to him. Perhaps we may suppose that he is in reality only collecting "contributions" towards the expenses of his sister's wedding-feast. Should he be discovered, however, he is liable to be beaten, or even ducked in the pond.

When things have been settled the young man, his bride-elect, and his procurator, have a meal together at the inn; and this is called the "cabbage-dinner" (*Krautessen*). When the *kraut* has been put on the table, the girl asks her future husband what he will give for it. "I want none," he says, but nevertheless bids a florin. "That is too little," she answers; whereupon the best man says he will give two, and so the bidding is kept up, until at last the betrothed one gets as much as eight or ten florins for her *kraut*.

A great variety of marriage customs prevails in

Switzerland. In some places a wedding is attended with full ceremonial, and many customs which have about them a strong flavour of the olden time. In others, where life is harder, perhaps, or the people poor, getting married is a very simple affair. In the valley of Anniviers (Canton Valais) only one in a family is permitted to marry, and thus the patrimony is never diminished. The family conclave decides which member shall perpetuate the stock. But the wedding furnishes forth no merry-making. At daybreak the pair come to church in their working clothes, and after the ceremony each goes back to work in the fields.

Swiss maidens have a good deal of liberty allowed them during the courting period, though their choice of a bridegroom is sometimes restricted to their own locality. In some of the villages in the Forest Cantons all the youths, as soon as they reach the proper age, join a society the object of which is to prevent lads from other villages coming to court the girls. The lovers of the village give the password, and climb to the windows of their fair ones at night unmolested. But the stranger who comes courting must somehow manage to find his way unobserved, or else fight his way through. Parents do not object to this somewhat unwise custom of nocturnal visits, which is known as the *Kirchgang*. Another custom closely connected with it is the *Maien-stecken*. In the Canton of Lucerne the lover anxious to do honour to his mistress plants before her home, on the first day of May, a small pine tree gaily ornamented with ribbons. This is regarded as a proof of great devotion, and the parents entertain him very hospitably. Less acceptable attentions are sometimes received by girls who spurn the young men of their own village. A straw puppet is suspended before the girl's window, or the farmer's best waggon is found to have been turned upside down on the green.

In the Canton of Lucerne weddings usually take place on a Monday in carnival time, and February is generally considered a lucky month. During the period between the publication of the banns and the marriage the powers of evil are supposed in many places to be unusually active. In consequence of this the bridal pair do not leave home after nightfall, or nobody knows what might happen. There is, however, much to be done indoors by way of preparations for the wedding. Invitations are sent round beforehand to all the guests. In Schaffhausen the bearer of these is the bridegroom's tailor ; in the valley of the Thur, the village schoolmaster. Armed with a red umbrella, and wearing on his hat a tinsel wreath, this important functionary starts on his rounds. At each house he delivers a set speech, to which every one crowds to listen, and at the end names the sum to be paid by a guest for his share in the entertainment given at the village tavern in celebration of the event.

Meanwhile the bride has been putting the last touches to the trousseau, and in the neighbourhood of Baden (Aargan) some days before the wedding the dowry-cart is driven, amid general rejoicing, to the bridegroom's house. The driver has a nosegay in his hat, and, in many places, the manes and tails of the horses are gaily decorated with red ribbon, save when the bridegroom is a miller or baker, then blue is the colour chosen for this purpose. A sympathetic crowd of wide-eyed villagers gather to watch the loading of the cart. Great care must be taken as to the disposition of the bridal furniture. Above all, the foot of the bed must be placed so as to point in the direction of the new home, or the young wife will soon return to her parents' house to escape the miseries of her married life. After setting forth the driver presently finds his course barred by the ropes the village lads have stretched across the roadway, and these demand toll of the bridegroom before they let the cart pass. Should he refuse they will indeed let him through, but with firing off of pistol and blunderbuss, and the niggardly youth has to submit to the shame of having his bride "shot away" from her native village.

A pretty custom is kept up by the maidens of Lucerne. They meet on the wedding eve at the bridegroom's house, and make buttonholes and nosegays for the lads they like best to wear on the following day. When the work is done each maiden leaves the gift at her favourite's dwelling. In Tagerfelden the making of the red kerchiefs, which are distributed among the wedding guests, is committed on that day to the girl companions of the bride. In some places the bride, in others the bridesmaid and groomsman, receive new shoes as a gift from the bridegroom.

The services of the orator who has borne the invitations are put into requisition early on the morrow. In the Thur Valley he accompanies the bridegroom to the bride's house, where they breakfast together, after which he makes a long speech to the father and mother, recounting to them all the noble qualities of the bridegroom, and beseeching them to give their daughter willingly away, as he is sure a long life of happiness is in store for her. A rival orator then "takes the word," and presents the reverse side of the shield, enumerates all the difficulties of the new position, and dwells on the virtues of the bride. When the time for the ceremony approaches, it is often a matter of some difficulty to get possession of the lady's person. At Sobrio, in Livenea, when the bridegroom and his companions come to her father's house to seek her, the parents offer as a substitute old hunchbacked women, or even large dolls. At Tagerfelden it falls to the lot of the orator to demand the bride. Guests and musicians are waiting, all is in readiness; but the lady, playing the old comedy of womanly reluctance, is upstairs locked in her chamber. The mother, however, is amenable to reason, and, after listening to the orator's delivery of the customary speech, and receiving a silver coin, called "The key of the bridal chamber," brings her daughter forth.

The bride then departs with her betrothed for church midst prayers, tears, and good wishes, while to keep up her spirits musicians cheer her with their songs. In the villages near Wiesen (Grisons) she is always dressed in black, and wears on her head a wreath of orange blossoms, while a pigtail of the same flowers reaches below her waist. Those of the wedding guests who wish to do much honour to the occasion also appear in black, and doubtless give to the wedding procession something of a funereal aspect. During the ceremony the bridal pair, say the people of Obwalden, must kneel so close together that no gap is left, and those behind cannot see when they join hands, a precaution taken, maybe, to ensure that no division may come between them in after life. Many eyes are meanwhile directed toward the two candles, one burning on each side of the altar. If either of them burns feebly or goes out, that betokens death to the one whose place is on the corresponding side. This curious superstition is remarkably similar to one in China.

An important *rôle* in the wedding functions is played by the "yellow woman," or *gelbe frau* (so called from the story of Ostara and the yellow slippers), a mistress of the ceremonies, often the godmother of the bride. She may be seen in Lucerne walking at the head of the women guests, bearing a basket filled with kerchiefs for distribution amongst the party. In return for these she receives, like the Tyrolese *Ehrenmutter*, the money presents destined for the bridal pair at the inn where the feast takes place. Hers, too, is the task of taking off and burning the wreath, symbol of the bride's virginity, during a special dance. If this is quickly consumed it is a happy omen ; should it smoulder a long time, there is trouble in store. So much is the smouldering dreaded that in Obwalden the young wife and her companion poke the fire fiercely to make it blaze, and then kneel down to pray for good fortune while the wreath is burning.

At Baumgarten the "yellow woman" has to perform a delicate office. During the wedding feast she wipes from the bride's eyes the tears which every well-trained and decorous maiden should shed at the prospect of leaving her parents' home. Whether she laughs or weeps, the bride of the Thur Valley comes off poorly at the wedding meal. She may only eat what the groomsman places stealthily on her plate, and she must beware of this friend's advances, and see that he does not in the meantime remove her shoe, or else the wedded couple will come in for a good deal of banter and merriment.

When the dancing, feasting, and merry-making is over, the neighbours prepare to accompany the bridal pair to their dwelling. Many quaint customs connected with the bride's home-coming once prevailed in French Switzerland, but have now fallen into disuse. On arriving at the bridegroom's house, which was bright with wreaths of roses and marigold, an old woman met her, hung the housewife's keys about her waist, and scattered three handfuls of wheat over her head. Then the husband, lifting her in his arms, entered the house, so that her foot never touched the oil-smeared threshold.

At Stilli, in the Aar Valley, according to an old and

THE BRIDE'S DEPARTURE FROM HOME, BLACK FOREST. *By* BENJAMIN VAUTIER.

By Permission of the Berlin Photographic Company.

now obsolete custom, the bridegroom and his parents left the inn a few minutes before the bride and guests. On reaching home they fastened every door and window, drew every bolt and bar, so that the house presented a very inhospitable front when the young wife and groomsman appeared before it. The groomsman rapped the door sharply with the "bridestick." "Who is there?" said a voice from behind the window-shutter.

"A young woman," answered the groomsman, "who wishes to be received into your house."

"That is a great deal to ask," said the father-in-law from within. "Is she virtuous, industrious, and orderly?"

The groomsman declared that she excelled in all these qualities.

"Can she cook, bake, wash, spin, sew, and knit?" persisted the father-in-law.

The groomsman assured him she was perfect in all these accomplishments, and then the door was thrown open by way of welcome, and the bride entered the house.

CHAPTER XIX

Italy, Spain and Portugal

THE good old custom of "keeping company," as distinct from being formally engaged, obtains among the gondoliers' families at Venice. When a young man finds that a damsel eyes his suit with favour, he informs a friend, and the two don their best clothes and make a ceremonious call upon the girl's father. If the parents are satisfied, a certain trial time of some months is arranged for, and the young people see what they can of each other, or "keep company" during this period. When this is past, if they have meanwhile discovered that their tempers are incompatible, the matter drops. If, on the other hand, all goes well, the young man, his parents and relatives, visit the girl's father and make a formal demand for her hand in marriage. A day or two later the betrothal is celebrated, when the lover presents his mistress with a wedding and other rings, which must all be returned should the lady prove fickle. Mr. Horatio Brown[1] says that in the province of Udine

[1] "Life on the Lagoons."

a jilt must present her former *fiancé* with a pair of shoes, as compensation for the time he has wasted in fruitless courtship.

The Venetian lover is exceedingly attentive; he makes certain regulation presents according to the season—at Easter a cake, on St. Mark's Day a buttonhole of rosebuds, at Martinmas roast chestnuts, at Christmas a box of almond paste and a jar containing a curious confection of fruit and raw mustard seed. The girl gives in return neckties and kerchiefs embroidered with his name, or two hearts, as a tribute of her affection. But both must beware of making presents which bring ill-luck, such as pictures of saints or books. To do so is to court misfortune. Neither should any person offer a comb, clearly because witches so often use one; scissors, not, as the northern people say, because they cut love, but because in Venice they signify a sharp tongue.

A Tuscan youth visits his *innamorata* on feast days, bringing as an offering a carnation or a rose. When poetically inclined he also composes verses in her praise. In due time the house-father (*capoccio*), who rules the bridegroom's family, demands the girl's hand for his kinsman, and a feast celebrates the conclusion of the business. A curious piece of conventionality hems in the Tuscan maiden. Just as among old-fashioned folk in England at the beginning of the century it was thought incorrect for a betrothed girl to visit her future husband's house, so the young Tuscan peasant of our day is ordered, as she values her reputation, never to approach her lover's dwelling, and even in her walks to avoid it (compare Melanesia, p. 161).

A valuer has meanwhile drawn up an inventory of the bride's belongings, and this paper is delivered to the *capoccio* of the bridegroom's house. Should the young man die without children, the widow receives back the full value of all she brought to her husband. Her dowry invariably consists of some clothes and linen, a bed, and a pearl necklace worth from £5 to £100; or if her family are too poor to buy pearls of this value she must be content with coral. In the north of Italy the dowry consists of gold ornaments, and a bride will sometimes have as many as twenty-three gold rings upon her fingers at the wedding. The Venetian *fiancée* knows that she must provide, if possible, the furniture of the household, but if her means are not adequate to such a purchase, the bed-room furniture, consisting of a bed of walnut wood, six chairs, two chests of drawers and a looking-glass. This is invariably expected of her. She brings also an array of copper pots, which hang from the beams of the kitchen roof. These become heirlooms and are portioned out to the daughters of the house as they marry. In many parts of Italy the dowry is brought with great pomp to the bridegroom's house the day before the wedding. A friend of the present writer met a cart drawn by white oxen, decked with gorgeous head-fringes, on the road between Scirollo and Loreto. The cart was laden with linen and household goods, two immense and gaily decorated pillows topping the pile. The bride's mother and friends followed, on their way to make up the nuptial bed.

Before the wedding-day the Venetian bridegroom must seek out a suitable "best man." This is not always an easy matter, for the duties of that functionary are heavy, and entail no little expense on any one who wishes to acquit himself of the task with *éclat*. On the day before the wedding he must send a box of bon-bons, on the top of which is a little sugar baby, to the bride's house, with two bouquets, one of real and one of artificial flowers, and a present of jewelry, a brooch or earrings. It falls to his lot to provide liqueurs and wine for the wedding supper, four candles for the wedding mass, four gondolas to convey the guests to the inn for supper, and satisfy the demands of beggars and children, who cry "*Evviva la sposa*," at the church door. A *compare's* hand is always in his pocket.

In Italy the dread of a wedding in May seems to be universal, and in Venice people marrying are very much restricted with regard to suitable days. When all is said, Sunday is the only time when the nuptial knot can be tied with any prospect of future happiness for the bridal pair. Saturday is indeed an exception to this rule, but then it is reserved for widows. "Marry on Monday and you are sure to go mad ; on Tuesday, and there is the prospect of endless suffering before you ;" while Thursday, as the witches' combing-day, is out of the question. There are no doubt equally cogent reasons why Wednesday and Friday should be rejected.

In Venice they prefer to be married at the earliest morning mass; in some parts of the Val d'Arno after sundown. The Tuscan bride wears a black dress, with a white bonnet or cap, while even in the coldest weather she carries a fan. No bridesmaids, but only married women accompany her to church, as no unmarried girl is allowed to witness a wedding. Her mother-in-law, or the house-mother (*messaia*) of her husband's house, also stays at home to give the new-comer the kiss of welcome on the threshold.

The Venetian bride walks by the canal side on the *compare's* arm, in her second-best wedding dress, for only the evening dance witnesses her best display of finery. The bridegroom and the *comare* follow in their wake, and thus they go to church in procession. The groomsman's services are frequently required during the ceremony; he kneels on a crimson faldstool beside the bridal pair, puts the ring on the lady's middle finger, pays fees when all is over, and scatters small coins among the waiting crowd for charity. Then he gives his arm to the bride, and all go merrily homewards. Still he is weighed down by a great responsibility during the remainder of the day. The bride is under his charge, and unless she is in her mother's keeping he must never let her go out of his sight.

After some slight refreshment the company separate to meet at four o'clock, when they adjourn to the tavern for supper. No formal invitations are issued, and all, save the parents and the *compare* and *comare*, pay their share of the bill. Supper lasts four whole

IMPROVISATORE AT AN ITALIAN WEDDING. *By* ARTURO RICCI.

By Permission of the Berlin Photographic Company.

hours; at dessert a cake of hardbake is placed before the bride with much ceremony; she breaks it and a bird flies out; the guests cry "*Evviva la sposa.*" Then the tables are cleared and they all dance. A curious feature of the wedding feast in Tuscany is the absence of the women of the bride's circle. It is true she sends them a basket of good things when the meal is over; but one would think she must miss them during the merriment.

On the whole the Tuscan wife knows that hers will be a hard lot. So many of her husband's family are gathered under the patriarchal roof. There is the frequently tyrannical *capoccio*, the *paterfamilias*, who orders the affairs of the whole family; there is the *messaia*, his mother or wife, under whose dominion the various women of the household, sons', brothers', nephews', and cousins' wives and daughters pass their lives. For the first week of her married life, the young wife, just to show her capacity, must rise early and prepare the meals for the male portion of her husband's household. This is a foretaste of her future labours. Working early and late, in the house and in the fields, we think as we watch these Tuscan women, grown old before their time, how abundantly in their case has the curse of Adam been added to the curse of Eve.

In Sicily the first step in arranging a marriage is for the young man's mother to call upon the mother of the girl selected by her son, in order to ascertain, in the first place, whether she approves of the proposed alliance, and secondly to find out the amount of her dowry. Should there be no objection on her part, and supposing that the girl also has no serious objection, the other mother usually presents an inventory of all the worldly goods she is able to bestow on her daughter. This seems to be the usual mode of procedure, but other ways are customary in certain districts.

About fifty years ago, in the province of Syracuse, the overtures were made in quite a different manner, which was less direct, and therefore possibly more polite. The young man's mother, when making the call, carried a certain kind of reed under her cloak, and inquired of the girl's mother whether she had a reed like it. If the latter said they had no such reed in the house, or refused to look for one, it was taken as a polite way of intimating that her family, or perhaps her daughter—were not desirous of receiving the young man as their son-in-law. This was considered final, and there the matter ended.

Mothers sometimes select wives for their sons ; they are naturally most anxious to find a steady and industrious girl who will be willing to work—not an idle flirt. The following method of selection may appear somewhat rough and ready, but there is something to be said for it. The young man's mother having some particular girl in view pays her a "surprise visit." Should the girl be found working (of course all good girls *ought* to be, among people in whose lives there is but little time for recreation) it is taken as a signal that she would make a useful wife, and her mother is interviewed at once. If, on the other hand, the girl is idling, it produces an unfavourable impression of her character, and no further steps are taken in that direction. How far such a method with its obvious defects is justifiable, it is not for us to say.

The betrothal customs of Sicily are curious. In the province of Trapani, the girl is placed in the centre of the room; her future mother-in-law then enters, parts her hair, places a ring on her finger, gives her a handkerchief, and finally kisses her. In the province of Catania the young man presents his *fiancée* with a red ribbon, which she wears in her hair until the day of her marriage.

This custom is observed in many parts of the island. The red ribbon being a sign of betrothal, serves as an announcement of the fact that a girl is "engaged"; and sometimes the young men merely present it to her, instead of making a formal proposal—which apparently requires more courage. As soon as a maiden is betrothed, her lover must consider what kind of present would be most acceptable to his future wife. In bygone days, young men gave tortoise-shell combs, silver needle-cases, silk handkerchiefs, rings or gloves according to their means. Nowadays there is less variety in these matters; a ring, a silver ornament for the hair, or a small gold cross, is usually given.

The valuation of the maiden's property, especially of her trousseau, is an important ceremony. Friends and relatives come to satisfy their curiosity. The garments are either laid out on a bed, or hung on cords stretched across the mother's bedroom. Amongst other things are tables, chairs, and various articles of furniture. A professional valuer, always a woman, determines the worth of each article, and an accountant makes the entries in a book. Should the woman be inclined to make her estimates too high, the young man's mother may protest, and sometimes quarrels arise in this way.

There is a civil marriage as well as a religious ceremony, the latter being considered the more important of the two ; the bridegroom, in fact, does not really consider himself married until after the latter has taken place. It is a very festive occasion ; and the ceremony frequently takes place at night, hence torches are used. According to tradition the bride used in old times to arrive at the church door on horseback.

In Spain when a young man desires better acquaintance with a maiden, he appears at her house-door and asks for water. If invited to sit down the lover rolls up a cigarette, and asks for a light. This gives him an opportunity to observe the lady, and, if his impressions are favourable, he finds excuses for subsequent visits. Having made up his mind to demand her in marriage he makes overtures to the damsel's father. The latter, like a true Spaniard, is in no haste. "Go," he says, "and make inquiries concerning me, so that you may learn who I am. I, for my part, will make inquiries concerning you ; come again after a certain interval, and you shall learn my decision." If, however, before this stage is reached, the lady has decided that the swain is not to her liking, she hands the crestfallen youth a pumpkin, and by that he knows that his hopes are dashed to the ground. But if the fair one is not averse to the match, and the father is satisfied, the lover is allowed to pay more frequent visits. A Murcian courtship is, however, a very decorous affair ; the damsel receives the youth under her mother's eye. They do not shake hands, and kissing is not allowed. And it is only in the larger towns of Andalusia, where the strictness of these customs is somewhat relaxed, that a lover may offer his mistress an arm when they are out walking together in the streets.

Among Spanish lovers, especially in Valencia and Andalusia, the serenade is a favourite method of courtship. The suitor, accompanied by two torch-bearers and musicians, stands, on an evening prearranged, underneath the lady's balcony, and tells his love through the mouth of a *trovador*, who has skill in improvising and singing verse. After much entreaty the lady vouchsafes to appear on the balcony, and first making a show of maidenly reluctance, is sometimes so overcome by the *trovador's* pleading, as to throw down the wreath from her head, and promise the lover to be ever faithful to him. Naturally this is all a comedy, even if a very graceful one, the lover having obtained the consent of the parents, and of his mistress, some time before this public display of his affection takes place.

If the girl's parents are obdurate, and refuse to countenance his suit, the Spanish youth has a sure remedy; he appeals to them three times, and after a third refusal, applies to the authorities. A local official (*Alkalde*) appears in a carriage in full uniform, and demands either the father's consent to the union or the person of his daughter. Should the former be denied, the girl is, without further parley, carried off, and placed in a respectable family until the wedding, which is sure to take place unless the youth is of questionable character.

In Castille the bride wears a white flower in her bosom; in Andalusia a wreath of pinks and red roses fastened on her head. In Cadiz no ring is given in marriage, but the distinction between a married woman and an unmarried girl is that the former wears a flower on the right side of her hair. Poor girls in Madrid wear a flower but do not always know on which side to put it. Hence the young men are sometimes at a loss to know what it means. Sometimes they say to a girl, "Are you married? You have a flower on the right side!"

In the neighbourhood of Madrid a curious custom, though not without its parallel in other lands, is still preserved. Two youths stand at the door of the bride's house on the wedding-day, and when all the children and idlers of the neighbourhood are gathered round, they begin an oratorical dispute. One points out the

Signing the Marriage Contract, Spain. *By* S. Viniegra.

From a Photograph by the Photographic Union, Munich.

bride's faults and failings, the other, loud in her defence, extols her virtues. Sometimes the orators are so carried away by excitement that they come to blows, and knives have been used at times. In the same district the bridegroom, if he is a native of another place, must buy with gifts of wine, meat, and good things, permission from the lads of the village to take away his bride—another form of ransom.

In Barcelona only the relations accompany the pair to church; the remaining guests meanwhile assemble at the parents' house, where the feast is to be held. The members of the different sexes have tables laid for them in two separate rooms, and while the gentlemen are well supplied with meat and wines, the ladies have daintier dishes, such as pyramids of candied fruits and sweetmeats of the most enticing description. At the close of the meal the bridegroom appears among the lady guests, who, seated in a semi-circle, hold out their dresses to receive the bon-bons he scatters from a basket into each lap. They are veritable children in the matter of sweetmeats, these sedate ladies of Spain.

After the meal is over the company dance, and as an interlude make gifts to the bride. This is, in a Spanish father's eyes, a most important item; for as he is obliged in many places to provide the whole of the furniture and household goods as well as the house itself, for the young couple, he can seldom spare his daughter a further dowry. Where the *seguidillas mancheqas*, as the popular dance is called, finds favour with the guests, each man, woman, and child takes a few turns with the bride and makes her a present, which usually consists of money. In the villages of Salamanca they place a pie and knife on a table at one end of the room, and every guest that dances with the bride comes up afterwards, cuts the pie with the knife and put inside a piece of money.

When at midnight the young Valencian husband tries to steal away with the bride from among the throng of guests, her girl comrades strive with all their might to keep her back, and he is forced to call in the aid of his friends. When at last they make their escape, the young people retire to the terrace on the house-roof, where a bower of flowers has been prepared. Truly they manage things poetically in Spain! In no other nation does (ostensible) courtship begin with music of the serenade under the stars, and married life begin with a bower of flowers!

In Portugal enamoured bachelors have to make the best of very slender opportunities for making love. A young man paces before the fair one's window until he has aroused her attention, and then must contrive to make some pretty speeches before being observed by the passers-by. He is sure to find her at mass, and so becomes constant in attendance at her favourite church. If the duenna is not too vigilant, it is always possible to slip a love letter, expressive of his deep admiration, into the fair lady's hand. They may be lucky enough to meet at dances; but, alas! how little can there be said, when decorum requires that the young lady should be led back to her chaperon the moment a dance is over.

It is a Portuguese custom for the priest literally to bind the hands of the bridal pair together with the end of his stole, before he puts on the ring. Directly the service is over, it rains bon-bons, and if the officiating priest is hit by any of the shower intended for the young couple, there is much laughter and merriment.

CHAPTER XX

France, Holland, and Belgium

THERE are many ways of encouraging or discouraging a lover's attentions besides saying in so many words that he is welcome or had better be gone. The Dauphiné maiden is past mistress in this art. When a swain's visits are pleasing to her, she makes his soup thick with grated cheese; if the contrary, he will find a handful of oats in his pocket. Should he still persist, she will turn the blackened ends of the firebrands towards him, a sign there is no mistaking. The peasant girl admits a favoured lover to a *parlement*, which corresponds to a consent to "keep company," as we say in England. The swain is now allowed to dance with and call upon her, and to make himself useful in a thousand little ways. Should no better suitor come forward, the two will probably become man and wife. But Frenchwomen have a shrewd turn for business, and, if a richer lover comes across her path, the chances are Jeannette will not let him sigh in vain. So Jean, who has been admitted to a *parlement* at the New Year, finds his privileges withdrawn at Easter; while Jacques, who has a larger vineyard or expectations from a rich uncle, now carries her basket and chats with her at the well.

But with the better classes there is little opportunity for courtship. In Paris young unmarried girls go out occasionally into society; in the provinces this is not allowed. The *jeune fille bien élevée*, who as an ideal of innocent and ignorant girlhood quite surpasses the "young person" of our own island, has no social intercourse outside her own family. The late Mr. P. G. Hamerton, whose long residence in the country made him intimately acquainted with French habits, states that a young man rarely catches sight of his *fiancée* until she is promised to him in marriage. In one of his charming books [1] he tells a story of an acquaintance who was engaged to one of two sisters, neither of whom he had previously seen. When first presented to these ladies the young man applied to his mother, who had doubtless arranged the affair, to know which of the two was to be his wife!

When a young man resolves on matrimony, and hears of a lady whose family and circumstances are in every way suitable, he makes informal inquiries, through a priest or some lady of her circle, about the girl's domestic qualities—and amount of dowry. This last particular is of the highest importance. It is rare for dowerless girls to marry in France, though the portions which wives, even of the comfortable middle-class, bring their husbands, only consist of some hundreds or at most two or three thousand

[1] "French and English."

pounds. On receiving satisfactory information the suitor, who wishes to do the thing in a decorous manner and avoid the unbecoming suspicion of being "in love," does not attempt to see the young lady of his choice, but commits the affair to some elderly woman, perhaps his mother or aunt. This good lady hastens to acquaint the girl's family with the offer, and in her turn informs them of the suitor's unimpeachable character and good circumstances. Should the business prosper, they may be married in two or three weeks. In orthodox families the clergy frequently act as ambassadors, and are said by anti-clericals to be very clever at securing large dowries for the faithful sons of the church.

Mr. Hamerton was once asked to negotiate a match between a friend of his and a certain young lady whom he also knew. She was domesticated, sensible, pleasant, and very beautiful. "I don't wonder," said he, "that you admire such an admirable young lady. She becomes more and more beautiful every day." "Is she pretty?" was the reply. "I have never seen her. Some people say she is pretty." Mr. Hamerton's feelings, "as an Englishman believing in love, and an artist believing in beauty, being outraged by this answer," he quickly rejoined, "Then for what reason on earth do you want to marry her?" It was the suitor's turn to be surprised. After opening his eyes in astonishment, he said, "I have reached the time of life when men take wives. I have made careful inquiries, and, from all I can learn, this young lady would make me a good and suitable wife. They say she is well brought up, and can manage a house, and has good manners. I know that she has a suitable property, which is essential."

Here was the matter in a nutshell. And the young man laid the greatest emphasis on the last and most important item. The essential thing was truly the "suitable property." French people have a wholesome dread of anything like a *mésalliance.*

At La Sologne, near Orleans, when a young couple marry without the means of commencing housekeeping, the contributions of the neighbourhood are always forthcoming to supply the deficiency ; the mode of collecting these is whimsical enough. Five young peasant girls, dressed, of course, in their best *costume de fête*, proceed to beg among the assembled company, which consists for the most part of nearly the entire population of the parish. They conduct their operations in the following manner. The first holds a distaff and spindle in her hands, which she presents to each of the company, while she sings a song telling how the bride has no hemp to spin her trousseau with. The second damsel receives the offerings produced by this appeal in the husband's drinking cup. The third acts the part of Hebe and pours out a draught of wine, which she offers to each contributor to the store. The fourth carries a napkin, with which she wipes the mouth of each guest after his draught, and thus prepares the way for the performance of the duty entrusted to the fifth, always the prettiest of the party, that of rewarding him for his generosity with a kiss.

Many of the ancient customs of the Bretons are rapidly dying out, but in certain out-of-the-way corners of Lower Brittany some still survive. Here a young peasant who is in love confides his passion to the village tailor. The latter then seeks out the damsel in question and speaks to her privately, laying before her the swain's suit. If the girl is willing, the respective parents are consulted. On a certain fixed day, the tailor, with a white rod in his hand, and with one purple and one red stocking on his legs, accompanies the youth and his father to the house of the future bride. Here the parents discuss "ways and means," while the young people enjoy a long private and uninterrupted conversation. The meeting over, they join the old people, and partake together of white bread, wine and brandy, using the same knife between them and eating from the same plate. On another day the "view" (*velladen*) is held at the same house.

On this occasion there is much display, every one appearing in holiday costume, and the conditions of the marriage-contract are then fixed. The guests inspect the trousseau.

The bride must choose a bridesmaid, and the young man a groomsman. These, accompanied by an inviter, or "bidder," as the person is called in Wales, who bears a white wand, go and invite people to the wedding. On so important an event as a wedding nobody is forgotten, however humble his condition in life may happen to be ; and nowhere in the world are the ties of kindred stronger than among the people of

Lower Brittany. A thousand persons have been known to assist at the wedding of a prosperous farmer! The friends and acquaintances are so many that the task of "bidding" often occupies several days. On the previous Sunday every one who has accepted the invitation is expected to send some present to the young couple. In the case of a farmer, the bearer of the present is one of his farm labourers, very carefully dressed, in order to produce a great impression of his master's consequence. Sometimes the gifts are of considerable value, but they usually take the form of some article of domestic use or something for the feast.

At an early hour on the wedding-day, the young men of the village assemble near the bride's house, where the bridegroom meets them. As soon as a sufficient number have gathered together they depart in procession, preceded by the "Ambassador of Love" (*basvalan*) with a band of music—the bag-pipe being conspicuous—to take possession of the bride. But parents do not give away their daughters too easily, and so pretend at first to refuse. Accordingly, when the procession has arrived at the farm, there is profound silence—except for the barking of savage dogs. The doors are closed, and the place appears to be deserted; but even a hasty survey of the homestead reveals the fact that preparations are being made for an approaching festivity—chimneys and cauldrons are smoking and long tables have been arranged in every available place.

Long and loudly does the ambassador knock, until

at length there appears an envoy of the bride's family. This person, with a branch of broom in his hand, replies in verse, pointing to some neighbouring *château*, where he assures the *basvalan* such a glorious train as his is sure to find a welcome on account of its unparalleled splendour. But this polite excuse is foreseen; the *basvalan* answers his rival, verse for verse, compliment for compliment, saying that they are in search of a jewel more brilliant than the stars, not hidden away in the *château* but *here* in the farmhouse. Upon this the family envoy retires, and presently leads forth an aged matron, and presents her as the only jewel they have got. "Of a truth," replies the ambassador, "a *most* respectable person; but it appears to us that she is past her festal time. We do not deny the merit of grey hair, especially when silvered by age and virtue. But we seek something far more precious. The maiden we demand is at least three times younger. Try again; you cannot fail to discover her from the splendour which her unparalleled beauty sheds around her!" But even after this it is not correct to produce the true bride; so first the man brings an infant in arms, next a widow, then a married woman, and then one of the bridesmaids. These candidates are all rejected very politely, so as not to wound their feelings, until at last the dark-eyed blushing bride is led forth arrayed in her wedding dress. The bridegroom's party then enter the house; the family envoy, falling on his knees, slowly utters a *Pater noster* for the living and a *De profundis* for the dead, and asks the family to bestow a blessing on their daughter. Then the scene assumes a more affecting character; sobs are heard, and tears fall while the man is speaking. There is generally some sad episode in connection with these rustic festivals. Perhaps the thoughts of both father and mother are led to the memory of a dear one whom they "have loved long since and lost awhile." But, in any case, there is the sad present trial of parting with their jewel. When the procession is about to start for church the mother severs the end of the bride's sash, and addresses her as follows—

"The tie which has so long united us, my child, is henceforward rent asunder, and I am compelled to yield to another the authority which God gave me over thee. If thou art happy—and may God ever grant it—this will be no longer thy home; but should misfortune visit thee, a mother is still a mother, and her arms ever open for her children. Like thee I quitted my mother's side to follow a husband. Thy children will leave thee in turn. When the birds are grown the maternal nest cannot hold them. May God bless thee, my child, and grant thee as much consolation as He has granted me!"

The wedding procession is interrupted on its way to the church by groups of beggars, who climb up the slopes bordering the roads—which are very deep and narrow, like Devonshire lanes—in order to bar the passage by means of long briars, or to hold up prickly thorns in the faces of the party. The groomsman removes the barriers, and scatters coins among the mendicants. When the distance is considerable, the number of such barriers is often great; but the groomsman must patiently remove each one, never losing his temper for a moment, and always liberally throwing the money.

After the religious ceremony comes the feast; the multitude of guests form a lively and variegated picture. The arrival of the newly-married couple from the church is announced by the firing of muskets, and the sound of bagpipes; pipers, fiddlers, and single-stick players head the returning procession; then come the bride and bridegroom, followed by relatives and guests. The neighbours who have stayed to help in the cooking desert their posts and rush from the kitchen, or the yard, where fires are burning, to watch the arrivals. Presently, when the confusion has subsided, the guests find their places at the long narrow tables formed of rough planks, supported by stakes driven into the ground. They eat soup from wooden bowls; meat is cut up and eaten in the hand, or as they say, "upon the thumb."

Beer and wine are served from rough earthenware jugs, and cups are shared. It is considered polite to hand one's cup to a neighbour, so that he may assist in emptying it; and a refusal would be considered extremely rude. The bridegroom and his relations wait on their guests, pressing each one to "take care of himself." Compliments are showered upon them, and they drink from time to time the cups that are offered to them. The feasting is not continuous, but goes on at intervals. After each course the musicians play, and all rise up from the tables. One party gets up a wrestling match—for the Bretons are famous wrestlers like their Cornish brethren. Others play at single-stick, or run races, while some dance, and beggars partake of what has been left on the tables.

Then games and dances give place to another course of eating and drinking ; and so they continue till midnight.

In some parts of Brittany the two tailors, representing the bride and bridegroom respectively, hold a quaint dialogue at the house of the bride, to which the young man comes with his friends on the wedding day to demand hospitality. The lady's poet replies that possibly the party are vagabonds, and had better pursue their way. At last the man's poet declares the real object of his visit and sets forth his friend's good qualities. How he can plough as much in a day as three hired labourers. How he can set up a cart that has been overturned ; what a champion he is at wrestling matches. The other one then dwells on the lady's good points, enumerating her many perfections of body and mind. "She is as light and supple as the blossom-covered branches of the broom," &c. "But," he adds, "she has unfortunately left her father's house !" Of course the bridegroom's man refuses to believe this, and insists that the fair one must be somewhere within. "Young girls," he says, "are made to grace the home of a husband. Do not drive us to despair ! Lead hither the one whom we desire, and we will place her at the wedding feast near the bridegroom, under the eyes of her friends."

Among the Dutch peasants (Boers) a young man goes courting on a Sunday, being too busy on other days. He must call at the house where the young woman lives. Should her parents offer him a chair, he may conclude that his presence is welcome. The elders then retire, leaving him to speak for himself. If, however, the young woman herself feels coldly towards him, she tells him plainly to make for the door, and there is an end of the matter. In certain parts of Holland, when a youth takes a fancy to some girl, he stands at the door of her house and asks for a match to light his pipe. Should he repeat the visit, her parents have no further doubt in their own minds that he intends to propose marriage. On his calling a third time they inform him whether his suit is viewed with favour or no. Should they be willing to accept the lover for a son-in-law, they ask him in, and the match which he asked for is given; but if not he must retire, and light the pipe with a match from his own pocket.

Those who are betrothed must enter their names in a book at the Town Hall (*Stadhuis*) at least a couple of weeks before the marriage, in order to allow any one who has the right to make an objection the opportunity of doing so. The bride-elect and her betrothed send out printed circulars to their friends and hold receptions at which they themselves sit in chairs on a platform under a canopy decorated with evergreens. Parents and relations arrange themselves on each side, making a "family circle." The visitors entering in small parties, from time to time, make little formal speeches and retire to partake of the refreshments that are always provided on a liberal scale. "Bridal sugar" (*bruid suiker*), a kind of sweetmeat, and spiced wine, called "bride's tears" are offered to all the visitors.

The door of the bride's house is painted green, and flowers are scattered near it by the wedding guests, as the bride and bridegroom leave for the Town Hall, to be married before the Burgomaster with civil rites.

Formerly it was the custom to invite the guests through two bachelors, who went, armed with gaily-decorated wands, to every house and repeated a number of verses.

According to another custom, which appears to have died out, it was usual for newly-married couples to provide themselves with planks of elm, from which their coffins might be made when they were dead; and a bride's trousseau usually included a cap and a shroud. At the marriage feast there is much merriment, together with singing and dancing. A large silver bowl, filled with brandy and raisins, is handed round to the guests. One of their favourite songs, beginning with the words,

> "How sweet it is where friendship dwells,"

is invariably sung on these occasions.

In Belgium they print their wedding invitations on a double sheet of paper, one containing an invitation from the parents of the bride, the other from those of the bridegroom. These are paid for by the bridegroom, but the bride has to provide the funds for the wedding mass, the church decorations, and beadles in splendid uniform. The man and the woman are enthroned before the altar in two big chairs while the Mass proceeds, the bride's veil being spread out behind her. Certain acquaintances of their respective families sit with them as witnesses, and these are always the most important people of their acquaintance. An interesting feature in these marriages is the collection for the poor, made by the bridesmaids, under the usher's escort. The money is thrown to the beggars at the church door as the marriage party leaves the building. The happy pair usually take a drive in the park, and then pay a visit to the photographer. The wedding breakfast takes place at some hotel.

CHAPTER XXI

England and Wales

WE have reserved our account of the customs of our country to the end, in order that the reader may be in a better position to understand the origin and meaning of those observances which have been handed down from a more or less remote antiquity. There are more survivals in our present marriage customs than one would think, as may be shown by answering a few simple questions. Thus: "Who was the 'best man,' and what did he do?" To answer this we must go back to the days of "marriage by capture," for, as has been shown by writers on the history of marriage, the "best man" was the friend or comrade who helped the bridegroom to catch his bride. How few and simple are his duties at the present day, compared with what these once were! They call for no special exertion, and certainly are unattended with danger—if we except the danger of falling in love with a pretty bridesmaid. But in those early days what might he not have to do, from murder downwards? We may picture him prowling round the hut, spear in hand, eyes and ears alert, to see whether the coast were clear, and then with stone-axe, knife or club helping to keep the family at bay while his friend carried off the damsel in spite of her cries.

Nor is this the only relic of the most ancient of human institutions; for what was the honeymoon? It was not merely a pleasure trip as now, but a rapid and hurried flight of bride and bridegroom, rendered positively necessary by the anger of an outraged father. And so for at least a month the newly-married couple deemed it advisable to keep out of his way. After that time perhaps his wrath would have partially subsided, and then it might be possible, by making handsome presents, to reconcile him to the situation, and persuade him to accept a *fait accompli*.[1]

Presents to the bridesmaids form another interesting link with primeval days. They were originally a form of toll, and we have described above the custom still existing in Central India, where Kurku girls go through the form of preventing the removal of the bride. They pelt the young men—formerly the attacking party—with balls of boiled rice. Then they make a last stand at the door of the house, and, finally, only suffer the bridegroom to enter and take away his bride, after paying toll in the form of presents all round; in fact they are bribed, and their resistance is more or less assumed for appearance sake. Throwing old shoes after the bride and bridegroom on their going away

[1] The Norse for Marriage is *Quan-fang*, or wife-catching, and the old German *Breit-loufti*, or bride-racing.

is possibly another relic of the same kind; but there are two interpretations of this custom. According to one view it may be taken as a symbolic act on the part of the father of the bride who, in throwing a shoe, meant to signify that from henceforth he gave up all authority over the bride. The other explanation refers it to "marriage by capture," when a fight at the bride's house was part of the proceedings, and shoes might be thrown in anger when nothing else came handy.

The ceremony of lifting a bride over the doorstep is of ancient date. The Romans had this custom, and it may still be traced in widely distant lands, among the Red Skins of Canada, the Chinese, the Abyssinians, and also in Europe. Its origin is somewhat obscure; most writers, apparently, consider it as merely a necessary incident in "marriage by capture." Another suggestion, already mentioned, is that the bridegroom took up the bride in his arms when they arrived at his house, and lifted her over the doorstep lest she should be so unlucky as to stumble, which would be a bad omen for her future happiness. There is something to be said for this view; but the writer prefers an explanation mentioned in Brand's "Popular Antiquities of Great Britain" (1849, vol. ii. p. 114), where evidence is adduced to show that in old days a Roman bride was expected to manifest the greatest reluctance to step over the door of her husband's house, because to appear to do so willingly would have shown a want of true maidenly modesty (compare Arabia, Persia). We can well imagine that in some countries it was the custom for brides to stand there a long time, until at last the impatient bridegrooms could wait no longer, and put an end to the delay by lifting up their brides and carrying them over.

The bride-cake, still cut by the bride's own hand, is one of the most interesting relics embedded in the strange mosaic of our present marriage customs. As the reader who has followed our previous accounts will have noticed, the taking of food or drink together by the contracting parties may be said to be the principal, and sometimes the only ceremony among primitive peoples. And still it has not died out with more civilised races. The Jews drink the consecrated wine; Chinese take tea; Japanese drink *saki*; Malays and others eat betel nut, and so on. The ancient Romans had three forms of marriage, but the strictest was the *confarreatio*, or eating together. It was jealously restricted to patricians and accompanied with awful religious rites. Hence, in Europe, the bride-cake plays an important part at marriages.

The throwing of rice, wheat, or other seeds was clearly symbolic of fertility, and expressive of the hope that the bride would in time be a happy mother of children. Abundance may be a secondary meaning.

It appears that, in the time of Edward VI., marriages were performed in the church porch, and not in the building itself. Selten states that dower could be lawfully assigned only at the door, and another writer says, "When he cometh to the church door to be married there, after affiance and troth plighted, he endoweth the woman of his whole land, or of the half, or other lesser part thereof, and there openly doth declare the quantity and the certainty of the land she shall have for her dower." The reader will easily perceive that the object of formally investing a bride with her endowments at the church door was that it might be a public act witnessed by all who chose to assemble there. The custom is older than Edward VI.'s time, for Chaucer, in the time of Edward III., makes the wife of Bath say—

"Husbands at churche door have I had five."

As in other countries, so in England, there was much joyous feasting on the occasion of a wedding. This is clearly shown by the very word "Bridal," which is simply another form of "Bride-ale" (or Bride-feast), the latter word being commonly applied to a feast. Originally it meant only the carousal, or drinking, in honour of the bride; and, indeed, "bride-ale" is still, in the Cleveland dialect of Yorkshire, the word applied to the draught presented to the wedding party on its return from church. There were also "Bid-ales," when the guests were "bidden," or invited; and "Church-ales," or Church-feasts, not to mention others.

Publicans used to make a good deal of money by these wedding-feasts. The amount of beer which other people might brew for a wedding was limited by law, so as to protect the publican.

In many countries, as previous pages have shown, the neighbours made presents in kind, as contributions towards the expenses of a marriage. The same custom prevailed in England.

Owen, in his "Welsh Dictionary," says, "The poor people in Wales have a marriage of contribution, to which every guest brings a present of some sort of provision, or money, to enable the new couple to begin the world." According to the same authority, it was customary for poor women newly married to go to farmers' houses to ask for cheese. In the North of England, after a public wedding of the kind here referred to, presents continued to come in for some days. The value of all the various contributions was sometimes as much as £200. A servant girl who had been with the same mistress for seven years, was entitled upon her marriage to a copper kettle holding from four to six gallons. If a young couple were very poor, they sent round a cart (wain) and horse to their friends to beg of them corn or whatever they could give. The corn was often used to sow the first crop. This explains the word "Bride-wain."

About a hundred years ago it was still usual to celebrate a marriage with "open house," to which all the inhabitants of the district were bidden. The county of Cumberland was specially famous for these "Bidden Weddings." The invitation took the form of a public announcement. Here is a sample of the year 1789—

> "Suspend for one day your cares and your labours,
> And come to this wedding, kind friends and good neighbours.

"Notice is hereby given that the marriage of Isaac Pearson with Frances Atkinson will be solemnised in due form in the parish church of Lamplugh, Cumberland, on Tuesday next, the 30th May inst., after which the bride and bridegroom, with their attendants, will proceed to Lonefoot, in the same parish, where the nuptials will be celebrated by a variety of rural entertainments."

Some families, however, were not rich enough to entertain their friends and neighbours in such a liberal manner, and so, in course of time, the cost of the entertainment came to be defrayed by subscription among the guests. Hence the origin of "The Penny Wedding," at which each guest contributed a few pence, and whatever was over went towards starting the happy couple in life.

As the Scotch lads used to "run fir the Kail," and Welsh ones for a jug of beer, so we find that in parts of England, they used to ride for the bride-cake; only this took place when the bride was brought to her new home. A pole was erected in front of the house, with the cake stuck on the top of it. The moment that the bride left her old home, a company of young men started off on horseback; and he who was fortunate enough to reach the pole first, and knock down the cake with his stick, had the honour of receiving it, from the hands of a damsel, on the point of a wooden sword. With this trophy he returned to meet the bride and her attendants, who, on arrival, was presented with a posy of flowers, while others decorated with garlands the horses' heads. Sometimes, instead of racing for the bride-cake, the young men engaged in a trial of strength, and threw heavy bars of iron. This game or contest was known as "throwing the quintal." Yorkshire men used to run a race in front of the house where the feast was held, and the victor claimed a kiss from the bride. In some parts of Essex the bride used to take a seat near a table, her husband standing by her side while the guests came up in turn and gave presents of money, the piper exhorting them to be liberal. Whoever gave the most received a pair of gloves, with a ribbon attached, and could claim a kiss from the bride.

According to the following old rhyme the middle of the week was the best day for getting married; and the last three days were considered unlucky.

> "Monday for wealth,
> Tuesday for health,
> Wednesday the best day of all;
> Thursday for crosses,
> Friday for losses,
> Saturday no luck at all."

In some parts of Lancashire a man must never go courting on Friday, and if he is caught with his sweetheart on that day he is followed home by a noisy band

THE MATE'S WEDDING. *From a Painting by John R. Reid.*

of roughs playing on tin-pots, or anything that comes handy.

An uneven number of wedding guests was a thing to be avoided, or one of them might die before the year was over. In the North, green, the fairies' colour, was not to be worn. The country folk also said that if a grave were open in the churchyard through which the party walked, the wedding would be sure to prove unlucky.

The following table gives the popular names of the various anniversaries of the Wedding Day :—

Year.	*Anniversary.*	*Year.*	*Anniversary.*
1st . .	Cotton	15th . .	Crystal
2nd . .	Paper	20th . .	China
3rd . .	Leather, or Straw	25th . .	Silver
4th . .		30th . .	Pearl
5th . .	Wood	40th . .	Ruby
6th . .		50th . .	Gold
7th . .	Wool	60th . .	
10th . .	Tin	70th . .	
12th . .	Silk and Linen	75th . .	Diamond

In Eastern countries, as our previous pages have frequently testified, women, as a rule, do not receive the respect and honour naturally due to them ; and a man buys a wife pretty much as he would buy an ox or a horse. But our readers will probably be surprised to learn that, even in England, wives have been purchased even in recent years. The strange belief that such a summary mode of divorce is according to law is not quite extinct. The writer remembers a case recorded in a daily newspaper only about ten years ago. And, if we go back a little further, it will be found that the practice was formerly not very uncommon. An old Devonshire farmer once thus addressed the friends assembled to celebrate an anniversary of his wedding—"I guv three pun' ten for my Missus three and thirty years ago this very day, and I wouldn't take it for her now!" In the year 1744, the second Duke of Chandos bought his second wife from her husband, an ostler in Newbury, who was offering her for sale as the Duke passed through the town!

The strange custom whereby a condemned criminal could be saved from death by marriage once prevailed in England and France. Early in the seventeenth century, an English ballad celebrated the story of a merchant, born at Chichester, who was saved from hanging by a gallant maiden, who married him at the place of execution. In 1725 a widow petitioned King George I., offering to marry a man under the gallows if a reprieve should be granted to him. In the United States similar cases were not unknown. We have not been able to ascertain the date of the last case of this kind in England.

According to Pinkerton, a certain criminal preferred death to marriage at the foot of the gallows.[1] The event was thus recorded in rhyme:—

"There was a victim in a cart
    One day for to be hang'd,
And his reprieve was granted,
    And the cart made for to stand.

See Browning's "Muckle-Mouthed Meg" for a similar tale.

"'Come, marry a wife, and save your life,'
The judge aloud did cry.
'Oh, why should I corrupt my life?'
The victim did reply.

"'For here's a crowd of every sort,
And why should I prevent their sport?
The bargain's bad in every part,
The wife's the worst—drive on the cart.'"

In the year 1725 it is recorded that nine young women, dressed in white, each with a white wand in her hand, presented a petition to his Majesty George I. on behalf of a young man condemned at Kingston for burglary, one of whom offered to marry him under the gallows.

One cannot help feeling that there is something to be said for this "ancient and laudable custom," although its revival in the present day would not be desirable. Nevertheless it showed a belief in the redeeming power of a good woman, so well illustrated by the story of Tannhaüser.

It is difficult to believe that the disgraceful and often fictitious marriages called "Fleet Weddings" were made less than a hundred and fifty years ago. They take their name from the Fleet Prison, where many of the couples were united, the officiating parsons being disreputable and dissolute men, often prisoners for debt, who were willing, for the sake of a fee, to unite any persons in marriage at a moment's notice. They asked no inconvenient questions, only stipulating for so much payment in money, or a given quantity of liquor wherewith to drink the health of those whom they thus unlawfully joined together. It was by no means a rare thing for the parson, bridegroom, and bride all to be in a state of intoxication while the ceremony took place. These disgraceful members of the sacred calling had their "plyers," who addressed men and women as they passed along the streets, asking them whether they wanted a parson to marry them. One of the most notorious of these scandalous officials was a man of the name of George Keith, a Scotch minister, who set up a marriage office in May Fair, and subsequently in the Fleet. His business in this line became so extensive and scandalous that the Bishop of London found it advisable to excommunicate him. One morning during the Whitsuntide holidays he and his "journeyman" united a greater number of couples than had been married at any ten churches within the bills of mortality. The man was a bare-faced profligate, but lived to the age of eighty-nine years. Many of the early Fleet weddings were really, as a matter of fact, performed at the Chapel of the Fleet Prison. But, as the practice extended, it was found more convenient to have other places "within the rules"; and thereupon many of the Fleet parsons and tavern-keepers in the neighbourhood fitted up rooms in their respective lodgings, or houses, as a Chapel. The parsons took the fees, allowing a portion to their "plyers"; and the tavern-keepers, besides sharing in the money paid, derived a profit from the sale of liquors which they supplied at the wedding parties. Some of these innkeepers kept a parson on the establishment at a weekly salary of twenty shillings, who entered the names of the parties married in registers kept at these taverns. Sign-boards were hung out of the windows in order to attract passers-by, with the enticing words, "Weddings performed cheap here!" One of these men, a Fleet parson of the name of Walter Wyatt, lived to see the gross error of his way, and certain entries made in a pocket-book show how bitterly he repented his misdeeds. "May God forgive me what is past," he says, "and give me grace to forsake such a wicked place, where truth and virtue cannot take place unless you are resolved to starve." His earnings were very considerable.

It need hardly be pointed out that these matrimonial facilities gave rise to many grave evils, the consequences of which were far-reaching. Parsons were frequently bribed to make false entries in their registers, to ante-date weddings, to give fictitious certificates, and even to marry persons unwilling to declare more than the initial letters of their names! Widows who were involved in debt could easily cheat their creditors by pretending to have been married before their debts were contracted: it was only necessary for the widow to pay a small extra fee to the parson, who found some man to act as bridegroom for a few shillings. Blank spaces were left in the registers, and so the names could be inserted in such a way as to make it appear that they had been married several years before! Entries could be obliterated for a fee! Sham bridegrooms, under different names, were married many times over; children born out of wedlock could be made apparently legitimate.

All kinds of people flocked to these unholy places—runaway sons and daughters of peers, Irish adventurers and rich but foolish widows, footmen and decayed beauties, soldiers and servant girls, boys in their teens, and young heiresses brought thither by force and compelled, against their wills, to be brides. The parson who solemnised an irregular marriage was liable to a fine, but such a penalty had no terrors for a man who was already in the Fleet Prison. The evil was abolished at last by making these irregular marriages invalid.

Many of the churchwardens and overseers of that day were in the habit of getting up marriages between paupers in order to throw the burden of their relief on other parishes. The *Daily Post* of July 4, 1741, reported the following case:—"On Saturday last the churchwardens for a certain parish in the city, in order to remove a load from their own shoulders, gave forty shillings, and paid the expense of a Fleet marriage, to a miserable blind youth, who plays on the violin in Moorfields, in order to make a settlement of the wife and future family in Shoreditch parish. To secure their point, they sent a parish officer to see the ceremony performed. One cannot but admire the ungenerous proceeding of this city parish, as well as their unjustifiable abetting and encouraging an irregularity so much and so justly complained of as these Fleet matches. Invited, and uninvited, were a great number of poor wretches, in order to spend the bride's parish fortune."

In the Society of Friends, or Quakers, a wedding is conducted with the greatest simplicity, as will be seen from our reproduction of an excellent picture exhibited in the Royal Academy, 1896, by our friend Mr. Percy Bigland (himself a Quaker), who has kindly allowed us to engrave it. Marriages are only entered into after much careful consideration, and with a due sense of the importance and solemnity of the contract. They mostly marry among themselves, "outside" marriages being discouraged. The Friends' *Book of Christian Discipline* contains the following injunction :—

"Friends are advised against running into excessive, sumptuous, or costly entertainments at marriage dinners; a great part of the cost of which would be better employed in relieving the necessities of the poor."

Friends intending to marry declare their intention at the monthly meeting of which they are members, the parents or guardians declaring their consent, if present, or, if absent, sending a signed certificate to the effect that their consent has been given. The meeting then appoints two men and two women to inquire if the contracting parties are free from other marriage engagements, &c. If no impediment appear, then a subsequent monthly meeting grants the parties leave to enter the married state. Marriages are solemnized at a usual week-day meeting, and at the meeting-house to which the woman belongs. There is no further ceremony than is here described. "After the meeting has been held a seasonable time, the parties are to stand up, and, taking each other by the hand, to declare in an audible and solemn manner to the following effect; the man first, viz.: '*Friends, I take this my friend D.E. to be my wife, promising through divine assistance, to be unto her a loving and faithful husband, until it shall please the Lord by death to separate us*' and then the woman in like manner, '*Friends, I take this my friend A.B. to be my husband, promising through divine assistance, to be unto him a loving and faithful wife, until it shall please the Lord by death to separate us.*'"

The parties also sign a certificate, and so do the witnesses. There are certain other rules laid down among Friends with regard to marriage, for example, that engagements may not be broken, as their Book of Christian Discipline says:—"And further, that such friends as have with serious advice, due deliberation, and free and mutual consent, absolutely agreed, espoused, or contracted upon the account of marriage, shall not be allowed, or owned amongst us, in any unfaithfulness or injustice one to another, to break or violate any such contract or engagement: which is to the reproach of truth, or injury one of another. And where any such injury, breach or violation of such solemn contract is known or complained of . . . we advise and counsel

A QUAKER WEDDING. *By* PERCY BIGLAND.

that a few faithful friends, both men and women, in their respective meetings to which the parties belong, be appointed to inquire into the cause thereof, and to report to a succeeding monthly meeting the result of their inquiry, that it may use its discretion as to the due exercise of the discipline in the case. And, further, we advise and exhort that no engagements made without honest endeavours to obtain, or due regard first had to, the counsel and consent of parents, relations, and friends, be countenanced; that so all foolish and unbridled affections, and all ensnaring and selfish ends, be not so much found among us on any hand."

Parents are to discourage the marriage of their children outside the society. Those that are married by a priest, or in any manner "contrary to the established rules of the said society," are to be dealt with "in the spirit of Christian tenderness, agreeably to our known discipline; all friends are also earnestly besought to prevent such marriages, and parents or guardians permitting or encouraging them are to undergo the discipline of the society. Parents, guardians, overseers and elders are likewise exhorted to check among young people all desire to form connexions *outside* the society, which so often lead to the solemnization of marriage *by a priest*, which, as being a violation of our testimony against a hireling ministry . . . we, as a people, have always believed it our duty to testify against."

With the Jews there are considerable differences in

the ways in which marriages are celebrated in the different countries where they are now to be found, and the following description deals only with Jewish marriages as they are celebrated in London of to-day. It was the author's good fortune to witness recently a marriage in the New West End Synagogue, and his thanks are due, not only to the Chief Rabbi, Dr. Herman Adler, for his courteous invitation, but also to the Rev. J. L. Geffen, of the New West End Synagogue, for his kind help in giving the information necessary for this brief account.

Jewish marriages are solemnized between the hours of 1 and 4 p.m.; the bride and bridegroom on that day partaking of no food or drink. Until quite recently, the marriage ceremony was preceded by the ordinary daily afternoon service; but now this is discarded, and the service begins with the chanting by the reader and choir of the following verses from the Psalms.

"How goodly are thy tents, O Jacob: Thy dwelling places, O Israel." (Numb. xxiv. 5.)

"Lord, I love the habitation of Thy house, and the place where Thy glory dwelleth." (Psa. xxvi. 8.)

In front of the reading desk is placed the canopy or *chuppah*, supported by four slender posts and beautifully decorated with white flowers and green leaves. Here the bridegroom waits while the reader pronounces the three following verses.

"Blessed be he that cometh in the name of the Lord: we bless you out of the house of the Lord." (Psa. cxviii.)

"O, come let us worship and bow down ; let us kneel before the Lord our maker." (Psa. xcv.)

"Serve the Lord with joy ; come before Him with exulting." (Psa. c. to the end.)

The bride then enters, led by her father, or, in his absence, by her nearest relative, such as a brother. She is followed by the mothers of the bride and bridegroom, the bridesmaids, and page-boy, if there is one, as is generally the case at fashionable weddings. The bride stands on the right hand of the bridegroom, while the two fathers are on his left, and the two mothers on the right of the bride. The reader pronounces the following benediction. "He who is mighty, blessed and great above all beings, may he bless the bridegroom and the bride." An extemporaneous address is then delivered by the senior minister, a cup of wine is handed to him, and he pronounces the following grace.

"Blessed art Thou, O Lord, our God, King of the universe, who hast sanctified us by Thy commandments, and hast given us command concerning forbidden marriages, who hast disallowed unto us those that are betrothed, but hast sanctified unto us such as are wedded to us by the rite of the canopy, and the sacred covenant of wedlock. Blessed art Thou, O Lord, who sanctifiest Thy people Israel by the rite of the canopy and the sacred covenant of wedlock."

The cup is then handed to the father of the bridegroom, who gives it to the bridegroom to drink. It is then handed to the mother of the bride, who gives it to the bride to drink. To do this, she lifts up the bride's long white diaphanous veil which covers her head and most of her dress. And now the wedding ring is produced and placed by the bridegroom on the forefinger of the bride's right hand, while he makes the following declaration. "Behold thou art consecrated unto me by this ring, according to the law of Moses and of Israel." Next, the marriage-contract is read out by one of the officiating ministers, first in Hebrew and then in English —it was signed before the service began by both the bridegroom and officiating ministers. A contract of this kind reads as follows:—

"On this——day of the week, on——day of the Hebrew month——in the——year,[1] the holy covenant of marriage was entered into in London between the bridegroom A. and the bride B. The said bridegroom made the following declaration to his bride. 'Be thou my wife, according to the law of Moses and of Israel. I faithfully promise that I will be a true husband unto thee, I will honour and cherish thee, I will work for thee, I will protect and support thee, I will provide all that is necessary for thy due sustenance, even as it beseemeth a Jewish husband to do. I also take upon myself all such further obligations for thy maintenance, during thy lifetime, as are prescribed by our religious statutes.' And the said bride has plighted her troth unto him in affection and sincerity, and has thus taken upon herself the fulfilment of all the duties incumbent

[1] The present year 1897 is reckoned as the year 5657, from the supposed date of the Creation of the world.

upon a Jewish wife. This covenant of marriage was duly executed and witnessed this day, according to the usage of Israel."

The cup is refilled, and the last seven blessings are read, after which the goblet is again given to the bride and bridegroom, who drink from it as before. The glass having been placed on the ground, the bridegroom shatters it into many pieces by stamping on it with his foot. This breaking of the glass is an important piece of symbolism, for it is meant as a sad reminder to all present of Zion's shattered crown of glory. Mr. Geffen informs the writer that for the same reason decorations in private houses, as well as in the Synagogue, are always left incomplete in some way, signifying that there can be no perfect rejoicing, not even on the happiest occasions in life, so long as Zion is unrestored to Israel. The minister then pronounces the benediction from Numbers vi. 24–26. The service concludes with the singing by the choir of Psalm cl.

In Wales, the ancient festivities connected with marriage were still retained some forty or fifty years ago; but since the introduction of railways into quiet mountainous districts many changes in manners and customs have taken place. The day having been fixed, "bidding papers" were despatched to friends all round the country side. The squire was sure to find one on his table, and usually responded by a liberal subscription. The feast was held at the bride's home, in most cases. When she appeared in bridal costume among the assembled guests, friends proceeded to hide her away, so that the bridegroom might have some difficulty in finding her: this was part of the fun. Then the four or five groomsmen advanced to the house-door, and on behalf of their friend, demanded the bride from her father, and her spokesmen made reply, thus reminding one of the curious little scene that takes place in Brittany. All the stock of wit possessed by either party was exhausted, until, amid much laughter, the claimants were admitted and began their search. Sometimes she was so well hidden that it was nearly noon and yet they had not found her! This was serious, because it would be too late after twelve o'clock (the law was only altered a few years ago). A friend then came forward to act as a guide, and her discovery was announced with loud acclamations.

In some parts it was the custom to ride full speed to the church. Thus Malkin[1] says, "Ill may it befal the traveller who has the misfortune of meeting a Welsh wedding party on the road. He would be inclined to suppose that he had fallen in with a company of lunatics escaped from their confinement. It is the custom of the whole party who are invited, both men and women, to ride full-speed to the church-porch; and the person who arrived there first, has some privilege or distinction at the marriage feast. To this important object, all inferior considerations give way, whether the safety of his Majesty's subjects who are not going to be married, or their own, be incessantly endangered by

[1] "Tour in South Wales, Glamorganshire," p. 67.

boisterous, unskilful, and contentious jockeyship. The natives, who are acquainted with the custom, and warned against the cavalcade by its vociferous approach, turn aside at respectful distance ; but the stranger will be fortunate if he escapes being overthrown by an onset, the occasion of which puts out of sight that urbanity so generally characteristic of the people."

Meanwhile the bridegroom awaited her at the church; but even then there might be further delay, for there took place a kind of mock ceremony of capture, and the poor girl often came in for some rough handling. It was nearly noon before the marriage-service had been read. No sooner had the clergyman given the blessing, than the men who were on horseback began a furious race to see who could first bring to those waiting at home the intelligence that the service was over. The rider who came first received a pint of ale. In Scotland the prize is a bowl of broth (*brose*).

The rest of the proceedings consisted of feasting and dancing, very much as in Brittany.

CHAPTER XXII

Scotland

THE old Scottish custom of the "Penny Wedding" has been thus described:—"When there was a marriage of two poor people who were esteemed by any of the neighbouring gentry, they agreed among themselves to meet and have a dance upon the occasion, the result of which was a handsome donation, in order to assist the new-married couple in their outset in life." [1]

Another writer says:—"A Penny Wedding is when the expense of the marriage entertainment is not defrayed by the young couple, or their relations, but by a club among the guests. Two hundred people, of both sexes, will sometimes be convened on an occasion of this kind." [2]

In the same work the Minister of Monquitter, speaking of the time of "our fathers," observes:—"Shrove Tuesday, Valentine Eve, the Rood-day, &c., were accompanied by pastimes and practices congenial to the youthful and ignorant mind. The market-place

[1] *The Gentleman's Magazine*, 1874.

[2] "Statistical Account of Scotland," vol. iv. 86

was to the peasant what the drawing-room is to the peer, the theatre of show and of consequence. The scene, however, which involved every amusement and every joy of an idle and illiterate age was a Penny Bridal. When a pair were contracted they, for a stipulated consideration, bespoke their wedding at a certain tavern, and then ranged the country in every direction to solicit guests. One, two, and even three hundred would have convened on these occasions to make merry at their own expense for two or more days. This scene of feasting, drinking, dancing, wooing, fighting, &c., was always enjoyed with the highest relish, and, until obliterated by a similar scene, furnished ample materials for rural mirth and rural scandal. But now the Penny Bridal is reprobated as an index of want of money and of want of taste. The market-place is generally occupied by people of business. Athletic amusements are confined to schoolboys. Dancing, taught by itinerant masters, cards, and conversation, are the amusements now in vogue; and the pleasures of the table, enlivened by a moderate glass, are frequently enjoyed in a suitable degree by people of every class." [1]

Of the parish of Avoch, co. Ross, it is said:—"Marriages in this place are generally conducted in the style of Penny Weddings. Little other fare is provided except bread, ale, and whisky. The relatives, who assemble in the morning, are entertained with a dram and a drink gratis. But, after the ceremony is

[1] "Statistical Account of Scotland," vol. xxi. 146.

performed, every man pays for his drink. The neighbours then convene in great numbers. A fiddler or two, with perhaps a boy to scrape on an old violoncello, are engaged. A barn is allotted for the dancing, and a house for drinking; and thus they make merry for two or three days, till Saturday night. On Sabbath, after returning from church, the married couple give a sort of dinner or entertainment to the present friends on both sides: so that these weddings, on the whole, bring little gain or loss to the parties." [1]

Jamieson, in his Etymological Dictionary, quotes an Act of the General Assembly, 13th February, 1645, for the restraint of Pennie Brydals.

The following account, taken from a story [2] published in the earlier part of the present century, will give the reader a fair idea of the way in which a Penny Wedding used to be celebrated in Scotland:—

Johnny Stewart first saw Jeannie Buie at the kirk, when she excited lively emotion within him. He afterwards met her at Elgin fair, and gave her a bumper of drink, while her master was discussing the price of cattle. He saw her a mile or two on the road home that night. The next year it was arranged they should be married when Martinmas came round.

Jeannie left her place on Whitsunday so that she might have time to spin her wool for blankets, and lint for sheets, before she got married. Three weeks before the wedding the bride and bridegroom went the round

[1] "Statistical Account of Scotland," vol. xv. 636.

[2] "The Penny Wedding," by John Grant. Edinburgh, 1836.

to invite their friends. On the eve of the marriage-day the friends all came to the Feet-washing. They drank a good deal "of mountain dew in its original state," and by ten o'clock they were very merry and insisted that Jeannie should have her feet washed. A tub filled with hot water was placed in the middle of the room, and a ring from the finger of a married woman was thrown into it.

Jeannie, blushingly, removed her stockings and plunged her feet into the water, and the lads and lasses crowded round the tub that they might wash the bride's feet and, perchance, find the ring, for the person that finds it will be the first to get married. When this ceremony was over, and the company had had some pulls from the "Tappit Hen" (a large bottle containing four quarts), they became exceedingly jovial, and one member of the company after the other was called upon for a song. An admirer of Jeannie's sang :—

> "There's mony lasses round about
>   To charm the heart and please the e'e ;
> But Jenny dings them out and out,
>   The bonny bride of Fallowlea.
> For O the bride's a bonny lass
>   And happy will her Johnny be,
> When she gaes o'er to keep the house
>   That stands beside the Fallowlea."

The grandmother also sang about the "good old times" and the sad alterations of the present day, whereupon the men got into a heated discussion about the "march of intellect." This being stopped, they drank "the health of the King—God bless him," and after a final glass of Glenlivet the company separated.

On the wedding morning Jeannie packed her wardrobe in a chest, and a cart was loaded with her belongings. The bride's party set out after breakfast for the manse, where the ceremony was to be performed.

One of the young men, who escorted the bride, carried a bottle of whiskey, out of which he must fill a glass for the first person the party met on their way; this person—called "the First Foot"—must also turn back and walk a mile or so with the wedding party, be his business never so urgent.

The bridegroom's party was waiting at the manse, and the wedding took place without delay. Both parties mixed, and proceeded to Fallowlea, the home of the young couple, the bagpiper playing "She's woo'd an' married an' a'," and the company singing the song on their way. At the cross-roads numerous people joined the party, for many intended being present at the wedding. When they arrived at the cottage the grandmother threw a number of pieces of bride-cake over the young couple's heads, "as a token that Jeannie Stewart was welcome to a house with plenty in it." Just before she entered the house a lad came up, claimed and took a kiss from the bride, to which he had a good right, as he had been successful "in running for the Kiles." For when the company were about 200 yards from the house, a number of young men started to run to the house, and whoever reached the homestead first, claimed the kiss.

The bride then took her place at the head of the table among her relations ; the rest of the company took their dinner in the barn. The fiddlers fiddled away during the meal to their hearts' content, and when it was over " two decent middle-aged men " went round, one with a glass of whiskey for every person, and the other with a basin to receive the shilling that each paid as the price of the meal.

Then the bridegroom led out the bride to the green, and they, with another lad and lass, danced the " Shamit Reel " before the company. This reel was called the " Shamit " because it was considered that it would take away the bashfulness under which the bride laboured before so many people.

Dancing was kept up in the house and barn with great spirit until the evening ; for every lad that chose to give a " bawbee " to the fiddlers could have what tune he liked played a dozen times over. When the fiddlers made a pause the lads cried " kissing time," it being the custom that every lad should then kiss his partner. They kissed one another right heartily and made " the roof and rafters dirl " with the sound.

At twelve the bride went to bed, and after a short time had elapsed her husband entered the room accompanied by a noisy troop of friends. She then threw her stocking in the air, and all present scrambled to clutch it, for the virtue in the stocking was, that whoever gained possession of it would be the first to be married. The best man presented whiskey to the married couple and the company, and then all departed, the best man locking the door of the bedroom. The rest of the party kept up dancing until six o'clock. At nine o'clock next morning the married couple were presented with a glass of whiskey before they got up.

During the next two days the dancing was kept up, and on Sunday about forty couples accompanied the bride and bridegroom to church.

It may be mentioned here that, at Scotch country weddings, not very long ago, the bridegroom's men and others ran, as in Wales, straight from the church to the bride's house, in order to see who could first bring the intelligence that she had been duly married. Nor was the feat without danger, for in every village where they might be expected the young men were received with shots from pistols and guns, and if any men stumbled, or were somehow upset, there was great merriment. At the bride's house a bowl of broth was prepared for the winner of the race. Hence the expression "running for the brose." It appears that sometimes these races took place on horseback. A Scotch newspaper, *The Courier*, of January 16, 1813, records a case in which a young lady came in first:—"Immediately after the marriage, four men of the bride's company started for the broos, from Mauchline to Whitehall, a distance of thirteen miles; and when one of them was sure of the prize, a young lady, who had started after they were a quarter of a mile off, outstripped them all, and notwithstanding the interruption of getting a shoe fastened on her mare at the smithy on the road, she gained the prize, to the astonishment of both parties."

In Great Britain, as in some other countries, May used to be considered unlucky for marriages, especially May 14th. The 13th was old May Day, and no doubt the festivities connected with May Day celebrations were often marred by much unseemly license, being survivals of old Heathen observances. The Christian Church, in refusing to countenance certain practices, probably caused the whole of this month to be avoided for formal and proper unions.

In the Orkney Islands they prefer to marry only during the waxing moon, or at flood-tide. A bright day is generally a good omen: "Blest is the bride the sun shines on" is a well-known saying.

The Fairies, or "little-folk," so skilful in magic, are supposed to be active at these times; hence no green should be worn at weddings among the Lowland Scotch, for green is the fairies' colour, and whoever wears it will be overtaken by ruin. They would even go so far, in some cases, as to banish green vegetables from the meal. In the Highlands, the bridegroom must put on his shoe without horn, or lace; otherwise the witches may play their evil tricks. Also, the people were careful to let no dog run between the bridal pair.

CHAPTER XXIII

Ireland

AMONG the peasants in many parts of Ireland the match-maker conducts all matrimonial preliminaries, both "affairs of the heart," where the messages she conveys are dictated by true love, and affairs fostered by calculating parents, who consult rather their children's interest than their inclination.

The most successful match-makers are mid-wives and "cosherers." The cosherer is a very respectable and well-treated female vagabond. She goes from the house of one relation to that of another, and is always hospitably received. She sews, knits, retails the news, tells old stories and (incidentally) doctors the children. The "senachie" is the male counterpart of the cosherer, but infinitely her inferior in the art of match-making; he concerns himself chiefly in prophecy and genealogies. Mr. Carleton, the novelist, knew a cosherer (by name Mary Murray) who was highly successful in the task of match-making, which indeed requires astuteness of no common order, and a fine instinct for a bargain, so shrewd and provident are the Irish in the matter of marriage. Many a time have marriages been broken off, because one party refuses to give his son "a slip of a pig," or another his daughter "a pair of blankets"; and it was no unusual thing for the match-maker to say, "Never mind; I have it all settled but the slip."

Mary Murray often met a young girl quite accidentally, and in the course of conversation would bring in the one important subject—in this fashion.

"Cirra, Biddy Sullivan, how are you, a-colleen?"

"Faix, bravely, thank you, Mary. How is yourself?"

"Indeed, thin sorra a bit o' the health we can complain of, barrin' whin this pain in the back comes upon us. The last time I seen your mother, Biddy, she was complainin' of a *weid* (bad cold). I hope she's betther, poor woman?"

"Hut! bad scran to the thing that ails her! She has as light a foot as e'er a one of us, an' can dance 'Jackson's mornin' brush' as well as ever she could."

"Throth, an' I'm proud to hear it. Och! och! 'Jackson's mornin' brush!' and it was she that could do it. Sure I remimber her wedding-day like yestherday . . . an' how the Squire himself an' the ladies from the Big House came down to see herself an' your father, the bride and groom, dancin' the same 'Jackson's mornin' brush!' . . . An' is there no news wid you, at all, at all?"

"The sorra word, Mary; where 'ud I get news? Sure it's yourself that always on the fut (foot) that ought to have the news for *us*, woman alive."

"An' maybe I have too. I was spaikin' to a friend o' mine about you the other day."

"A friend o' yours, Mary! Why what friend could it be?"

"A friend o' mine—ay, an' o' yours too. Maybe you have more friends than you think, Biddy . . . an' friends that e'er a girl in the parish might be proud to hear named in one day wid her. Awouh!"

"Bedad we're in luck, thin . . . Cen' who may these great friends of ours be, Mary?"

"Faix, as dacent a boy as ever broke bread the same boy is, 'and,' says he, 'if I had goold in bushelfuls, I'd think it too little for that girl'; . . . 'I'm afeard,' says he, 'that she'd put scorn upon me, an' not think me her aiquals' . . . Poor boy! throth my heart aches for him!"

"Well, can't you fall in love wid him yourself, Mary, whoever he is?"

"Indeed, an' if I was at your age, it would be no shame to me to do so, but . . . the sorra often ever the likes of Paul Heffernan came acrass me."

"Paul Heffernan! Is that your beauty? If it is, why, keep him and make much of him."

"Oh wurrah! the differ there is between the hearts an' tongues of some people . . . Well, well, I'm sure that wasn't the way he spoke of you, Biddy, an' God forgive you for runnin' down the poor boy as you're doin' . . ."

"Who? me? I'm not runnin' him down. I am

neither runnin' him up nor down. I have neither good nor bad to say about him—the boy's a black stranger to me, barrin' to know his face."

"Faix, an' he in consate wid you these three months past, an' intends to be at the dance on Friday next, in Jack Gormby's new house. Now, goodbye, alanna; keep your own counsel . . . It's not behind every ditch the likes of Paul Heffernan grows . . . My blessin' be wid you."

Next day, by a meeting similarly accidental, she comes in contact with Paul Heffernan, who, honest lad, had never probably bestowed a thought on Biddy Sullivan in his life.

"How is your father's son, ahagur?"

"My father's son wants nothing but a good wife, Mary."

"An' it's not every set day or bonfire night that a good wife is to be had, Paul—that is a *good* one, as you say; for, throth, there's many o' them in the market, sich as they are. I was talkin' about you to a friend of mine the other day—an', trogs, I'm afeard you're not worth all the abuse we gave you?"

"More power to you, Mary! I'm oblaged to you. But who is the friend in the manetime?"

"Poor girl! Throth! when your name slipped out on her, the point of a rush 'ud take a drop of blood out o' her cheek, the way she crimsoned up. 'Ah, Mary,' says she, 'if ever I know you braith it to man or mortal, my lips I'll never open to you to my dyin' day.' Trogs, when I looked at her, an' the tears standin' in her purty black eyes, I thought I didn't see a betther favoured girl, for both face and figure, this many a day, than the same Biddy Sullivan."

"Biddy Sullivan! Is that long Jack's daughter of Carga?"

"The same. But Paul, avick, if a syllable o' what I tould you——"

"Hut, Mary! honour bright! Do you think me a *stag*, that I'd go and inform on you?"

"Fwishper, Paul: She'll be at the dance on Friday next in Jack Gormby's new house . . . Think o' what I bethrayed to you."

Thus did Mary very quietly and sagaciously bind two young hearts together, who probably might otherwise have never for a moment thought of each other. Of course, when Paul and Biddy met at the dance on Friday, the one was the object of the closest attention to the other; and each being prepared to witness strong proofs of attachment from the opposite party, everything fell out according to their expectations.

As a rule Mary was received everywhere with the greatest kindness and hospitality. Every one knew that what she did, she did always for the best; and if some small bits of execration were occasionally levelled at her, it was not more than the parties levelled at each other. All marriages cannot be happy; and indeed it was a creditable proof of Mary Murray's sagacity, that so few of those effected through her instrumentality were unfortunate.[1]

According to Mr. Arthur Young,[2] there was a very strange custom in the interior of Ireland last century. A number of country neighbours among the poor people fixed on some young woman that ought, as they thought, to be married; they also agreed upon a young fellow as a proper husband for her. This determined, they sent to the fair one's cabin to inform her that on the Sunday following she was to be "horsed," that is, carried on men's backs. She must then provide whiskey and cider for a treat, as all would pay her a visit after mass, for a hurling match. As soon as she was "horsed" the hurling began, in which the young man appointed for her husband had the eyes of all the company fixed on him; if he came off conqueror, he was certainly married to the girl; but if another was victorious, he most certainly lost her, for she was the prize of the victor.

If a young woman's *fiancé* dies it is a common practice among the peasantry for her to solemnly "give back her promise." "We had given one another a *hand*-promise," said an old woman, speaking of her dead lover, "and I had to go, when he was dead, an' take him by the right hand afore witness, to give back my promise."

A belief in the fairies, once so prevalent, still

[1] Characteristic Sketches of Ireland and the Irish, by Wm. Carleton. 1845.

[2] Young, "Tour in Ireland," 1798.

lingered on in some parts of the country not long ago. As an example of this kind of folk-lore, we may mention here that the country people used to say that if a man, at his marriage, unbuttoned one button of the right knee, the fairies could not harm him in any way.

In some parts of Ireland, the "Mullet of Mayo," for instance, there is a strange survival, namely, the wedding dance with a straw mask, and in parts of Leitrim with a straw petticoat. On this subject the author consulted the Rev. W. S. Green, an authority on these matters, who writes from Dublin Castle as follows:—"The Wedding Masks to which you refer are used by the 'Strawboys,' or Clagheras, at weddings. A gang of nine visits the home in the evening of the wedding. The 'captain' dances with the bride, and the others with the other girls. They leave in a short time, and another gang arrives. It is unlucky if their identity is recognised. In the west of this county it is still much in vogue, but dying out in other parts. I have heard that a similar custom exists in Wexford." Masks of straw are sometimes used on other occasions, such as Saints' Days.

As a good example of Irish humour we submit the following story:—

"Though the Irish are so prone in general to early and improvident marriages, no people are closer in their nuptial barter when they are in a condition to make marriage a profitable contract. Repeated meetings between the elders of families take place, and acute arguments ensue, properly to equalise the worldly goods to be given on both sides. Pots and pans are balanced against pails and churns, cows against horses, a slip of bog against a gravel pit . . . a little lime-kiln sometimes burns stronger than the flame of Cupid, the doves of Venus herself are but crows in comparison with a good flock of geese, and a love-sick sigh less touching than the healthy grunt of a good pig.

"A marriage bargain was once broken off because the lover could not obtain from the father a certain brown filly as part of the dowry. He afterwards met the lady in a tent at a fair, and being newly stirred by the sight of her charms, asked her to dance, but was astonished at her returning him 'a look of vacant wonder,' which said '*Who are you?*' as plain as looks could speak.

"'Arrah, Mary,' exclaimed the youth.

"'Sir!!!' answered Mary, with great disdain.

"'Why, one would think you didn't know me!'

"'If I ever had the honour of your acquaintance, sir,' answered Mary, 'I forget you intirely.'

"'Forget me, Mary?—arrah, be aisy—is it forget the man that was courtin' and in love with you?'

"'You're under a mistake, young man,' said Mary with a curl of her rosy lip. . . . 'No one was ever in love with *me*. . . . There was a dirty, mane blackguard, indeed, once *in love with my father's brown filly*, but I forget him intirely.'"

In Ireland degraded clergymen, known as "Couple Beggars," sometimes perform irregular marriages.

The ancient custom of seizing wives by force and carrying them off had not died out towards the end of last century. A remarkable instance occurred in the year 1767. A Kilkenny farmer's son, being refused a neighbour's daughter of only twelve years of age, took an opportunity of running away with her; but, being pursued, the girl was brought back and married by her father to a lad of fourteen. But her former lover, determining not to lose her, procured a party of armed men and besieged the house of his rival. In the fight which took place her father was shot dead, and several of the besiegers mortally wounded, and so the would-be husband retired without his prize.

CHAPTER XXIV

The Gipsies and the Mormons

IN Spain, a gipsy girl is generally betrothed at the age of fourteen to a youth chosen by her parents, and the marriage takes place two years after. During the period of betrothal they must never appoint a rendezvous at a distance, or converse with one another save as mere acquaintances. The wedding festival is a very costly affair, the bridegroom often involving himself in difficulties for life in order to provide an entertainment worthy of the occasion. In that country they are very strict with their daughters, and any lapse from virtue on the part of a betrothed girl may be punished with death. Mr. George Borrow, who witnessed a marriage at a church, thus describes what followed. "When the wedding party returned, singing and dancing began. Sweatmeats nearly a ton in weight strewed the room to a depth of three inches. The bride and bridegroom began to dance on them, the company followed suit. To convey a slight idea of the scene, is almost beyond the power of the words. In a few minutes the sweatmeats were reduced to a powder, or rather to a mud, and the dancers were soiled to the knees with sugar, fruit, and yolk of eggs. Still more terrific became the lunatic merriment. The men sprang high into the air, neighed, brayed and crowed; whilst the Gitánas snapped their fingers in their own fashion louder than the castanets."

In one corner an old convict gipsy produced demoniacal sounds from a guitar. The festivities lasted three days.

The gipsies in some parts of the continent have a curious custom. The chief breaks a pitcher crowned with flowers, and from the fragments foretells the fortune of the bridal pair.

According to Mr. C. G. Leland and others,[1] the most valuable gifts are contributed by the girls, probably in order to show that they are not quite penniless. They will hide money they have earned and bake it in a cake, which, at some fitting opportunity they throw over the hedge to their lovers. A Romany song says :—

"I told a lady's fortune
 In that big house hard by ;
No gipsy could have done it,
 More cleverly than I.
I promised that she'd marry,
 A lord with heaps of gold ;
She filled my hands with silver,
 As much as I could hold."

The following lines allude to the cakes thrown to lovers :—

[1] "English Gipsy Songs."

"Oh, Rommanis are coming!
  I know what I'm about;
I hid away the money,
  Where no one found it out.
I bought some flour last evening,
  I bought it secretly;
Come, now the cake is ready,
  And nobody to see.
Meal so white, money bright,
  Baked together here;
All for you, love, all for true love,
  All for luck, my dear."

"Marrying over the tongs" is a Scotch gipsy custom referred to by Mr. J. M. Barrie in his well-known "Auld Licht Idylls," who says it "is a thing to startle any well-brought-up person, for before he joined the couple's hands, 'Jimmy' (the gipsy king who officiated as priest) jumped about in a startling way, uttering wild gibberish, and after the ceremony was over, there was rough work with incantations and blowing on pipes." The parties, it appears, stood on either side of the tongs, or in some cases it was a broomstick. Until recent years British soldiers frequently married "over the sword."

Scotch gipsies had also a curious ceremony of divorce. The man and woman who were about to separate for life led forth an unblemished horse, and chose a priest (by lot) who walked several times round the animal, extolling its good qualities, and repeating the names of its possessors. It was then let go and caught again, when the priest stabbed it. Then the man and woman joined hands over its dead body; they walked three times round it, halting at last at the tail, where they shook hands and went off in opposite directions. The woman received a token made of cast iron, which she was made to wear for the rest of her days. They never allowed her to marry again, and she was liable to be put to death if she endeavoured to pass for an unmarried woman. The horse was buried, all but the heart, which was taken out, roasted, and eaten by the husband and his friends.

The Mormons of Utah have their own peculiar marriage rites and customs. In the early days of the sect they seem to have borrowed their forms and ceremonies from other religious bodies, only adding here and there terms of an original character. The ceremony was performed by the President himself in the Temple; but in some cases he deputed a competent elder to take the office, in which case the ceremony took place at the officer's house.

Disputes arose continually between the various courts as to the legality of such elders' performance of the rites, but these they settled amongst themselves. When, however, the Church became more organised, it was ordained that the ceremony of marriage might be performed in a public place, the office being taken by the highest or the lowest dignitary, as the occasion served. In fact the restrictions became less and less, and those in the church were permitted to employ the usual outside agencies for the marrying of their children, without fear of censure or reproof.

Of the religious aspect of marriage the Mormon seems more tenacious, interpreting Scripture to show the error of uniting with unbelievers, and generally giving to the ceremony an air of solemnity which must have been impressive to the thoughtful mind. The concluding words of the priest are: "In the name of the Lord Jesus Christ and by the authority of the holy priesthood, I pronounce you legally and lawfully husband and wife for time and for all eternity. And I seal upon you the blessings of the holy resurrection with power to come forth in the morning of the first resurrection clothed with glory, immortality and everlasting lives, and I seal upon you the blessing of thrones and dominions and principalities and powers and exaltations, together with the blessings of Abraham, Isaac, and Jacob, etc.," after which follows the registration, a few friends also signing their names as witnesses. When the man already has a wife the first wife stands to the left of her husband, and the bride at her left hand. The president then asks, "Are you willing to give this woman to your husband to be his lawful and wedded wife for time and for all eternity? If you are, you will manifest it by placing her right hand in the right hand of your husband." The right hands of the husband and bride being thus joined, the wife takes her husband by the left arm, and the ceremony then proceeds as described above.

The church, in addition to such benediction, secures other privileges for the initiated. Thus, by the additional ceremony of "Spiritual Marriage," eternal salvation and permanent positions of spiritual rank may be attained. For say they, "One woman can save one man only; but a man can be instrumental in the salvation of an indefinite number of women."

Brigham Young, in a discourse delivered forty or fifty years ago, gave the following dictum: "And I would say, as no man can be perfect without the woman, so no woman can be perfect without a man to lead her. I tell you the truth as it is in the bosom of eternity; and I say so to every man upon the face of the earth, if he wishes to be saved he cannot be saved without a woman by his side."

The first wife, according to the view generally taken amongst polygamists, is *the* wife, and assumes the husband's name and title; the others are called "sisters," and stand to the first wife's children in the relation of aunts. The first wife is married for *time*, the others sealed for *eternity*. The age at which girls marry is about sixteen, or a little more, and this seems to meet with approval by the bachelors. Divorce is not much sought, because the man is ashamed that he cannot keep order in his house; only in case of adultery, cruelty, desertion, or neglect of a flagrant kind. Then wives are allowed to claim to be free. The too literal interpretation of Scripture has seemingly led the Mormon to commit polygamy. Thus Abraham's descendants were to be as the stars and the sands of the sea, and in his seed all the nations of the earth were to be blessed. And they, believing themselves to be Abraham's children, seek to perpetuate the same design. The theory that "the man is not without the woman, nor the woman without the man," they interpret as an absolute command that both sexes should marry, and that a woman cannot enter the heavenly kingdom without a husband to introduce her. "Nature is dual," say they, and an unmarried man or woman is, and for ever must be, an imperfect creature. A celestial marriage is a marriage of God, and those thus joined can never be divorced except by the power of God.

In justice to the Mormons, we may add, in conclusion, that they have other codes which appear less open to objection than some of those we have alluded to above. Their polygamy has lately been made illegal by the United States Government.

INDEX